IDENTIFY YOURSELF

IDENTIFY YOURSELF

THE 50 MOST COMMON
BIRDING IDENTIFICATION CHALLENGES

BILL THOMPSON III
EIRIK A. T. BLOM
JEFFREY A. GORDON
GEORGE ARMISTEAD
MARSHALL ILIFF
and JULIE ZICKEFOOSE

ILLUSTRATED BY

JULIE ZICKEFOOSE

HOUGHTON MIFFLIN COMPANY
Boston   New York
2005

For information about permission to reproduce selections from
this book, write to Permissions, Houghton Mifflin Company,
215 park Avenue, New York, New York 10003.

Visit our Web site: www.houghtonmifflinbooks.com.

Library of Congress Cataloging-in-Publication Data

Identify yourself : the 50 most common birding identification challenges / Bill
Thompson III ... [et al.] ; illustrated by Julie Zickefoose.
p. cm.
Includes bibliographical references and index.
ISBN 0-618-51469-4
1. Birds — North America — Identification.   I. Thompson, Bill, 1962–
QL681.I35 2005
598'.07'2347—dc22   2004062901

Book design by Anne Chalmers
Typefaces: Scala, Frutiger, Officina Sans, Book Serif, Caflische Script

Printed in the United States of America
QWT 10 9 8 7 6 5 4 3 2 1

CONTENTS

ACKNOWLEDGMENTS

THE CREATION OF THIS BOOK AND ITS CONTENTS is the result of the work, knowledge, and field experience of a number of contributors. The idea for an identification column in *Bird Watcher's Digest* (the material this book draws on) came from a meeting between myself, birding expert and field guide author Eirik A. T. Blom, and bird artist Julie Zickefoose in our basement guest room in the winter of 1996. *BWD* needed an identification column, so the three of us came up with a laundry list of bird identification challenges to explore over the coming months. I've never worked with a more effective team. Adding greatly to my enjoyment was the fact that Rick was one of my best friends and Julie, well, we had liked each other enough to get married back in 1993.

From that meeting in late 1996 until Rick's death in December 2002, Rick always handled the writing, Julie created the art for the bird ID plates, I handled the editing and publishing, and the three of us together came up with the identification challenges. This book's foundation is built squarely on the expert contributions of Eirik A. T. Blom. Its publication fulfills a promise I made to him and is dedicated to his memory.

Our team of contributing authors, without whom this book would not be possible, are

George Armistead, whose favorite areas of bird identification fit perfectly with our needs for this book.

Jeffrey A. Gordon, who took the reins of the "Identify Yourself" column in the spring of 2003 and helped us craft and cull the contents of this book. His vast birding experience has proven invaluable time and time again.

Marshall Iliff, a lifelong birder and a tour leader for Victor Emanuel Nature Tours.

Julie Zickefoose. While the text required the hard work of many people, this book's artwork was created by one remarkable artist.

At *Bird Watcher's Digest* we wish to thank Deborah Griffith and Heather Lynch for their editorial and production support, as well as Andy Thompson, Elsa Thompson, Helen Neuberger, Ann Kerenyi, Susan Hill, Linda Brejwo, Nate Wooley, David Schiemann, Velinda Graham, Laura Kammermeier, and Joyce Abicht for holding the fort and cheering us on. John and Durrae Johanek helped make our material look good and read well. Bob Ayers and Cheryl Reid at Publication Design made an excellent design come to life. Thanks to Al Zimdars, Laurie Allen, and all at Times Printing for their speedy pre-press scanning help. Russell Galen not only catalyzed our vision, but challenged us to think big. Special thanks to John Rakestraw, whose bird identification articles initially caught the attention of our readers and made us realize we might be on to something. Kim Eckert made important suggestions to improve the book's text. Computer whiz and bird artist Michael DiGiorgio fine-tuned the digital files of several illustrations just before this book went to press. Susan Zorn's proofreading was invaluable.

This book project would not have been possible without the support and expert guidance of Lisa White at Houghton Mifflin. Lisa and her assistant Elizabeth Kluckhohn redefined my understanding of the editing process, and all of us are grateful for their input. Anne Chalmers at Houghton Mifflin created the book's lovely and compelling design.

Julie Zickefoose is grateful to David Willard of Chicago's Field Museum for cheerfully entrusting her with the loan of their beautiful study skins. Without his help, these plates could not have been painted. Nancy Merrill, Tom and Donna Sheley, and Dr. Arthur Frock denuded their walls to graciously loan original plates back to us for scanning and reproduction. Bill Thompson III knew before anyone else that this would be a good book, and his love and support kept the paintings rolling off the drawing board.

Finally we'd like to thank Bill Thompson Jr. and Elsa Ekenstierna Thompson for having the vision and courage to launch America's first magazine for bird watchers in 1978. Without *BWD* and it loyal readers, we'd be just another bunch of anxious birders worrying about those confounding and confusing fall warblers.—*Bill Thompson III, April 2005.*

A complete list of the authors of each chapter appears on page 376. All artwork contained in this book is by Julie Zickefoose.

FOREWORD

BY KENN KAUFMAN

PHILOSOPHERS SOMETIMES SAY that names have no importance, or that these labels actually distract us from the reality of things. In one sense this may be true, but it's also true that knowing the names for things can change our perceptions of them for the better.

Consider the way we react to birds. Anyone may take passing notice of some bird that is especially colorful, or large, or notable in some other way. But there's a critical point at which a person is intrigued enough by this notable bird to say, "Hmmm, I wonder what *kind* of bird that is?" When someone asks that question, the answer is going to be a name. When someone cares enough to find out the name of a bird, he has started down the road toward becoming a bird watcher.

Knowing the names of birds opens up the possibility of learning more about them. We have a couple of bright yellow birds that are common across much of North America in summer and seem to disappear in fall. If you know their names, you can look up information about them and find out that the one called "yellow warbler" has flown south to the tropics, while the one called "American goldfinch" is still around and simply has molted into duller hues for the winter. You can read further and learn that the yellow warbler had to migrate to a warmer climate because it eats insects (hard to find in the north in winter), while the goldfinch can find plenty of food in cold weather because it feeds on seeds. Thus the names of birds can lead to more insight into the world around us.

Most birds are easy to recognize, and a glance at the pictures in any good field guide will yield their names. However, some — a sizeable minority — are more difficult. When I was getting started in bird watching, I hated sparrows, gulls, terns, flycatchers, and female ducks because they were so confusing, so variable, so similar to their relatives. After I had been at it for a while, I loved these birds for the very same reasons. The pleasure of being able to tell all these birds apart was more than

> *There always will be challenges in identifying birds, and frankly, that's the way I like it.*

worth the effort, the learning process, that it took to get to that point.

That's the kind of thing that this book is about: the learning process. Its focus is not on the quick-lookup types, like a red bird with black wings being a male scarlet tanager. Its focus is on things like that tanager-shaped greenish bird with slightly darker wings, but maybe not dark enough for a female scarlet tanager . . . okay, just how big was its bill? What color was its tail? What was the exact shade of greenish? Did it give any call notes? Identifying birds like this will take some care, some learning of subtle differences. That process of learning can be tons of fun, if it's done in the style of *Bird Watcher's Digest*.

For more than a quarter century, *Bird Watcher's Digest* has been one of my favorite publications. I have looked forward to every issue, knowing that it will be informative, interesting, and above all entertaining. This remarkable magazine has been, all along, a project of the equally remarkable Thompson family. Any time spent with the fun-loving Thompsons is sure to be a swirl of birds, good music, bad jokes, zany imagination, and more birds. They mostly keep the bad jokes out of the magazine, but the sense of fun comes through. It's no wonder that Bill and Elsa Thompson, their sons Andy and Bill III, and Bill III's wife, Julie Zickefoose, are among the most respected and best-loved members of the bird watching community.

They're also modest, though, and quick to point to other talented people who have contributed to the success of *BWD*. Chief among the latter is the late Eirik A. T. Blom, "Rick" to his many friends, a brilliant and prolific writer on all things bird-related. It was Rick Blom who began the column "Identify Yourself" in *Bird Watcher's Digest* as a way of helping people to improve their field skills. Each column was beautifully illustrated by Julie Zickefoose, but the heart of the column was Blom's detailed text. In each installment he would examine some difficult pair or group of birds and take the time to explain, to clarify, to give his readers real understanding of what they were seeing. The column quickly became one of the most popular items in the magazine.

So popular, in fact, that readers were soon agonizing over whether to cut up their magazines to make their own collection, or to carry their whole *BWD* library with them in the field. The obvious solution was a volume like the one you are holding now. There were some important groups of birds that Rick had not covered before his untimely death in 2002, so sections were contributed by other top-notch bird experts such as Jeff Gordon, Marshall Iliff, and George Armistead. Penning several additional chapters and pulling all the material together for publication was the work of Bill Thompson III, editor of *BWD*, a master of birds and words.

There always will be challenges in identifying birds, and frankly, that's the way I like it. If the birds all wore name tags, if it never took more than a glance to identify them, a little bit of the pleasure would be gone. When we learn to tell these birds apart, when we unravel the clues and solve the mysteries and identify more of these creatures, the sense of accomplishment just adds to the fun. And no one knows more about the fun of bird watching than the people at *Bird Watcher's Digest*. I salute them for giving us this fine new volume. And I recommend this book to bird watchers at all levels of experience, as an essential guide for making their time in the field more rewarding.

INTRODUCTION
Why You Need This Book

THERE ARE MANY PEOPLE who are content with seeing birds and thinking, "Look, there's a bird," and they leave it at that. Then there are those of us who aren't content unless we can identify the birds we see down to species, sex, and plumage. This is the essential core of bird watching: the desire to *know* what a bird is — to be able to properly identify it, give it a name. We birders often find ourselves watching birds whose identities we can't quite pin down. What makes bird watching so thrilling is the element of surprise — you never know what birds you'll encounter. But you know that you'll do just about anything to identify them . . .

BEYOND THE FIELD GUIDE

Binoculars and a field guide are the two essential tools for any bird watcher. Without them, a walk in the park is just that. With them, a walk in the park — or anywhere else — becomes a bird watching adventure. But there are other tools and resources, more gear and gadgets, that can greatly enhance your enjoyment of birding. This book, *Identify Yourself,* is to your field guide what a spotting scope is to your binoculars — it provides you with a more detailed, in-depth view.

Field guides help you identify bird species by detailing their field marks and notable characteristics. They rely heavily on pictures — photos or paintings — and the text supports the images with short descriptions of plumage, habitat, and behavior. A field guide needs to be small enough to be carried into the field, preferably in a pocket for quick access. This usually means the text it offers on each species is limited to telegraphic sentence fragments in a language that might be referred to as "field-guide-ese." These books are very handy to have in the field for quick reference, but they can't always go into the kind of detail you need to tackle many of the more difficult identification challenges.

Identify Yourself has both a hearty helping of text and excellent large color illustrations; it is not meant to be carried into the field on your birding excursions, but you might want to keep it in your car for quick reference.

Between the information in a birder's well-thumbed field guide and his or her own actual bird watching experiences, there is a vast uncharted sea of unfamiliar birds encountered and identification tips, techniques, pointers, and tricks to be learned and remembered for each and every one of them. It can all be very confusing and frustrating—even disheartening. *Identify Yourself* is designed to help you distill and absorb all of this information in a way that makes bird identification not only easier, but also more fun.

Our goal is to provide beginning and intermediate-level bird watchers with a clear and logical path by which to navigate each identification challenge.

WHAT'S IN, WHAT'S OUT

In this book, we've collected fifty of the most commonly encountered bird identification challenges in North America and explored each of them with the intention of taking you beyond the field guide. Many of these challenges concern birds that you won't find on the same page of your field guide, but they are birds that are confusingly similar in the field.

We do not cover every one of North America's toughest identification challenges in this book. There are other resources available for separating the dowitchers in winter or for discerning the silent *Empidonax* flycatcher from its kin. Rather than cover all of the small confusing shorebirds, or "peeps," we cover the basics of shorebird identification and the confusing shorebirds you'll encounter *before* you're ready to tackle the peeps. As we selected the bird groupings for this book, we left out similar species that would be confusing, but they are rarely, if ever, found together. In these cases, the normal range and distribution of a species can be used to determine its identity.

OUR GOAL

In creating this material—much of which originally appeared in the "Identify Yourself" column in *Bird Watcher's Digest*—we've selected real-world bird identification conundrums and matched them with our team of experienced field birders. Our goal is to provide beginning and intermediate-level bird watchers with a clear and logical path by which to navigate each identification challenge. The text and illustrations were created in an effort to make their combined impact both useful and memorable to you when you need them most. When you need more information than your field guide offers, *Identify Yourself* will be here on your bookshelf, in your car, on your table, waiting.

GETTING STARTED
Top 20 Rules of the Bird Identification Game

BIRD WATCHERS EVERYWHERE know that identifying birds can be either easy and intuitive or the hardest, most confusing thing they've ever attempted. Different people become birders in different ways and for different reasons, but what never changes are the basic techniques that maximize your chances of getting your identifications right. Chapter by chapter, *Identify Yourself* spotlights confusingly similar species and gives you useful pointers for telling them apart; most of these pointers make use of at least one, and often more, of these techniques. To give you a head start on the journey ahead, we've broken them down into the Top 20 Rules of the Bird Identification Game.

You'll certainly come up with your own versions of some of these rules. They are not intended to be set in stone; think of them as guidelines, meant to be adapted to fit your circumstances. The idea is to give you the tools you need to enjoy the bird identification process more, and let fewer birds get away from you unidentified.

WHAT TO LOOK FOR

1. LOOK AT THE BIRD, NOT AT THE BOOK. Roger Tory Peterson, the father of American bird watching, once said, "Birds have wings and tend to use them." How right he was. Birds have wings — books do not. Unlike the bird, your field guide will stay right where you left it. When you have a mystery bird in sight, resist the urge to dive into your field guide and start flipping through the pages for a matching image. What if all you noticed in your brief look was that it was a yellowish warbler, or a streaky sparrow? There are dozens of birds in your guide matching these descriptions. It's tempting to reach for the guide, especially if you're excited about an unusual bird — but resist. Watch the bird for as long as it lets you. The longer you look, the more you'll notice and remember about the bird's field marks and behavior. Then, when you do open your field guide, you'll be better prepared to make your identification.

2. START AT THE TOP AND WORK DOWN AND BACK. If you've managed to follow the first rule, you're taking a long careful look at your mystery bird. The next step is to look at the bird in an organized way. The head is the best place to start, provided you can see it; many North American birds can be positively identified by the shape of and markings on their heads. Start at the crown, work down toward the breast, and then back toward the tail. By the time your eyes get to the bird's tail, you will probably have noticed at least three key field marks, and these should be enough to nail an identification.

3. SHAPE SAYS A LOT. The flight silhouette of a chimney swift, the bill of an American avocet, and the tail of a scissor-tailed flycatcher are a few examples of birds whose shape alone is enough for a positive identification. Though the shapes of other birds may be less immediately identifiable, it is nonetheless an important clue. First, try to get an impression of a bird's overall shape. Then look specifically at head shape (is it peaked, flat, rounded, or crested?); tail shape (is it long, forked, fanned, or pointed?); bill shape (is it decurved, upturned, pointed, blunt, thick, tiny?); and finally at wing shape (are they short, long, broad, pointed, angled, or straight?). The descriptive terms you use may vary from those in the field guides, but the point is to give yourself a general impression of how the bird is put together.

4. SIZE SOMETIMES LIES. Small dark birds can look larger than they actually are on overcast days. Young birds might appear larger than their parents. The effects of temperature might also alter how big a bird looks. A cold bird puffs its feathers, looking considerably larger than a sleek bird. Still, size is an important clue to its identity. When judging size, it's often more useful to compare your bird to other nearby birds or objects than to try to gauge its size in inches. Noting its size in relation to familiar species — "It's larger than a robin, but smaller than a crow" — can be very helpful. Judging the size of distant birds, like soaring raptors, is much more difficult. In those cases it's better to rely on other clues, such as shape and behavior, in working toward an accurate identification.

5. COLOR CAN MISLEAD. Most beginning bird watchers (and even some experienced ones) focus too intently on a bird's color when attempt-

ing to identify it. Perhaps this is because color is such an obvious clue. Or perhaps it's because as birders, we tend to get more excited about the really colorful birds. (Go ahead, try to remain calm while watching a male painted bunting.) Color is certainly important in bird identification, but overemphasizing its importance can lead us astray. Accurate bird identification relies on several clues—it's not a puzzle with just one piece. Factor color into your identification process—it certainly can be diagnostic, not least for the male painted bunting—but bear in mind that viewing conditions, seasonal molt, and individual variation make it an unreliable clue most of the time. And remember that sometimes even "plainness" can be a field mark.

First, try to get an impression of a bird's overall shape.

6. BEHAVIOR. Bird behavior (much like human behavior) centers around food and sex. Like humans, different birds pursue these objectives in different ways. Watching a mystery bird long enough to notice its specific behaviors—tail flicking, wing flapping, feeder hogging, and so on—vastly increases your chances of identifying it. As your bird knowledge grows, you'll be able to sort out familiar birds by their habits and behavior, even if you can't get a long careful look.

WHAT TO LEARN

7. LEARN THE ANATOMY. Words such as "crissum," "lores," "tarsus," "mantle," and "flank" may seem like a foreign language at first, but learning the parts of the bird that these words refer to will make you more fluent in field-guide-ese and give you the vocabulary you need to describe the bird very specifically. (One way to learn them is to study the bird topography diagram on page xxiv, then cover the labels and quiz yourself.) Don't be discouraged if you cannot remember the names of all the parts of the bird at first. Just knowing that they can be used in identification is half the trick to using them.

8. LEARN THE SOUNDS. Sound is often the first clue to a bird's presence. Listen to the dawn chorus on a spring morning, and you'll know how vital sound is to the birds themselves. Start by learning the songs and sounds of your familiar local or backyard birds, so that when a stranger adds its voice, you'll notice the difference. Finally, when your fellow bird watchers identify a bird by its sounds, ask them how they did it. Learning bird sounds takes time, field practice, and a good audio collection (see Resources on page 373), but it'll be worth it when your fellow birders start asking you how you do it.

9. KNOW WHAT TO EXPECT. British bird watchers pioneered the concept of "birding by habitat," in which a birder starts off by anticipating the bird species he or she is likely to encounter in a given location. Put simply, as you are approaching a particular place — say, an old farm field that's been left to its own devices for a few years — consider the habitat and season and make a mental list of the birds you could expect to see there. Knowing what to expect gives you an advantage in spotting something out of the ordinary. This technique also gives you the opportunity to sharpen your knowledge of bird ranges, habits, and preferences and makes finding sought-after species simply a matter of placing yourself in their preferred habitat — what a concept!

WHAT TO HAVE

10. GOOD OPTICS HELP. We are living in the golden age of bird watching. Excellent optics and birding gear are widely available and affordable. Of all the things that you can do to become a better bird watcher quickly, none will make you better faster than excellent binoculars. One day in 1984, I was struggling with my student-model binoculars to see *anything* birdlike in a certain bush. When I looked through a friend's top-of-the-line binoculars at the same bush, it was as if someone had shone a spotlight into the shady interior directly onto a skulking yellow-breasted chat. Within a week, I had upgraded my binoculars and I've never looked back. Buy the best optics that you can afford. Make sure they are comfortable, easy for you to use, and light enough to hold steady for several minutes at a time. Ask your friends for recommendations (or to try their binoculars!).

11. GOOD FIELD GUIDES HELP, TOO. As with optics, today's bird watcher has a rich array of field guides to choose from. Photographs or illustrations, worldwide, continental, or regional coverage, pocket-sized or reference-sized — there *is* a field guide for everyone. Buy several, and use them all. You'll find a favorite. The important thing is that you take it with you whenever you go birding — or wherever you might see a new bird. There are few things more frustrating than needing a field guide that's back home on the shelf.

WHAT TO DO FIRST

12. **USE MEMORY DEVICES.** Yes, bird watching requires you to remember a lot of information. Many birders find it easier to remember details if they use a memory device. I find this especially helpful for remembering bird songs — a silly, short phrase can perfectly remind me of a bird's song. ("Quick! Three beers!" from the olive-sided flycatcher. Or "I will see you. I will seize you. I will squeeze you 'til you squirt!" which reminds me of the warbling vireo's song.) The first mnemonic I learned as an eight-year-old bird watcher was "downy is dinky, hairy is huge" for telling these two similar woodpeckers apart. To help with ibis identification, one of our experts recommends using the sound of the bird's name — *eye-bis* — to remind you to check the color of the birds' eyes. Your memory devices may be just as pragmatic — or just as silly — as these, but you'll find they come in very handy.

13. **BIRD WITH OTHERS.** A good musician will tell you that he or she performs better when playing with other, more experienced musicians. It's true for bird watching, too. Take every opportunity to get out in the field with other birders. Go on bird-club field trips. Join the walks at the local nature center or community park. Birding has become such a popular pastime that it's almost impossible not to find people near you who share this interest, no matter where you are. You'll be a better birder for it.

14. **ASK QUESTIONS AND TAKE NOTES.** When you're afield with other bird watchers and someone identifies a distant speck or calls out the identity of an unfamiliar bird song, ask, "How did you know that?" Nearly every experienced bird watcher is willing to share his or her knowledge with others (and is usually flattered to be asked). Take notes on the information others share with you. I keep my notes right in the margins of my field guide, and over time I've found that I associate them automatically with the corresponding illustration. Don't be shy — if you want to know, ask.

15. **PRACTICE.** Whenever you can, wherever you are, practicing will make you a better bird watcher. The more time you spend watching (and listening), the more birds you'll see and identify. An hour spent watching wild birds is equal to three or more looking at pictures in a book — even if those birds are just house sparrows in a city park. Practice, practice. practice.

WHAT TO DO NEXT

16. **TAKE YOUR TIME.** It's great to be able to nail every identification within a few seconds, but we all know that this is sometimes impossible. If an unfamiliar bird is being cooperative, take advantage of the opportunity to watch it closely for as long as possible. If you've only had a brief glimpse of the mystery bird, it might be helpful to reflect a moment to try to recall everything you noticed about it. You might even want to take a few notes. Often these mystery birds reappear later and can be positively identified. Blurting out a guess at a bird's identity prematurely may lead to a misidentification (not in itself a tragedy, but occasionally mildly embarrassing if you're birding with a group); it also prevents you from making a more considered judgment that could lead you to a new bird.

17. **TRUST YOUR INSTINCTS.** As you become more experienced, your innate ability as a bird watcher will begin to take over. Learn to trust this instinct when you encounter an unfamiliar bird. In direct contradiction to rule 16, remember that your first guess will often be your most accurate one. (Well, we did say these were guidelines rather than rules.) Isn't this what our teachers told us before we took an exam in school? In technical terms, this method is sometimes referred to as "jizz," a mangled acronym for "General Impression of Size and Shape" (or GISS), which was developed in World War II as a way of identifying distant aircraft and ships. It works wonderfully with birds, too.

18. **BAD CALLS HAPPEN TO GOOD PEOPLE.** Everyone has done it. Made an embarrassingly bad call and announced it out loud, just as the bird proves itself to be another species. I seem to have a knack for really bad calls when I'm leading a group of bird watchers. It's nothing to be ashamed of. In fact, it's a rite of passage. You can't be considered a full-fledged bird watcher until you've made a backpack full of bad calls — the more embarrassing, the better. It happens to everyone.

19. **KNOW WHEN TO LET GO.** I'd be lying if I told you that I can identify every bird I encounter. Anyone who told you this would be lying. It's simply not possible. Some birds refuse to fully show themselves, some race past at Mach One, and some never appear at all, but call to us in unfamiliar voices from just out of sight. As a birder, you must accept this fact with Zenlike resolve. Some birds we must let go, forever unidentified.

WHAT TO DO LAST, AND ONE BONUS RULE

20. **CELEBRATE YOUR VICTORIES.** When you nail a really tough identification on a mystery bird, pat yourself on the back and celebrate a little. You've climbed the bird identification mountain and planted your flag at the top. Whatever your mode of celebration—I'm partial to hot fudge sundaes, myself—just do it. You deserve it.

21. **SEE MORE BIRDS. HAVE MORE FUN!** This may be the most important rule of all. We watch birds because they are fascinating creatures. We relish the identification challenges they present, with their changing plumages, confusing songs, odd behaviors, and extreme mobility. The more birds we see, the more fun we have. May there *always* be more birds for us to see.

Bird Topography: THE PARTS OF A BIRD

Bird watchers who know the basic parts of a bird will find it easier to describe and identify unfamiliar birds. The terms used to label this immature white-crowned sparrow are commonly used in this book, in most field guides, and even among bird watchers in the field.

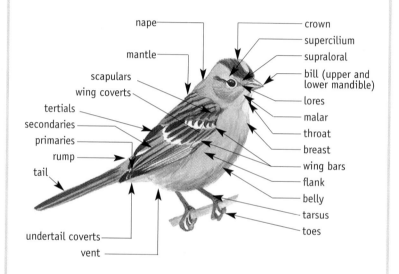

nape

crown

supercilium

mantle

supraloral

scapulars

bill (upper and lower mandible)

wing coverts

lores

tertials

malar

secondaries

throat

primaries

breast

rump

wing bars

tail

flank

belly

tarsus

toes

undertail coverts

vent

MERGANSERS

Find out how to identify

THESE FAST-FLYING FISH EATERS IN A FLASH.

WHEN YOU ARE WORKING YOUR WAY THROUGH A lakeful of ducks, no bird stops the eye more quickly than a male merganser, no matter which species you run across. They are among the most beautiful and startling of the waterfowl, both gaudy and intricate. The females, on the other hand — like the females of most waterfowl — are plainer, and they provide a greater identification challenge.

This chapter covers the North American mergansers, and although one always wants to be balanced, the focus is going to be on the females and birds in flight. Just to get them out of the way, let's start with the males.

MALE MERGANSERS

The greatest difficulty in identifying male mergansers is not confusing them with each other, or even with other ducks. In poor lighting or at great distances, the most likely sources of confusion are species that are not even closely related to mergansers.

Male common mergansers are only likely to be confused with distant loons. Both are heavy-bodied, low-slung birds that appear black and white at a distance. The most obvious differences are the common merganser's much thinner bill and its striking white sides. Most loons, in breeding or winter plumage, look dark almost to the waterline, and their bills are heavy, enhancing the big-headed look. Another useful clue is the generally solitary nature of loons. Except on rare occasions, they are usu-

WATERFOWL

red-breasted merganser
male

red-breasted merganser
female

red-throated loon in winter plumage

common merganser
female

common merganser
male

hooded merganser
male

bufflehead, male (left) and female

hooded merganser
female

ally seen in ones and twos. Even when there are more birds present, they tend to be spread out. Common mergansers are usually seen in bunches.

Telling male commons from male red-breasted mergansers is not hard because at a distance male red-breasteds are dark on the sides and reddish on the breast, which is why they are called red-breasted.

Male hooded mergansers are a strong contender, along with harlequin and wood ducks, for the most beautiful of the waterfowl. Their intricate plumage is not similar to anything else except distant male buffleheads. Even when the thin merganser bill is not evident, the dark sides contrasting with the white breast easily differentiate a male hooded from the white-sided and white-breasted male bufflehead. Sometimes, when the water is rough, the sides are not evident, but the white on the head of a male bufflehead goes all the way around the rear of the crown, while on a male hooded the white is bordered by black at the rear, so that no white is evident when the bird is facing away.

FEMALE MERGANSERS

Female mergansers are the birds most likely to cause problems. They are plain, low-contrast birds, and unlike males, they have no easy plumage characters that scream out the identification.

Female commons, even more than males, can be confused with winter-plumaged loons. The first clue is the common merganser's smaller bill, although red-throated loons do have fairly thin bills. Loon bills tend to be shorter, though, and have a slightly upturned look. The best character is the dark head and neck of female common mergansers that ends abruptly at the white breast, creating a strong contrast. Winter loons have pale throats and breasts that show little or no contrast, making them a plainer bird. The white chin patch of female common mergansers stands out from the dark head and is a field mark that no loon shares.

Female red-breasted mergansers are even more loonlike because the throat and breast are generally an even, dull color. Making the distinction requires more reliance on the merganser's thinner, proportionately longer bill and the exaggerated crest on the back of its head. Loon heads always appear sleek, and both male and female red-breasted mergansers nearly always show an obvious bushy crest trailing out behind the head.

Both female red-breasted and common mergansers have bushy crests; however, the red-breasted's is more unkempt and often appears divided.

Red-breasted females' heads are paler and duller than the heads of female common mergansers, which are a rich, dark nut-brown. The common's white chin patch contrasts nicely with this dark head color; no such clean patch is evident on a female red-breast. The female common merganser shows greater contrast between its head and white neck front; red-breasted hens are paler, with less contrast. One plumage that might cause confusion is juvenal. Here, look for two features — the smoother contours of the common's head versus the split, ragged crest of the red-breasted. In all plumages the common has a stouter, deeper bill base than does the red-breasted, whose bill looks pencil-thin all along its length.

The female hooded merganser may be the most frequently overlooked or misidentified of the diving ducks. It is a smallish, plain, almost patternless bird and can be misidentified as almost any of the smaller female ducks. It is the very thin bill and the shaggy crest that usually catch the eye first, characters that no other small duck shares.

The real problem with female hooded mergansers crops up when you see one alone. It is often difficult to determine size at a distance, and even though hooded mergansers are 50 percent smaller than red-breasteds, that is often not obvious at first. One clue on a single bird is bill color, sometimes visible at a surprisingly long distance. The bills of common and red-breasted mergansers are reddish, and they look pale in all but terrible light. Female hooded mergansers have mostly dark bills. Female hoodeds are also the darkest overall of the mergansers, with no pale area showing on the throat. Hooded mergansers ride very low in the water, usually with their necks well pulled in. Females have a long bushy crest that gives them a distinctive hammer-headed look.

Two pieces of information can be used as strong clues in identifying mergansers, although they are not absolutely diagnostic by themselves.

The first is the company they keep. When large numbers of waterfowl are concentrated in a small area you are apt to find any combination of birds, but in most situations it is unusual to find mixed flocks of mergansers. Even when all three are on the same lake, they usually clump together by species. Treating the tendency to hang around with their own species as diagnostic can cause you to overlook the occasional odd bird, but if a female merganser is seen in a flock of red-breasteds it probably is a red-breasted.

Habitat is also a key. If you see large numbers of mergansers on saltwater, they are almost always red-breasted or hooded. Common mergansers just seem to hate the stuff and shun even brackish water unless everything else is frozen. By contrast, in winter red-breasted mergansers seem to favor salt and brackish water and are generally scarce inland, though they do occur on the Great Lakes in winter. Hooded mergansers favor freshwater but can be found in coastal bays and inlets. They are also the merganser most likely to be found in wooded swamps and small lakes. Hoodeds are frequently found in shallow water and right along the shoreline, especially in areas where trees overhang the water, a situation the other mergansers avoid.

There is an oddity that many observers have noted about common and red-breasted mergansers that does not appear to be as true for hoodeds: the tendency to group by sex. It is fairly common to find flocks of female common or red-breasted mergansers, or flocks of males. Mixed-sex flocks are also seen, especially when the numbers are large, but single-sex flocks are more common, even in the spring. Finding hoodeds in single-sex flocks is much rarer.

It is fairly common to see single-sex flocks of common or red-breasted mergansers— all females or all males.

Identifying flying birds is harder. Actually, that is true of all ducks, not just mergansers. The first step is to recognize the birds as mergansers. Common and red-breasted mergansers in flight look strikingly loonlike, with long necks and long thin bills making them appear disproportionately front-loaded. They are swift and fairly agile flyers, however — much faster than loons — and you often have to be quick with the binoculars to get on the birds. Commons are the easiest because the dark head and neck contrast with the pale underparts, a field mark that works for both males and females.

Flying red-breasteds are more evenly colored, looking uniformly dusky overall in most views, with not much contrast anywhere. Males are easier to spot because of the large white patches on the inner wing and the white band on the throat, often obvious on flying birds. Females are harder because of the lack of contrast and the smaller white patch on the inner part of the wing. They are best recognized by the merganser shape and separated from commons by the black line dividing the red-breasted's white wing patch (the common has an undivided, square patch). The lack of

Female mergansers in flight

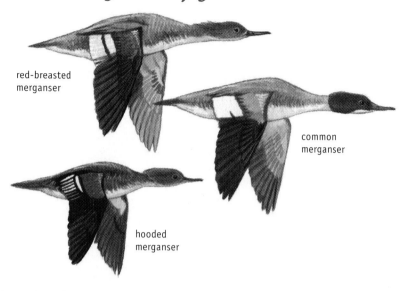

red-breasted
merganser

common
merganser

hooded
merganser

contrast between the red-breasted's neck and breast is another good clue.

Flying hooded mergansers are harder to identify. The white patch in the crest of males is hard to see on flying birds, although it often shows as a small white spot or line, reminiscent of the pattern on the head of a female bufflehead. The undersides of male hoodeds are almost uniformly dark, however, and the back is solid and dark, unlike the white on the sides and upper part of the back of a bufflehead.

Flying female hooded mergansers are the toughest call of all. They are basically small dark ducks with small white patches on the trailing edge of the wing. A lot of small fast-flying ducks seem to look just like that. The most diagnostic characters are the white belly, contrasting with the darker breast and upperparts, and the longer, thinner neck and bill. It is also typical to see female hoodeds flying with males, a useful clue when nothing else shows. Another hint is the very quick flight of hoodeds, with flocks apt to veer or change direction quickly, maneuvers their larger cousins rarely indulge in.

With a little practice, you will find that most mergansers are not hard to identify, and there are few pleasures for the avid waterfowl watcher quite like spotting all three on one day. That can happen almost anywhere on the continent if you keep your eyes open.

SCOTERS

Here's how to differentiate

THESE MOSTLY BLACK SEABIRDS, EVEN
WHEN THEY'RE FLYING AT A DISTANCE.

THE FIRST SCOTER I NEVER SAW WAS A FEMALE WHITE-
winged. I had checked the local park and found a nice flock of
ducks, mostly bufflehead and scaup with a canvasback or two and
a long-tailed duck (then called oldsquaw), a nice bird locally.

A friend called me excitedly that evening and told me he'd had a white-
winged scoter at the lake. "It was in a flock of scaup and bufflehead and
there was even an oldsquaw!" The bird must have come in right after I
left. I mentioned the black duck. "What black duck?" he asked.

The next morning most of the flock was gone, including my white-
winged black duck.

What caused me to miss the scoter was expectation, lightly seasoned
with inexperience. The lake was inland after all, and scoters don't occur
inland. If you want to see scoters, I reasoned, you go to the coast and
watch long lines of them streaming past in spring and fall. You do not
find them inland.

I know better now. Scoters do occur inland, although they are generally
scarce enough to be considered good local birds in most places. (The
exception is in the Great Lakes region, but these lakes are really just small
oceans; most of the rules that pertain to bird occurrence get thrown out
when you are talking about the Great Lakes.) Scoters, especially single
birds in mixed-species flocks, probably occur inland more frequently than
we think. Occasionally, small single-species flocks of scoters are seen
inland on lakes and rivers, and, as with mergansers, it is not unusual to
see single-sex groups, all males or all females and immatures.

Scoter identification can be divided into four categories: adult males,
females and immatures, birds in flight, and how-to-spot-a-scoter-when-

black scoter
adult female

black scoter
adult male

black scoter
immature male

surf scoter
immature male

surf scoter
adult female

surf scoter
adult male

white-winged scoter
immature male

white-winged scoter
adult female

white-winged scoter
adult male

you-are-looking-at-a-black-duck. The last category is one close to my own heart, so we will start there.

THE GENERIC SCOTER

Scoters are large, dark, heavy-bodied diving ducks. They are typically darker than the birds they are seen with. Males are black and females are dark to medium brown. Because they are diving ducks, they are chunky and usually ride lower in the water than dabbling ducks, such as mallards. Scoters are about the same size as the larger dabbling ducks and slightly larger than most of the other diving ducks they are seen with.

Other than overall size and darkness, two characters can be used to spot a scoter when it is in a mixed flock: the bill and the tail. Compared to most waterfowl, scoters have fairly heavy bills that taper quickly and look slightly pointed. On most other ducks, the bill appears more uniform and slightly broader at the tip. The scoter's tail is often cocked up, giving the appearance of a ruddy duck on steroids. On more than one occasion, I have nearly passed off a scoter as a ruddy duck until the obvious size difference kicked in.

These generic criteria are most useful when the bird is a female. Male scoters are usually much easier to spot, although in bad light or at a distance they can easily be passed off as just another dark duck. (When the light is bad enough or the distance great enough, almost all ducks fall into that group.)

In coastal areas scoter spotting is different. Here scoters occur in flocks, sometimes several hundred birds at a time. They can be seen flying just offshore anytime from fall through spring, and they gather in resting and feeding flocks just beyond the surf line, around jetties, and in sheltered bays and river mouths. It is common to see flocks of all males or of all females and immatures, but flocks of mixed sex and age also occur.

A scoter flock on the move is fairly distinctive. The formation tends to be single-file, bill-to-tail, close to the water, and moving fast. The overall darkness, heft, and speed separate them from most other ducks seen migrating along the coast, although in the northern parts of the continent they may be confused with eiders.

ADULT MALES

Adult male scoters are reasonably easy to identify. All three species are black, and each has at least one distinctive plumage character. No other duck looks like a male surf scoter. They have large white patches on the front of the face and on the nape. The white nape patch can be seen at a great distance, even when no other character is visible. Male surf scoters also have large bright orange bills, with a round black disc on either side.

Male black scoters live up to their name. They are black all over and would be nearly nondescript if it were not for the huge orange-yellow knob at the base of the bill. In good light the knob can be seen at a considerable distance. Black scoters also have smaller bills and more rounded heads than the other scoters, characters that are more useful on females and immatures than on adult males.

Male white-winged scoters are nearly as nondescript as male black scoters, but they usually have a noticeable white teardrop-shaped patch that starts at the eye and extends back and up. It is not large, but it stands out against the black head. At a distance it gives the bird a slightly goggle-eyed look.

All white-winged scoters have white in the wing. The secondaries are entirely white; on flying birds, the white is easily seen as a bright patch at the trailing edge of the wing, close to the body. Field guides usually show the white on sitting birds as a thin line or patch on the side, near the rear of the body. On many birds it shows just like that, but on some white-wings it is hard or impossible to see the white when the bird is resting on water. A visible white patch allows you to identify the bird as a white-winged. If you don't see the white patch, go to other characters before making the call.

FEMALES AND IMMATURES

Most of us are guilty of identifying female ducks by the company they keep. This works less frequently with scoters than with many other waterfowl because scoter flocks are so often single-sex. It also means overlooking many inland scoters because most of them (at least the ones seen singly) are females or immatures.

Females and immatures are grouped here because in the fall both young male and young female scoters look like adult females. By late fall and early winter, however, they begin to change, and the young males begin to acquire black feathering and some of the bill color of adult males. This can result in a messy-looking and troublesome bird, but they can almost always be identified. It requires mixing and matching characters from both male and female plumage. Except in rare cases, the characters will eliminate two of the three species quickly.

Female (and immatures of both sexes) surf scoters are plain brown birds. They almost always show two distinct white patches on the sides of the face. These, combined with a slightly paler brown cheek, give most female and immature surf scoters a distinctly "capped" appearance that can be seen at a considerable distance. Most immature males, and some females, also show a pale patch on the nape; if it is present, it quickly solves the identification problem.

The biggest identification challenge with female surf scoters is to avoid confusing them with female white-winged scoters. Assuming the white wing patch is not evident, the differences can be subtle. Many female white-wings show almost uniformly dark heads, but many have two white patches on the face, similar to those on the face of surf scoters, instead. The differences between them are not easy to see. The white patch at the base of the bill on female surf scoters is horizontal, a thin slash. On female white-wings it is oval, the same shape as the white patch on the rear of the face. Also, on female surf scoters, the top edge of the rear patch is sharply demarcated from the darker cap. On female white-winged scoters, the patch is less regularly shaped and tends to bleed out into the dark cap.

Despite the white patches on the sides of the head, the female white-winged does not show a distinctly capped appearance, mostly because the rest of the face is as dark as the crown. Be cautious of birds in bad light. The face patches of white-wings can sometimes appear to blend together at a distance.

Female black scoters present the least difficulty. Like the other two, they are dark brown birds, but the face and the front and sides of the neck are pale gray, almost white. The pale throat coloring ends abruptly at the breast, and the pattern is striking and diagnostic even at great distances.

BILL SHAPE

Bill shape is a helpful character under good viewing conditions. Surf scoters have a flat forehead and a distinctly canvasback-like profile. The head shape of white-winged scoters is slightly more rounded, and the feathering on the sides of the bill extends almost to the nostril, or about the middle of the bill. On surf scoters the feathering does not extend far at all, and as a result the bill seems to go farther into the face. The smaller, noticeably thinner bill and the steep forehead of black scoters result in a profile more like a dabbling duck than a scoter that is quite different from the other two species. These characters are often impossible to judge with certainty, however, and at best should be used only as indicators unless you have had the opportunity to study lots of birds at close range.

BIRDS IN FLIGHT

If you spend much time at the shore, most of the scoters you see are whizzing past in distant flocks, providing only limited views. If the water is dead calm, the look you get can be reasonably good, as long as the light is mostly behind you and the birds aren't at the horizon and shimmering through the haze.

The easiest of the flying scoters is the white-winged, because here is where the bird earns its name. The white secondaries are immediately obvious, shining against the all-dark wing and body. It also helps that although all three scoter species can be seen in mixed groups, either sitting or flying, white-wingeds are far less likely to be found in the company of the other two.

Male surf and male black scoters are not difficult as long as you know that you are looking at males. The white patch on the nape of male surf scoters can be seen at almost any distance, a gleaming white beacon that quickly identifies the bird. Male black scoters are the most uniformly black ducks you will see in flight. It is often possible to see the orange-yellow knob on the bill of flying birds, a single bright headlight that seems to be leading the bird across the water.

The real challenge is in identifying flying female black and surf scoters. The subtleties of these females' head patterns make them irrelevant on flying birds unless they are close. The best distinction on flying females is the pattern of the underside of the wing.

Black scoters, male and female, have a wing pattern very like a turkey vulture: the flight feathers (the trailing edge and the primaries) of the underside of the wing are silvery, contrasting with the black leading edge. The contrast is usually visible on flying birds. The underwing of surf scoters is uniformly dark, with no contrast.

Now this pattern, although frequently visible, is not a field mark that is easy to use the first time. It takes a few flocks before you start to become a true scoter-ologist. First, the birds are almost always flying low, barely above the water, and it is necessary to follow the flock for a while before you can be certain of what you are seeing. Second, scoters really work at flying, the wings beating rapidly, sort of like demented bumblebees. And then they disappear behind a wave.

Patience works. After a few flocks you begin to suspect you are consistently seeing the difference. A few more, or a few dozen more, and it starts to get easy.

Don't be unnerved if you see both patterns. It is not unusual to see mixed flocks of surf and black scoters flying past. In fact, the mixed flocks speed up the recognition process.

CAVEATS AND OTHER BIRDS

At dawn on the East Coast and in the evening on the West Coast, seabirds are backlit, and they all look all dark. There is no contrast, no pattern. In these conditions almost all scoters are black, as are other ducks, shorebirds, gulls, and terns. It is just one more example of why we should not get too attached to one field mark or too confident when the conditions are bad.

In the northern parts of the continent one has to separate the scoters from the eiders. Eiders are usually bigger, heavier, and much paler than scoters. Male eiders are gaudy, and tend to be much lighter colored than female scoters; female eiders are brown. In sitting flocks, eiders usually stand out because of their size and relatively pale plumage, but if you are in an area where eiders occur, double-check your identification.

Although scoters are the most noted and talked about of the flyby seabirds, others occur. Scaup can move along the coast in big numbers, and so can birds such as green-winged teal. So can loons. Do not assume that just because the birds going by are reasonably big and dark that they must be scoters. The differences are usually obvious if you let your brain sort through all the possibilities before focusing on the which-scoter-is-it problem.

All the scoters can occur inland, but white-wings are by far the most frequent, and blacks the least likely, to be found. Any scoter is possible, however, and you should never identify a single bird on the basis of probability.

You won't see many scoters at your local lake or pond, but if you are persistent, and don't overlook the one that does show up, your chances of spotting one eventually are fairly good. I learned a trick from an experienced local bird watcher that has dramatically increased the number of scoters I have found away from the coast — go out in bad weather.

Storms, fronts with showers, and ugly, rainy stuff drops birds out of the sky. Scoters fly overland and tend to stay high until they get to the coast, but if they hit bad weather they look for a place to ride it out. At a moment like that, any lake or river will do. The same weather that gets them down should get you up and out there looking.

GREBES

Horned, eared, and red-necked

EASIER AND HARDER THAN THEY LOOK

ALTHOUGH IDENTIFYING HORNED, EARED, AND RED-NECKED grebes in the spring and summer is not as easy as it may seem, given their bold breeding plumage, trying to identify these same species in winter plumage is even more challenging. But because most bird watchers in North America see these grebes in winter, we focus our attention here on their duller winter plumage.

RANGE

Range is less important as a clue in identifying grebes than it is for many species. On many field guide range maps, eared grebes are mapped as birds of the West; it should follow that any grebe in the East is a horned. The range maps are right, at least as far as the main ranges go, but they have little room for subtleties. There is more to the story of the eared grebe than the maps might tell you.

As bird watchers have become more aware of the field marks separating the two species, the number of eared grebes reported in the East has steadily increased. In fact, so many eared grebes have been spotted that the bird can be best described as rare but regular in the East.

Horned grebes breed from Alaska south to the United States–Canada border east to central Canada. They winter along both coasts and inland where there is open water. In migration they can be seen almost anywhere.

Eared grebes breed in the West from southern Canada south to the United States–Mexico border. They winter along the Pacific coast and along the western Gulf coast in small numbers. Most winter south of the

eared grebe
breeding plumage

eared grebe
winter adult

horned grebe
breeding plumage

horned grebe
winter adult

red-necked grebe
breeding plumage

red-necked grebe
winter adult

United States but can be found inland where there is open water. They are rare but regular throughout the eastern United States in migration and winter. You can find both species almost anywhere, and there is nowhere you can make the identification on range alone. This leaves us to focus on plumage and other field marks.

THE OTHER GREBES

First, make certain you are looking at a horned or eared grebe and not one of the other five species that occur in North America. In all but a few instances, this is straightforward.

Eliminating the two large grebes, western and Clark's, should be nearly automatic. Both are much larger, with long slender necks and long yellowish bills. You are more likely to confuse them with a loon than with a horned or eared grebe. But it's not that hard to confuse a winter horned grebe with a western grebe, until you really consider overall size: the western is 25 inches long and the horned is just 14.

The red-necked grebe is more similar to the horned and eared grebes than the swan-necked Clark's and western grebes are. Breeding-plumaged red-necked grebes have a rufous neck (as horned grebes do) but their pale silvery white cheek patch is striking. They lack golden ear panels or noticeable tufts. In winter, red-necked grebes fade to gray and white, sometimes with a trace of rust on the neck. The large cheek patch remains as a pale area behind the cheek. At a distance, the winter red-necked grebe has a dusky neck, as does the eared grebe; the horned grebe is overall a much whiter and cleaner-looking bird in winter plumage.

In structure, however, the red-necked grebe stands out. It's longer-necked, with a daggerlike bill. In overall shape and size, it looks almost loonlike. Compare its mostly yellow, heavy bill to the short, upturned bills of horned and eared grebes: the red-necked is a more substantial, considerably less cuddly-looking bird than either one. At close range, you can see the startling red eye that characterizes the horned and eared grebes; the red-necked's eye is dark.

Pied-billed grebes may give momentary confusion to the novice grebe watcher. With experience, however, pied-billed grebes become instantly recognizable. Their heads have a distinctive square, blocky look, accentuated by their distinctive short, thick, black-banded bills. Overall, pied-billed grebes are uniformly charcoal gray, lacking any white or pale zones on the throat or head. Take a good look at the next few pied-billed grebes you see, and these characteristics should add up to a watertight identification, even in low light.

The last species, the least grebe, is a tiny all-dark bird. It's limited in range to the lower Rio Grande Valley of Texas. It is even smaller and darker than the pied-billed and the adult least has a startling yellow eye. There's no mistaking the least grebe for anything else, though juvenile pied-billeds resemble them for a short while in their first fall.

GENERIC HORNED AND EARED GREBES

Horned and eared grebes are structurally similar. Both are fairly small, compact birds with relatively thin bills. Both have fairly short necks and often ride low in the water. Each feeds by diving and can disappear in the blink of an eye. When actively feeding, both can be hard to follow. They can travel surprising distances underwater, and it is impossible to predict where they might pop back up. Often they will surface for only a second or two, and, if you are not looking at the exact spot when it happens, you may get the impression that they are spending five or ten minutes at a time underwater and traveling hundreds of yards. Keeping track of a diving grebe frustrates even the most diligent observer.

In the West, eared grebes can sometimes be found in flocks numbering a million or more.

Both species can be found singly or in small flocks. Groups of horned grebes may seem more like loose assemblages than cohesive flocks. They congregate in decent-sized clumps at favored feeding sites, though counts of a hundred or more are fairly rare. Eared grebes, on the other hand, can sometimes be found in flocks numbering a million or more in their core range in the West, especially at California's Salton Sea. In the East, eareds are typically found in ones and twos, with flocks of a dozen or more much rarer.

SEPARATING THE TWO

The most useful differences between horned and eared grebes in non-breeding plumage are the pattern of the head and throat and the size and shape of the bill. There are other minor differences, but they are rarely instrumental in identification.

The first thing to look at is the pattern of the head and throat. The horned grebe in winter usually has an entirely white throat and chest that contrast sharply with dark gray sides, upperparts, and especially the sides and back of the neck. This bright white front is obvious and is usually visible at great distances, especially when the bird is facing you.

Eared grebes show almost no contrast on the breast and throat. The area is dingy gray, and only slightly lighter than the back, sides, upperparts, and back and sides of the neck. They are overall plain gray birds. They do, however, have a distinct pale area at the rear of the face. It is often rounded in a half-moon shape and sometimes extends to include more of the face or even the chin. This pale area is often a dingy white and lacks the high contrast visible on the horned grebe. The overall grayness of the face also reduces the contrast with the blackish crown, which comes down to slightly below the eye on eared grebes. The blackish crown on horned grebes ends at the eye and contrasts sharply with the white of the lower face.

If all this makes it sound like the two are fairly easy to tell apart, it's because many birds are. Some individuals that seem intermediate may be more difficult to identify, but they are exceptions, not standard.

YOUNG BIRDS

The birds most likely to cause trouble are juveniles in the fall and adults molting from breeding to winter plumage in the fall or back again in the spring. Horned grebes in these plumages can be similar to winter-plumaged eared grebes. They can usually be identified using other characters and by taking timing into account.

Juvenile horned grebes have a variably dusky throat and lack the bright contrast of adults. They usually have more white in the face than eared grebes, though, and the amount of contrast between the face and the dark cap is still different enough to be useful. More important, this juvenal plumage is gone by early November at the latest, which is about the time that horned grebes begin to show up outside the breeding grounds. As a result, this is a plumage few bird watchers even get a chance to see, let alone be confused by. The same is true for adults in transition from breeding to winter plumage in fall: seeing one is rare enough that most bird watchers won't get the opportunity to be confused by it.

MIGRATION TIMING

The timing of fall migration is actually a clue to identification. In general most birds seen south of the United States–Canada border before November are most likely eareds, even in the East. Eared grebes start their southerly fall migration about two months before horned grebes do.

In spring, eared grebes start north a bit later than horneds, but the differences are not as great and timing is not an important clue. In spring, both species begin molting into breeding plumage, and birds in transition can be seen almost anywhere. These are the birds most likely to cause confusion. Both have variably dusky necks, and the amount of white in the face varies, too — from a lot of white to almost none. For these birds you need to rely on other field marks, principally head and bill shape, as well as any evidence of breeding plumage that might show.

BILL SHAPE

Once you have seen a few of each species, the difference in bill shape becomes the most useful field mark separating the two. Experienced grebe watchers identify birds hundreds of yards away using only bill shape, even in bad light. And the birds often swim closer, confirming the identification.

Horned grebes have relatively straight, short, thin bills. Eared grebes have slightly longer and definitely thinner bills that angle slightly upward. This may not sound like much of a difference, but it is surprisingly easy to see in the field. The eared grebe's bill looks razor-thin and the slight upturn is usually obvious. The difference in length is emphasized by the yellow tip on the horned grebe's bill, which often can't be seen unless the bird is quite close. If you can see the yellow tip, then you are looking at a horned grebe. The eared grebe's bill is entirely dark.

HEAD SHAPE

Head shape can also be a useful mark, but is a little harder to judge. The heads of eared grebes appear peaked, with a distinct "bump" at the highest point of the head, right over the eye. This bump and the thin bill give them a delicate, steep-foreheaded look. The head of the horned grebe is fairly flat by comparison, with no peak above the eye. On many birds the difference in head shape is clear, but be careful: birds actively feeding and diving can have almost any head shape imaginable; head shape is more of a clue than a diagnostic field mark in those cases. Birds molting into breeding plumage are also hard to identify using head shape. Both horned and eared acquire bright yellowish feathers on the head that distort the shape. Head shape is most useful on birds in the fall and winter when they dive less often — which describes most of the grebes you will see anyway.

OTHER FIELD MARKS

There are several other smaller differences that can be used to confirm your identification, though you will almost certainly have decided which species it is before you can see them.

The first of these is the small yellow tip on the bill of the horned grebe mentioned above; it is present in all seasons. Another is the white spot between the eye and the base of the bill on winter-plumaged horned grebes. This area (the lores) is white on most horneds — if it is, you've got your identification. The absence of these marks may mean you're looking at an eared, but you need to use other field marks to be certain. Both are hard to see at any distance or in bad light, and some horneds lack the white spot.

One useful, though subjective, character is the relative thickness and length of the neck. Eared grebes have slightly longer, thinner necks than horneds. This difference becomes very obvious with experience. The eared grebe's longer, thinner neck, combined with its thinner bill and more peaked head, gives it a decidedly delicate and elegant look, especially in profile. The thicker, shorter-necked horned, with its flatter crown and stubbier bill, looks squatter, more compact, and, well, dumpier by comparison.

The standard cautions apply when looking at structural and relative field marks. Horned grebes on alert, with their necks stretched up, look slimmer. An eared with its head tucked down looks less elegant. First impressions should be supported by second, third, and even fourth looks. And if you just can't decide whether or not the bird is "elegant" enough to be an eared grebe, forget about impressions and look at the field marks.

BREEDING-PLUMAGED BIRDS

Going by the pictures, you would assume that separating the breeding-plumaged eared and horned grebes is a snap. Most of the time it is. It is not always as easy as it looks, however, and there are pitfalls that it helps to be aware of. Except in good light, the red throat of a horned can look as black as any eared. And what about the eared grebe's "ears" — those fine golden filoplumes on the sides of its head? They are very different from the solid yellow patch (the "horns") on horned grebes, but in the field they don't often look as different as a picture might lead you to believe. At any distance, both birds look essentially the same — like dark grebes with yellowish patches on the head. It can be even harder to spot the differences on birds that have been diving and have wet heads. The rest of the field marks will still be there, however, and you should always check them to confirm your identification. A lot of bird watchers are fooled by breeding-plumaged horned and eared grebes seen at a distance, and it is always a good idea to double-check your identification. Head and bill shape are good clues for sorting out the breeding-plumaged grebes, from the tiny, pointy heady and bill of the eared grebe to the streamlined head and daggerlike bill of the red-necked.

The next time you see a smallish grebe on your local pond or lake, give it a closer look, no matter where you are on the continent. Don't take any grebe for granted. ⌐

RING-NECKED DUCK AND SCAUP

The scoop on scaup

AFTER THE LEAVES HAVE TURNED, FALLEN, AND BEEN raked up, bird watchers often turn their attention to waterfowl. Small lakes, city parks, ponds, reservoirs, rivers, and creeks — all host ducks in fall and winter. One of the pleasures of waterfowl is that many are easy to identify, but even experienced bird watchers struggle with the identification of ring-necked duck, greater scaup, and lesser scaup.

Identifying these small ducks of the genus *Aythya* is challenging because there are not many useful plumage characters. This leaves size and shape, field marks that are hard to use without experience. Still, using shape as a field mark — especially the shape of the head and bill — is not as hard as you might think.

Many bird watchers deal with females in this group by using the first rule of duck identification. To identify female ducks, learn the field marks for the males. When you find a female, check which male is closest and call it that species. This works most of the time, but you will occasionally overlook the unexpected species. It is worth giving the females a closer look, though; for scaup several of the field marks for females (head shape, amount of white in the wings) are exactly the same as they are for males.

DISTRIBUTION

Scaup and ring-necked ducks are some of our most widespread waterfowl and at the right season can be found almost anywhere on the continent. Ring-necked ducks breed from eastern Alaska across central Canada and in the northern tier of the United States. They winter along the coasts from Canada south to the southern edge of the United States, and occasionally farther north in the Southeast and Southwest, where there is open water. Greater scaup breed from Alaska east across north central Canada to Hudson Bay. They winter along both coasts from Alaska to southern California and the Maritimes south to northern Florida, and in the Great Lakes. They are the rarest of the three to spot inland, but can occur anywhere during migration. Lesser scaup breed from Alaska south to Colorado, Minnesota, and Nevada. They winter from the United States–Canada border south through Mexico, avoiding the interior West. They are common inland, though they are limited by the availability of open water.

The same lake often hosts a mixed flock containing all three species, even though each has its favorite habitat. Ring-necked duck is almost exclusively a freshwater species and typically shuns brackish bays and estuaries. They seem to have a preference for wooded swamp habitats and smaller lakes. Lesser scaup usually prefer mid-sized lakes and ponds and avoid smaller bodies of water. They may be found in the fresher parts of bays and estuaries but often stick close to shore. Greater scaup are primarily coastal and occur in greatest numbers in bays, inlets, and estuaries of the Northeast. Inland, they are found on larger lakes and rivers, including the Great Lakes. Exceptions are common, though, and habitat is only a rough guide. Any one of these species may be found anywhere there is open water.

THE BASIC BIRD

As is true with almost all ducks, there are two basic plumages to deal with, male and female.

Known to hunters as bluebills or blackheads, male scaup (both lesser and greater) are boldly patterned with dark glossy heads, black breasts, flashing white flanks, and pale blue-gray bills. Male ring-necks are similar but are duller on the sides and easily separated by other characters.

Female birds of all three species are brown overall with whitish bellies, some white at the base of the bill, and backs that are slightly darker than the sides. Eye color is bright yellow.

With the exception of male ring-necked ducks, the key characters are

greater scaup
female

greater scaup
male

greater
scaup
male

lesser scaup
female

lesser
scaup
male

lesser scaup
male

ring-necked
duck
male

ring-necked duck
female

ring-necked duck
male

head shape, bill shape, body size, and wing stripes, and these particular characters are the same for all plumages.

Identifying scaup and ring-necks is often a comparative process because, at least in migration, they are regularly found together. Scaup are obliging, and you can often find greaters and lessers side by side, providing the opportunity to compare size and shape. A word of advice: practice helps, but make sure that the impressions you form are right from the start. If you misidentify the first lesser scaup as a greater, you'll throw off your whole day. Be sure to take advantage of occasions when you have both species available for comparison, and study the field marks. Males and females have the same shape, and if you learn the shape by looking at the easier-to-identify males, the females will become easier as well.

MALE RING-NECKED DUCKS

All three of these species have dark glossy heads, black breasts, bluish bills, and backs that are darker than the flanks. The easiest challenge in this group is separating male ring-necked ducks from male scaup.

Even at a distance, you can tell that ring-necked ducks have black backs compared to the whitish or grayish backs of male scaup. Scaup backs are actually finely barred with black, but at any distance the backs appear whitish or dusky, slightly darker than the gleaming white flanks. The flanks of the ring-necked duck are not gleaming white, but smooth gray, which means that the birds show less overall contrast. The key field mark is the stark finger of white that separates the black breast from the grayish sides. This field mark is unique and, under decent conditions, shows at great distances. If you see it on a distant black-and-white bird, you are looking at a male ring-necked duck. (Male green-winged teal show a similar white mark but they do not appear black and white even under the worst light conditions.)

Bill pattern is also useful in separating male ring-necked ducks from

It's important to study the head shape of the male ring-necked duck, because the female's is identical.

ring-necked duck
male

ring-necked duck
female

scaup. The bill of ring-necked ducks is blue-gray and has a thin, sharply defined white border at the base. The tip is black, bordered by a prominent white ring. Scaup lack the white border at the base of the bill and have a much smaller black patch on the tip of the bill. The area of black on the tip is referred to as the "nail" in most guides.

Because identifying most male ring-necks is easy, it provides a wonderful opportunity to study their shape — a key when it comes to identifying females. Concentrate on the high peak at the rear of the head, the fairly slender triangular bill, and the skinny neck. Lesser scaup, which more closely resemble the shape of ring-necked ducks, have a shorter peak on the head, a wider bill, and a thicker neck.

FEMALE RING-NECKS

Bill pattern is the best way to identify females. The bill is slightly duller than the bill of the male but in most conditions looks identical. The bold white ring near the tip is slightly smaller than on males but is still easily seen.

Female ring-necks also have a distinctive face pattern. Female scaup have mostly plain faces with clean-cut extensive white patches at the base of the bill. Female ring-necks, on the other hand, have a diffuse whitish area at the base of the bill which does not contrast nearly as much with the paler face. Because the face is pale and the top of the head is dark, they have a distinctly "capped" appearance, not found in scaup, that can often be seen at a considerable distance. At close range, note the small white eye-ring and the thin white line going back from the eye. At a distance, or in poor light, female redheads and ring-necked ducks might be confusing. Female redheads are uniformly plain and warm brown overall, while female ring-neckeds are grayer and show a dark cap and back. Female ring-neckeds also show areas of white in the face.

greater scaup
female

lesser scaup
female

The same structural differences that apply to males also apply to females. Ring-necks of all ages and plumages show a very high peak on the rear of the crown, making the head appear almost triangular. The shape is quite distinctive once you are used to seeing it. Less obvious, but worth looking for, is the thinner, more triangular bill, and the longer, thinner neck of the ring-necked.

SEPARATING THE SCAUP

Telling the lesser and greater scaup apart is one of the great challenges in waterfowl identification. Even experienced bird watchers sometimes have to throw up their hands and walk away from an individual bird. The key field marks are head shape, bill shape and pattern, and, on flying birds, the wing stripe. Less useful, but worth looking at, are the size and thickness of the neck. There are also a few characters that apply only to males, which will be discussed later. The following field marks apply to both males and females.

The challenge depends in large part on where you are. If you are inland, the trick is to find the one or two greater scaup in the flock of lessers. If you are along the coast, the situation is frequently reversed. It is *usually* safe to assume that inland flocks are almost all lessers. It is *always* wise to double check, however.

HEAD SHAPE

Head shape is by far the most reliable field mark for differentiating between sitting scaup. There are pitfalls, however, and experience and practice are crucial. Almost all field guides tell you to look for the rounded head on greater scaup and the pointed or peaked crown on lesser scaup. This is the key field mark, but it's important to understand exactly what it means. On greater scaup, the head appears blocky. The crown rises almost vertically from the base of the bill. There is a peak at the forward part of the slightly rounded but mostly flat crown, and a smoothly rounded corner at the rear of the head. The result is a bird with a steep forehead and an almost square head shape.

Lesser scaup have a head that is more angular, less rounded. The forehead rises at a sloping angle from the base of the bill toward the middle of the head. Just behind the middle of the head is a small tuft of feathers, which often forms a slight peak, and sometimes forms a tuft that sticks out at the rear of the crown. The back of the head slopes gently down to the neck. Although the head is peaked at the rear like the ring-necked duck's, the peak is not as prominent and the head not as distinctly triangular as the ring-necked's. The overall impression is of a peaked, roughly triangular, slightly tufted head on lesser scaup.

Caveat time. Anyone watching feeding scaup will notice that head shapes seem to change with every posture the duck assumes. The most striking of these head shape changes occurs just before a dive, when both species sleek their heads down to be as streamlined as possible. Under these conditions, lesser scaup can look every bit as round-headed as greater scaup. Conversely, a preening greater scaup, with its head feathers all fluffed up, may assume an almost peaked appearance to the crown. If you are comparing the relative head shapes of scaup in a flock, make sure that the birds are in similar poses and doing similar things.

The lesser scaup has a peaked, triangular, slightly tufted head compared with the rounded head of the greater scaup.

Many experienced birders prefer to watch sleeping scaup. When they aren't diving, milling about, or sleeking and unsleeking their heads, their head shape is easy to gauge. The peak at the rear of the crown of the lesser scaup tends to stick out especially far when the birds are sleeping, and it looks like a folded-over tuft. Greater scaup retain their round or block-headed shape and never show a peaked or tufted look while asleep.

Another caveat here is that though using head shape as a field mark makes greater scaup the easy one to pick out, it can make ring-necked duck harder to spot, because the peaked head shape of the ring-necked duck closely resembles that of lesser scaup on sleeping birds.

NECK SHAPE

The head of greater scaup seems enormous, but it is not proportionately larger than the thick neck. The lesser scaup has a relatively skinny neck, and its triangular head seems to sit on its scrawny neck a bit like a golf ball on a tee.

SIZE

The greater scaup averages 10 to 15 percent larger in body size than the lesser scaup and this difference is readily apparent in direct comparison. When birds are not present for comparison, though, size is useless, and trying to guess at size relative to other species is fraught with problems.

WING PATTERN

The wing pattern is most easily seen on flying birds, but it can sometimes be glimpsed when a swimming bird sits up high and flaps its wings. If you watch a flock of scaup long enough, most birds will eventually sit up and flap.

Both species have pale wing stripes that run along the trailing edge of the wing, formed by white bases on the flight feathers (primaries and secondaries). On greater scaup the wing stripe is white from the body to the end of the wing, although the size of the white stripe is reduced at the tip; the wing stripe narrows. The key is that it is all one color. On lesser scaup, the inner half of the wing stripe (closest to the body) is bright white, but the outer half is gray. The result is a distinctly two-toned wing stripe. Under less than optimum conditions the outer end of the stripe is hard to see, making it look like the bird has half a wing stripe or a white patch on the inner half of the wing.

greater scaup
male

lesser scaup
male

The wing stripe is the only easily used, completely reliable plumage difference between greater and lesser scaup, and it applies equally to males and females. If you are at all uncertain about the identification of a bird based on other characters, try to hang in there until it flaps or flies.

The ring-necked duck's wing stripe is entirely pale gray in all plumages.

BILL PATTERN

Bill pattern is the single best field mark in separating the ring-necked duck from scaup, and it can help in separating scaup from each other as well. The difference between scaup bills is subtle and requires good head-on views and an understanding of bill shape. Both species of scaup have mostly pale bills with a small protuberance on the tip, like a fold-over tab for holding sheets of paper together. This small tab, the nail, is black in both species and in all plumages. On greater scaup, however, it is almost twice as large as it is on lesser scaup, and thus proportionately much larger relative to overall bill size. Furthermore, on greater scaup, the black bleeds off the sides of the nail to the area around the bill tip. On lesser scaup, the black is confined to the tip and can be hard to see, especially if the bird is not facing you.

BILL SHAPE

Harder to gauge, but easier to see at a distance, is the difference in bill shape between the two species. In addition to the proportionately larger head, neck, and overall body size, greater scaup also have a proportionately larger bill than lesser scaup. The tip is broad and slightly spatulate, and the base of the bill is thick and substantial when seen from above or from the side. The result is somewhat reminiscent of the bill of blue-winged teal. Lesser scaup have a much smaller bill that tapers to a less spatulate tip.

ADDITIONAL FIELD MARKS
FOR ADULT MALE SCAUP

These field marks are of use only for separating adult male scaup in breeding (non-eclipse) plumage. They are of little use for immature male scaup, so be sure that the birds observed have glossy heads, well-defined black breasts, whitish sides, and finely barred whitish backs. Immature male scaup invariably have some brown feathering, which is not present on adult males in breeding plumage.

Flank color. In addition to the striking flank (side) pattern which distinguishes male ring-necked ducks from scaup, flank pattern can also be useful for telling adult males of the scaup species apart. Greater scaup have much whiter sides than lesser, especially on the upper flanks, where greater scaup show a sharp definition between the white sides and the finely barred back. The upper sides of lesser scaup are very finely barred. The result is that the side plumage appears to blend gradually into the back, lacking the sharp distinction between sides and back shown on greater scaup.

Back pattern. Back pattern is also of use in separating the scaup, although it is not a primary field mark. Greater scaup appear to have a whiter back, the result of finer black lines over the white back. Lesser scaup have thicker bars on the back, making the birds look slightly darker above. Not surprisingly, it requires a close view to be certain of the difference.

Head color. Useful only on adult males and often more misleading than it is helpful, head color is one of the most frequently mentioned field marks in field guides. Iridescent colors, such as those of a scaup's head, are highly influenced by light conditions, which can make usually green heads look purple. Study a male mallard's head to see how tricky iridescence is. The mallard's head is much more intensely green than the heads of scaup, but it is not at all hard to pick up purplish or bluish reflections on the head of a mallard in the right light. With this in mind, remember that scaup heads are essentially blackish with a faint cast of iridescence in perfect light.

With that said, we can repeat what the field guides say: lesser scaup and ring-necked duck heads usually look purplish, and those of greater scaup look greenish — but unless you have a close look at the bird from every angle, don't use head color as diagnostic.

Notice the trend in the above field marks: greater scaup are "greater" in every respect. Greater scaup are larger, their bills are larger and wider, the nails on their bills are larger, their wing stripes are larger, they have more white on their sides, and their heads have more area (being rounder).

The next time you go duck watching you may find ring-necked ducks to be fairly straightforward, even the females. If you are still vexed by scaup, though, do not be surprised. This is one of the toughest identification problems in North America, and it remains an issue for even the most experienced birders. Concentrate on really studying birds of known identification, learning their shapes, and studying the two species when you have them together. Eventually, with enough careful looking, the big round-headed birds will stand out like pink flamingos on a lawn . . . well, almost. And once you have learned the difference, you may find that at least some of the birds on the local pond are not what you expected.

TEAL

How to identify our appealing teal — male and female

LATE FALL AND EARLY WINTER ARE IDEAL TIMES TO GO out and look at ducks, at least in much of North America. By early December the mature males will be in their fancy breeding dress while many other bird families are still wearing their cryptic winter plumages, and will be for months.

Ducks are a good group to study for a number of reasons, beginning with the fact that they tend to be out in the open where you can really watch them, especially if you have access to a spotting scope or live near a park or protected area where you can see them at close range. Such leisurely views are a refreshing contrast to the glimpses we typically get of songbirds as they flit between leaves and other cover.

Among our North American ducks, the three commonly observed teal species — *Anas crecca, A. discors,* and *A. cyanoptera* — stand out. They are better known to most of us as green-winged teal, blue-winged teal, and cinnamon teal, respectively.

Note that these three species aren't necessarily more closely related to each other than they are to other "dabbling ducks" (their relatives in *Anas*), including mallard, black and mottled ducks, gadwall, pintail, the wigeons, and northern shoveler. "But wait," I hear many of you saying, "Isn't teal a blue-green or green-blue color?" Well, yes it is, as even a quick perusal of the L.L.Bean catalog will demonstrate. And, yes, the teal have blue or green in their wings (cinnamon and blue-winged have both), but so do many other ducks. The northern shoveler has a wing pattern that looks nearly identical to that of blue-winged and cinnamon teal, for example. It seems every bit as similar to them as they do to the green-winged teal, which has quite different wing markings. Still, names are powerful things, and because three of the dabblers share the English moniker "teal," they are strongly associated in most birders' minds and make a useful grouping.

DICHROMATIC DUCKS

One of the striking characteristics of most dabbling ducks, including our three teal, is their pronounced sexual dimorphism (or, more specifically, dichromatism): the males and females look dramatically different from each other. But while most of the adult males (drakes) have unique plumages that fairly shout their specific identity, the females (hens) look so similar that many birders rarely attempt to identify them. After all, there's usually a drake lurking nearby, so why bother?

It makes sense that female ducks are a classic identification problem.

Like so many things in life, from cleaning the house to getting out for a brisk walk, you'll feel better once you do. Not only will you increase (probably more than twofold) your chances of turning up something unusual, but you'll also be better able to interpret and enjoy the fairly complex social behavior of ducks.

THE DRAKES

Before we plunge into those streaky brown female/immature/eclipse teal, let's spend just a moment looking at the drakes — the adult males in breeding plumage. You don't need any help to tell these three apart — they are as different in appearance as cardinals and blue jays — but I would encourage you to look beyond the most obvious field marks.

The only thing many of us know about the blue-winged teal is that it has a white facial crescent and dark blue-gray head. But there's a lot more going on. Look at the many tiny black dots and bars that lend a lovely, almost wood-grained appearance to the beige sides, and how those sides are separated from the black undertail by a startling patch of

common teal
male

green-winged teal
male

green-winged teal
female

cinnamon teal
male

cinnamon teal
female

blue-winged teal
male

blue-winged teal
female

pure white. And what about the cinnamon teal's glaring red eye, or the way that the green eye patch on the green-winged teal glows purple-blue in certain lights? All of these beautiful details are lost to those who stop at the most obvious field marks.

Looking closely at a group of drake green-winged teal is likely to net you another nice surprise, at least in some regions. You might find a bird that doesn't have a white vertical spike jutting up into its breast, but instead has a horizontal white line where its sides meet its back. Versed as you will have become in drake teal, you might also note that its green face patch has thicker whitish outlines, and it has a paler area where the gray flanks meet the black and buff undertail. This would be the Eurasian, or common teal (or just "the teal," as the British call it), *Anas crecca crecca*. Considered by many to be a distinct species, this form is worth noting and reporting whenever and wherever it appears.

It makes sense that female ducks are a classic identification problem. They have evolved cryptic, visually disruptive plumages that help them escape predation, especially at the nest. Note, too, that juveniles of both sexes, and even drakes during their post-breeding molt (which renders them flightless for several weeks), also wear henlike camouflage. In drakes, this relatively brief period of summer drabness is called "eclipse plumage," a term that often causes considerable head scratching among new field guide users. It's the female teal that pose the real identification challenge, and once you've got them down, the other age and sex categories will present you with few problems.

FACE PATTERN

Many of the female puddle ducks have variations on the same face pattern that you can observe on female mallards at any local park. A plain brownish gray face, on close inspection consisting of many small dark streaks against a paler background, is crossed by a rather bold dark line. This line runs from the base of the bill across the eye to, or, as in the mallard, toward the nape. Above this eye line is a pale line (the superciliary), which is usually the same tone as the cheeks. The crown is dark, accentuating the eyebrowed look.

Blue-winged and green-winged teal are good examples of this classic female *Anas* face pattern. The blue-winged adds an extra touch, sporting whitish eye crescents. The cinnamon teal has a suggestion of face pattern, but it is considerably clouded, like that of the wigeon and pintail hens.

WINGS AND BODY PLUMAGE

Both blue-winged and cinnamon teal hens share sky blue "shoulders" or lesser coverts and dull greenish speculums. With such similar wing patterns, it's best to rely on other cues, such as overall body size and bill shape. Green-winged teal of both sexes have a brilliant speculum that flashes like a green neon sign, proclaiming their identity.

Green-winged teal have a unique field mark: a pale streak, usually buffy, that runs along the sides of the undertail coverts. Green-winged drakes have a dark frame around the buff, making it more noticeable, but it is also present on all green-wingeds. Oddly, birders often refer to the undertail region of ducks as the "butt," an anthropomorphism that I can recall being used only with ducks and gallinaceous birds.

BEHAVIORAL CLUES

Compared with blue-winged and cinnamon, the green-winged teal is notably smaller, with a shorter neck and smaller bill. It often forms good-sized flocks of several dozen birds and is regularly seen walking about on mud flats and shorelines. The other teal appear to prefer swimming and commonly travel in groups of a few pair. Green-wings beat their wings quite rapidly and do a good deal of twisting as they fly, showing their backs, then their bellies (which are white), then their backs, and so on. The other teal fly more steadily and slowly, giving a fairly constant view of their profile.

Of course, behavioral marks like these are more fluid than feather details and would not, by themselves, be a firm basis for an identification. But that doesn't make them less useful in practice, and noting such distinctions will increase your skill at identification and your enjoyment of bird watching.

Blue-winged teal are, in some respects, intermediate between green-winged and cinnamon, especially in their structure. The green-winged is compact and diminutive, whereas the cinnamon is more massive and rangy-looking. In fact, with its long, heavy, somewhat spatulate bill, the cinnamon teal looks more than a little like a miniature northern shoveler. The cinnamon's face pattern tends to be indistinct and reduced in extent; the blue-winged teal has the sharpest, most high-contrast face of the bunch.

Once you have a handle on teal, you'll find it easier to progess to deeper knowledge of all dabbling ducks.

Once you've got a handle on the teal, you'll find it much easier to progress to a deeper knowledge of all the dabbling ducks. Then you can go on to the various diving ducks and other waterfowl. Start looking more closely at ducks, both the handsome drakes and their more subtle companions — your efforts are bound to be rewarded. ✦

WINTER LOONS

Knowing that a bird is a loon
IS FAIRLY EASY. KNOWING WHICH LOON IS WHICH IN WINTER IS A BIT TOUGHER.

THE EERIE WAIL AND ABRUPT TREMOLO OF THE ADULT common loon could scarcely be mistaken for any other living thing. A silent juvenile common loon sitting on a lake in winter, however, can be mistaken for several things. Identifying a loon is easy enough with a little practice, but deciding which loon you are looking at can be difficult, because in most places in the United States at least two or three loon species are reasonable possibilities.

THE PLAYERS

North America has five loon species: common, red-throated, Pacific, Arctic, and yellow-billed. The first three are by far the most widespread and commonly encountered loons in North America. These large waterbirds are most common in winter, when their plumages are highly confusing.

Most North American loons spend the breeding season in the Far North; only the common loon's breeding range includes the northernmost fringe of the continental United States. In winter, though, this distribution changes. The Arctic loon is an accidental species in most of North America, and yellow-billed loons winter along the northern reaches of the Pacific coast. The Pacific loon's winter range extends as far south as the Baja peninsula in Mexico, and common and red-throated loons winter along both the Atlantic and Pacific coasts. Let's look more closely at these five loon species.

The common loon, as the name implies, is widespread and occurs throughout the United States in migration and along both coasts in winter. It's the only loon that's common in winter on the Gulf Coast and is the most frequently encountered species in North America. If you see a loon on any inland body of water, it is likely to be a common.

The yellow-billed loon is an Arctic breeder that winters from the southern coast of Alaska to northern California, though sightings in the southern end of this range are fairly rare. Although it vaguely resembles the common loon, it is easily distinguished from other loon species, first by its namesake yellow bill, and then by its size (it's our largest loon), structure, and plumage.

The red-throated loon is North America's smallest loon and regularly winters along both the Atlantic and Pacific coasts. It occurs sparingly inland, and can turn up just about anywhere in the lower forty-eight states, especially during migration.

The aptly named Pacific loon is found commonly along the Pacific coast during winter, but is also a rare vagrant along the East Coast and an even rarer one in between. Pacific and Arctic are both medium-sized loons and were, until recently, considered a single species.

The Arctic loon is primarily an Old World species whose range just barely spills over into western Alaska, but is accidental everywhere else on the continent. As you might guess with any recently split species, Arctic and Pacific loons are very similar in appearance, though the Arctic is larger than the Pacific, more angular, and exhibits a noticeable white patch at the waterline along the flanks in all plumages.

In this chapter, we'll examine the three most commonly occurring species, common, red-throated, and Pacific loons in winter and juvenal plumages.

LOON ID CHALLENGES

Loon identification can be difficult, not only because the birds are similar, but also because of the circumstances under which we observe them. Loons seldom swim close to shore, especially in winter, and even when they do they may be obscured by wave action. Diving and flying birds allow only brief views. At rest, loons may not always exhibit typical loon posture (an upward-tilting bill), which further complicates any attempt at

red-throated loon
juvenile

red-throated loon
adult,
nonbreeding

Pacific loon
adult, nonbreeding

common loon
adult, nonbreeding

identification. Combine these birds' unreliable behavior and appearance with any adverse weather conditions, and it should be little wonder that so many birds in this group are misidentified. In winter, these three species can give even experienced birders the fits.

START WITH SIZE

As with many identification challenges, the best place to begin is with the size of the loon in question. One's impression of a bird's size is usually formed concurrently with a sense of its structure or shape. This combined impression is often referred to as "giss," an acronym for "general impression, size, and shape," sometimes pronounced by birders as "jizz." When you encounter a winter loon, the first question to ask yourself is, "Is the bird large, medium, or small?" Even a general guess at the bird's size can be a good start. Here's how our three common winter loons are sized.

LARGE, MEDIUM, AND SMALL

The common loon has a big, thick bill and big, blocky, angular head with a thick neck and heavy chest. The angle of its forehead is quite steep, and the bird may look as though its head is double-peaked, with one obvious peak at the front, just behind the base of the bill, and another, less obvious, at the rear of the crown. These angles are what lend the common loon its block-headed look.

When you see a common, you should be immediately struck by the fact that it is a large bird. This impression can be a good way to rule out the noticeably smaller red-throated and Pacific loons.

The Pacific loon is the next largest of our three commonly encountered loons. It measures about the same as a red-throated loon in length and wingspan, but outweighs it by a fifth or so. At rest on the water, the Pacific affects quite a different shape than the common. Many birders think of the Pacific as being a "medium" — halfway between the heavy, chunky common and the small, delicate red-throated. The Pacific loon has a noticeably thicker neck, larger head, and thicker bill than the red-throated, but it has nothing like the hulking appearance of a common loon. The Pacific loon's rounded head and thick neck are its most obvious features.

The red-throated loon is the smallest of the three widespread loon species. At rest on the water the bird looks slender, with a narrow body and a rather long neck that is typically held straight. The head is small, with a peak located at the rear of the crown. The bill is thin and fine when compared to the bills of the common and Pacific loons, and has an upturned look not shared by the others. Overall, the red-throated loon is almost pin-headed in comparison.

LOONS IN FLIGHT

Flying loons are fast-moving creatures, so you need to think fast to make your identification. Two helpful field marks are overall shape and the thickness of the neck, head, and bill.

In flight, size and structure are easier to gauge, and the common loon becomes noticeably different from the red-throated and Pacific loons. You can see the common loon's large feet spread out and dangling behind the bird as it flies. The trailing legs, large head, and thick neck give it a flight silhouette that shows as much body in front of the wings as behind them.

The flight styles of the three loons differ as well. Common loons hold their wingtips more vertically, more perpendicular to their bodies than red-throated or Pacific loons, both of which keep their wings backswept in flight. Common loons have more deliberate and shallower wingbeats than the other two, and it is not uncommon to see them flying with their bills slightly open. Pacific loons in flight are less bulky than commons and noticeably bulkier than red-throateds. Pacifics also have a shorter, thicker neck than red-throateds, so they look heavier in the front and less pin-headed or fine-billed.

The red-throated loon's fine bill, small head, and skinny neck are fairly obvious in flight. The head appears merely as an extension of the neck and is only slightly wider. Winter adults show a distinctive white face and neck that are immediately recognizable. Red-throated holds its neck rather low in flight compared with the other species, which hold their heads out straight from the body. Furthermore, red-throated loons appear a little more agile, with thinner wings and faster, deeper wingbeats than either common or Pacific loons, and red-throated's wings are more swept back.

Winter loons in flight

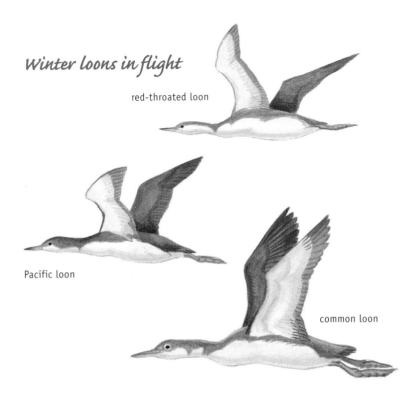

red-throated loon

Pacific loon

common loon

AGE AND PLUMAGE

If you have the opportunity to study a winter loon at length, then you may enjoy trying to figure out its age. The small and medium-sized loons — red-throated, Pacific, and Arctic — require two years to reach adulthood. The larger common and yellow-billed loons require three.

There are four plumages illustrated in most field guides for loons: breeding adult (held from spring through fall), nonbreeding adult (winter plumage, held from August or September through March or April), first summer (held by birds that are one or two years old, and not yet in adult plumage), and juvenal (worn by juvenile birds from fall until their first spring). All this information about plumages and age is at least confusing, if not intimidating, to most bird watchers. It can be difficult to remember the finer details of first-summer-plumaged Pacific loons — that's why we carry field guides. So let's boil things down to the most general terms.

During the nonbreeding plumage season, most North American loons are a combination of light and dark, with the lightest parts being white and the dark ones being anywhere from a pale gray to nearly black. The red-throated loon is typically the palest, appearing quite white in the face, with a paler appearance overall than the other species. Juvenile red-throated loons have a dusky neck, but still give an overall pallid impression. A smallish loon with a mostly white neck is likely to be a red-throated. Pacific loons in nonbreeding plumage always show the darkest or blackest backs and a distinct vertical contrast between the white throat and the black nape (or back of the neck). The dark "chinstrap" on a winter adult Pacific loon is another distinctive feature. Nonbreeding common loons show the messiest necks (the pattern is not as distinct as Pacific's), but almost always with a hint of the breeding adult's banded or collared neck. Many field guides point out the white around the common loon's eye, which is a good mark for birds nearby, but not visible on flying or distant individuals. Remember that all loons can show pale flanks and each species is known to hold the bill at an uptilted angle, so strict reliance on these clues can be misleading.

Should you encounter one of the two uncommon loons — yellow-billed or Arctic — it will most likely be in winter, or nonbreeding, plumage. If you should be so lucky (and you've eliminated common, Pacific, and red-throated loons as possibilities), consider the size of the bird first. The yellow-billed loon is a giant. If your bird is only mid-sized, look for the telltale white flanks of the Arctic loon. Then grab your camera to document the sighting and alert your fellow birders!

Flights of loons can be observed along both coasts during migration and in winter, and these times are wonderful opportunities to compare the shapes of two or three species. The first few hours of the day are the best times to see them. Even when the birds are far off, you can often spot the structural differences that separate them. A sea watch is a good way to learn the differences in size and shape between loons and cormorants and grebes, which often have similar appearances. 🪶

BROWN HERONS

Don't let the brown get you down!

WHAT, YOU ARE WONDERING, IS HE TALKING ABOUT?

There are white herons, blue herons, and green herons, even tri-colored herons, but there are no brown herons. Actually, there are three brown herons, and for most bird watchers they are as much of a challenge as the white ones.

The confusion comes because two of them are night-herons that are brown only in their first year, and one of them is the bittern, a member of the heron family often overlooked because of its name. Immature black-crowned and yellow-crowned night-herons and American bitterns of all ages look confoundingly similar in the field. It is a problem to which field guides tend to give short shrift. There are, however, fairly easy and reli-able field marks for both sitting and flying birds, and because the group is small, these clues are not hard to remember.

WHEN AND WHERE

Two of the species, American bittern and black-crowned night-heron, are widespread and can be encountered almost anywhere on the continent from central and southern Canada south. American bitterns breed south to the central United States. Most winter in the southern tier of states, but in migration they can show up anywhere, and a few winter well north of the mapped range. The same is true of black-crowned night-herons, although they breed to the southern edge of the country and beyond. The yellow-crowned night-heron is more restricted in its range, limited in summer primarily to the southeastern United States. They winter mostly

WADING BIRDS

yellow-crowned
night-heron
juveniles

black-crowned
night-heron
juveniles

American bittern
adults

in Florida and south, but a few stay farther north. Both night-herons wander after the breeding season, and yellow-crowneds have been seen well north and west of the breeding range in summer and fall. Almost anywhere on the continent that you encounter one of the "brown" herons, you need to consider all three options.

THE BASIC BROWN HERON

All three share characteristics that separate them from other birds. They are medium to medium-small (for herons), basically brown, proportionately short-legged and thick-necked, and have yellowish green legs. Both night-herons are quite distinctive in adult plumage and can be easily identified using any field guide. It is the first-year plumage of the night-herons that is so similar to the American bittern and to each other, and that is the focus here.

One other area of possible confusion is the juvenile green heron, which is also brownish, chunky, and streaked with brown below. The confusion should be only temporary. Green herons are small compared to the others; the bill is proportionately long and thin; the face is reddish; and the streaking on the underparts is darker and more of a contrast because of its white chest and belly. The key is size, however. Green herons, about the size of crows, are tiny, at least in the heron world.

TELLING NIGHT-HERONS FROM BITTERNS

The first step in the which-is-it process is to decide if you are looking at a bittern or a night-heron. On sitting birds this means looking at the bill, the head, the underparts, and the upperparts.

COMPARE BILLS

Compared with night-herons, bitterns have relatively long, thin, pointed bills, and in direct comparison, the difference is easily noticed. They also have mostly pale, yellowish bills, which eliminates the yellow-crowned night-heron, though it is similar to the bill of young black-crowneds.

CHECK THE HEAD AND FACE

When circumstances don't permit confident assessment of the bill, look at the face pattern. Bitterns have a strong dark mustache that borders the bottom of the face and goes down to the shoulder, a mark that is completely absent on night-herons. First-year bitterns have a slightly reduced mustache, both in size and darkness, but the pattern is still there.

UNDERPARTS

At first glance, the underparts of all three appear similar — basically buffy with darker brown streaks. On bitterns, though, the streaking is almost always more obvious and a little darker, broader, and cleaner looking than on night-herons.

UPPERPARTS

The quick and dirty way to tell the difference is the upperparts. On both night-herons the brownish upperparts are moderately to heavily spotted with white, and the upperparts of the bittern are finely mottled brownish with no white spots. One word of caution is needed regarding an otherwise easy-to-see field mark: some young night-herons, especially late in the year, become worn, and the white spotting is not as evident or extensive, although it should always be present. When a bird is seen from the side or from behind, the wingtips can be helpful, because on bitterns they are darker than the rest of the upperparts. On a sitting bird, the wingtips are the feathers that overlay the tail and are nearly blackish on most bitterns.

CHECK WINGS IN FLIGHT

Flying brown herons are harder to identify. Still, most of them can be identified if you get a half-decent look. If you see a flying brown heron, look first at the upperside of the wings. On bitterns, the outer half of the wing is very dark, almost black, and contrasts sharply with the browner inner half. Along the trailing edge of the wing, the dark plumage goes almost all the way to the body and the pattern is striking and obvious. On young night-herons the wings are much plainer, entirely medium to pale brown on black-crowneds, and darker with only a hint of bitternlike pattern on yellow-crowneds. While yellow-crowneds show darkish wing tips, the pattern is nowhere near as extensive or striking as it is on bitterns. In addition, young yellow-crowneds are much darker overall than bitterns, and they have chunky heads and the thickest, shortest bill in the group.

HABITAT AND BEHAVIOR

Habitat and habits can help separate bitterns from night-herons, but they are rarely diagnostic. Bitterns are definitely skulkers, rarely seen in the open. They are most often spotted at the edges of marshes, half in the reeds, often displaying the characteristic bittern pose: bill pointing skyward, body stretched out, unmoving. Any bird in this posture is almost surely a bittern, but I have seen bitterns feeding in the open (although this is rare), and once I even saw one standing in the middle of a mud flat, undoubtedly confused. Night-herons, despite their name and despite the fact that they are often active at night, can be seen at any time of day. Herons and bitterns share marshes, but birds along streams and feeding at the edge of open water are almost always night-herons rather than bitterns.

TELLING YOUNG NIGHT-HERONS APART

For a long time field guides made this seem harder than it is. The field marks usually emphasized were the slightly shorter, thicker bill and the slightly darker overall look of young yellow-crowneds, and the white spotting on the back and wings of sitting birds. Flying birds weren't even touched.

YELLOWS ARE DARKER

It is true, young yellow-crowned night-herons are slightly darker overall than young black-crowneds, and the white spotting on the back and wings of yellow-crowneds is smaller and finer looking. The focus on these field marks leaves a lot of bird watchers unable to decide which night-heron they are seeing. There are far better, quicker ways of telling the two apart.

BILL IS BEST MARK

The best field mark is the bill. Not only is the yellow-crowned's bill noticeably shorter and thicker, but it is a different color than that of the black-crowned. Size may be relative, but color is not, and the difference is usually easy to see even at a distance.

Young yellow-crowned night-herons have a black or almost all black bill. On some birds there is an area of yellow at the base of the lower mandible, but it is small and often hard to see even if it is present. Young black-crowned night-herons have a mostly pale yellow bill, with only a small area of dark at the tip and a thin line of dark running along the top edge. The dark spots are often hard to see, leaving the impression of a pale yellow bill. When you are uncertain about all other characters, bill color solves the problem.

OTHER FIELD MARKS

There are some other subtle differences between the two that can help. Yellow-crowneds are proportionately longer legged than their relatives, and they feed in deeper water than black-crowneds much of the time. The head of the yellow-crowned is slightly rounder and the neck proportionately longer and a little thinner. (These characters are not much help when a yellow-crowned has its neck pulled in, or a black-crowned is stretching.) The spotting on the upperparts is finer on yellow-crowneds, the throat and breast are usually darker, and the face seems to be streaked with fine white lines. The face of black-crowneds usually looks buffy with fine brownish, not white, streaks. Individual variations require that some caution be exercised in using these characters, although on the majority of birds the differences are obvious.

Separating flying young night-herons is the hardest challenge in this group. If you have seen a flying brown heron and have decided it is not a bittern, you are left with the two night-herons.

Overall darkness is a clue. Young yellow-crowneds are usually darker than young black-crowneds, and even in flight you can sometimes tell the difference. Distance and lighting can make it hard to be sure, however. The longer, thinner neck and the shorter, thicker bill and slightly rounder head can help as well, but these field marks are subjective and require practice with both species.

There is a subtle difference in wing pattern as well. Young yellow-crowneds have a hint of the bittern pattern, with slightly darker wingtips and sometimes a slightly darker trailing edge to the wing in flight. The difference is real but can be hard to judge and should be used as a supplement to other characters.

CHECK LEGS ON FLYING BIRDS

One characteristic that older field guides mention is the longer legs of the yellow-crowned. In flight, the whole foot extends beyond the tail and is often visible. On black-crowneds, the shorter legs do not extend beyond the tail, although the toes might. This field mark can be very useful — or completely useless — depending on the circumstances, but you should always check flying birds to see if the legs look proportionately long and stick out beyond the tail.

BILL COLOR IN FLIGHT

On flying birds the best field mark is often, surprisingly, bill color. Even at a distance, the pale bill of young black-crowneds usually shows, as does the black bill on young yellow-crowneds. I have looked at a lot of young flying black-crowned night-herons after being told about this field mark, and most of the time you can see the difference without much trouble.

The next time you spot a brown heron, or flush one from the edge of a marsh, make a quick check of the bill and wings. If the bird is cooperative and you get the chance to study the finer points, do so, but even if the look is fleeting you should be able to feel confident about the identification using these clues. ❱

WHITE HERONS

Sorting out the subtle differences among the white herons

WHAT DIFFERENTIATES A HERON FROM AN EGRET? NOTHING, really. They are all members of the family Ardeidae, which also includes the bitterns and night-herons. In a very casual sense, herons are dark and egrets are white, but as we'll see, there are lots of holes in this definition.

There are three species of long-necked wading birds in North America that are predominently white throughout their entire lives: great egret, snowy egret, and cattle egret. Little blue heron is white its first year, then dark thereafter. Another two species, reddish egret and great blue heron, include a number of individuals that are white at all ages, though most are always dark.

The white form of great blue heron, which has at times been considered a separate species, makes up a tiny, geographically restricted fraction of the population. Found primarily in saltwater habitats around the southern tip of Florida, the so-called great white heron is never encountered by the vast majority of North American birders. Be aware, though, that a few great whites have been found at scattered places up and down the Atlantic coast.

Turning to the five more widespread white wader species, there are several basic approaches to sorting them out. Most of us prefer to latch on to "field marks," in the most restrictive sense: literally how birds are marked or colored, either on their feathers or skin. This approach is easy and fast. When it works, it's great fun—you can dispatch your identification problems with the self-assurance of Harrison Ford shooting the

cattle egret

snowy egret
immature

little blue heron
immature

reddish egret
white morph

great egret

sword-wielding thug in *Raiders of the Lost Ark*. But, alas (and thank good-ness), things aren't always like they are in the movies.

Ask most birders how to identify a snowy egret, and 999 out of a thou-sand will mention yellow toes, or "golden slippers." Ask them how to identify a snowy egret with its feet under water or otherwise obscured, and an awful lot of them will be at a loss.

WHAT WE KNOW

First, let's list the field marks that might be called the least you need to know about white waders. Then we'll set about enlarging our vision of each member of the group, arming you for a much wider array of field situations.

SNOWY EGRET has golden slippers (and black stockings).
IMMATURE LITTLE BLUE HERON looks like snowy, but has greenish legs and feet.
CATTLE EGRET is small and stocky and has a yellow-orange bill; it likes fields where livestock are grazing.
GREAT EGRET also has a yellow-orange bill, but is very large, while still seeming graceful.
WHITE-MORPH REDDISH EGRET races around like a drunken, spastic clown.

In many ways, this is an admirable distillation of a huge amount of information into a half-dozen or so easily memorized facts. It closely fol-lows most birders' preference for ways to identify birds: go for colors and markings first; if those don't work, try structure, especially size; failing that, grab something from range, habitat, or behavior, or (if you're really stuck) voice.

Let's take a second look at each of our white waders and see where we can bolster our knowledge of the group.

SNOWY EGRET

Pity the poor snowy egret . . . blessed and cursed with a field mark so distinctive that many of us never see past it. One wonders if he might wish, however briefly, to have been born with black toes, or yellow tarsi —anything but the trademark combo he sports.

Actually, he was born with something else. Juvenile snowies have legs that are predominently greenish yellow, not black. Many, many birders misidentify juvenile and even nonbreeding adult snowies as immature little blue herons, especially if the bird in question is facing away from them. Relatively few birders seem to know that though snowies do have black stockings, those stockings have big yellow seams up the back. In fact, the stocking is often more like a thin black line down the shins of largely yellow legs. So if you suddenly start seeing a very high percentage of immature little blue herons at your favorite wetland in mid- to late summer and the number of snowies drops off, take a closer look.

While you're looking closely, you might notice a number of other things about snowy egrets. First, their bill shape is long and slim and straight, as formal as a cigarette holder. In fact, nearly everything about a snowy egret is graceful and refined. I'm talking about structure here — their harsh, grating croak of a voice isn't going to inspire many sonnets.

The bill on snowy egrets is usually black, but be careful. It can look surprisingly bicolored, too, with a mostly pale lower mandible that can approximate the pattern of a little blue heron's bill. But it still has that long straight shape.

If you've got a good view of a snowy, look at its face, or lores — the area between the eye and the bill. The snowy egret has yellow skin there, usually quite bright yellow. None of our other herons with black or dull-colored bills has yellow lores.

JUVENILE LITTLE BLUE HERON

Little blue herons change their appearance radically as they go from white juveniles to dark adults, with a brief, calico adolescence in between. But their shape is always just a little thicker, less elegant than their close cousin the snowy egret. This difference is most noticeable in the bill. The little blue's bill has a rather heavier base, and the culmen (the ridge of the upper mandible) droops abruptly as it reaches the bill tip. The bill looks overall heavy and blunt, but only when compared with the svelte bill of snowy.

The little blue heron's neck is a smidge thicker and shorter than that of snowy egret, but their favored feeding postures can obscure this difference. Little blues often forage with the neck fully extended, peering downward into the water, while snowies typically keep their necks tucked in like a snake ready to strike.

The little blue heron prefers freshwater habitats and often hunts among emergent vegetation. Snowy egrets gravitate toward more open water and seem equally at home in fresh, brackish, or saltwater. I've seen little blue herons catch frogs much more often than snowies, which I generally see with fish. Whether little blues actually prefer frogs and choose to hunt where they are common, or whether they like hunting a specific sort of habitat and take the prey most available there is a chicken and egg question. Either way, you can still factor habitat into your identifications.

A final point: juvenile little blue herons have dusky gray wingtips that can sometimes be seen when the bird is in flight. While I'd never rule out the species based on not seeing this field mark, if it's there — bingo!

REDDISH EGRET

The reddish egret is in many ways distinctive, but you can still see its close relationship to both little blue heron and snowy egret. It is best known for its active, seemingly deranged foraging habits, charging here and there, then stopping to peer into the shade of its suddenly outstretched wings. Other herons may occasionally mimic this behavior, and not all reddish egrets display it, but it is the stereotype.

But how do you identify a white reddish egret that isn't in a manic period? Size helps, since reddish egret is a good deal larger than snowy egret or little blue heron but is obviously smaller than great egret. Range and habitat are useful, too. White phase reddish egrets are birds of the Gulf Coast and are rarely seen away from saltwater. Though the species does have some tendency to wander, the majority of individuals are dark birds, so it would be a real coup for you to find a white one out of range. Be sure to let other birders know if you do!

The next time you spot a reddish egret, notice its almost outrageously long bill. It's straight but heavy, like a sword. In breeding adults, the bill shows a very pink base, but may be a dull pinkish orange color, or even darkish, in other ages and seasons.

The legs are fairly thick but also quite long, and they vary from dusky to distinctly bluish gray. Kenn Kaufman has pointed out that the tarsal joint, which most of us informally refer to as the "knee," is placed quite low on the reddish egret. This configuration contributes to the comic nature of its locomotion, giving it the look of a clown pedaling around on an undersized tricycle.

And while I don't think reddish egret is a bad name, it doesn't apply at all to the white phase. Perhaps we could redress that wrong by calling it "maned egret," in honor of its shaggy neck plumes, which it erects and flattens in a wonderfully expressive manner.

GREAT EGRET

The great egret, mascot of the National Audubon Society, is, perhaps even more than snowy, the embodiment of egretness. You could unreservedly call it statuesque, and its peerless form is recreated in thousands of lawn ornaments that grace the yards of every community within a half-day's drive of any body of water.

And really, it poses few identification problems. But that shouldn't dissuade us from taking the time to more exactly note its characters. The incredibly long neck, the finely tapered but broad-based yellow-orange bill, the long black legs, the black feet—all are worth our time to observe and describe. Not only will such exercises make you more ready to spot the one-in-a-million oddball vagrant that you may find, but they can also deepen your enjoyment and appreciation on a purely aesthetic level.

And if you've never noticed the gorgeous emerald green facial skin that great egrets sport for just a week or two at the height of their courtship season—well then, you haven't seen the whole bird.

CATTLE EGRET

At the other end of the egret spectrum, the cattle egret is short and stocky and not what most of us would call graceful, though its ability to ride standing up on the back of grazing mammals is impressive. A recent immigrant to these shores, cattle egrets arrived in the United States (from Africa, via South America) about the same time Elvis Presley began making records.

Cattle egret is well known for its preference for hunting in dry, often grassy locales, snatching grasshoppers and the like that are disturbed by roving animals or machinery. It's a good thing that its habits and squat, short-necked, short-legged structure are so distinctive, because it rarely stays in one place long enough for birders to tally up field marks.

White for most of the year, adults are broadly stained with buffy orange on the chest, back, and crown during the breeding season. The short bill is usually yellowish, but can be orange or even reddish at the height of courtship, and on recently fledged juveniles, it's black.

Leg color also runs the gamut, being black on juveniles, dusky to dull yellow on most birds most of the year, and reddish on breeding adults. So, for cattle egrets, you really have to rely on structure and habits.

A FINAL NOTE

Of course, it's hard to put all this information, with its exceptions and variations, into the tidy sort of summary with which we began. Boil it down to a few key points (leg color, bill color, size, behavior, habitat) and the white herons will prove less confusing wherever you find them.

DARK IBISES

Check the faces, check the eyes of the dark ibises.

THERE ARE FEW BIRDS MORE RECOGNIZABLE THAN AN IBIS.
Ibises are a fine example of how the physical structure of a bird can be its most revealing character. A standing or feeding ibis, with its long decurved bill, long legs, skinny neck, and small round head, is distinctive at almost any distance.

Ibises are gregarious birds that are usually found in small groups (and sometimes rather sizeable flocks) in wetland areas, where they mingle with herons and shorebirds. They are active feeders, using their long bills to methodically probe mud and shallow water for insects, crustaceans, snails, frogs, and worms. Marshes, ponds, rice fields, impoundments, and other wet areas make good ibis habitat. They nest and roost in trees, often as part of large heron or egret colonies. These habitat preferences make these birds faithful to certain locations, and thus relatively easy for bird watchers to find.

There are three North American ibis species: glossy ibis, white-faced ibis, and white ibis. (A fourth species, the scarlet ibis, is a South American species closely related to the white ibis and is occasionally seen in Florida as an escapee from zoos.) Each of our native ibises is distinctive in adult breeding plumage; the younger birds of all three species are more problematic. We'll focus here on the two always-dark ibises, the white-faced and glossy, and on the juvenile white ibis, which is mostly dark.

Range should be your first clue. In fact, the location where you see a dark ibis is your first, and perhaps best, indicator as to which species it is. The ranges of glossy ibis and white-faced ibis overlap very little. While both species are known to wander, white-faced ibis is really a species of

glossy ibis
breeding plumage

glossy ibis
immature

white-faced ibis
breeding plumage

white-faced ibis
immature

white ibis
immature

the interior western United States, whereas the glossy ibis is a bird of the immediate Atlantic and Gulf coasts. Seeing a white-faced ibis east of the Mississippi River is very rare, but as our collective field knowledge improves, more white-faced ibises are being spotted in the East. West of the Mississippi, glossy ibis becomes rare, and it is accidental west of the Great Plains.

In the interior northeastern United States and in Canada, ibises are a rarity, and any ibis you encounter deserves a careful look. As a rule, identifications should never be based entirely on range; however, probability is a good guide.

ADULT DARK IBISES

Dark ibises in breeding plumage (held from about March through August) are pretty straightforward. Adult breeding glossy and white-faced ibises are less distinctive than white ibis, but if you manage to get a decent look at head pattern and leg color, telling glossy from white-faced is not too difficult.

FACE IT

The white-faced ibis in breeding plumage is aptly named, having a distinctive white border around the edges of its reddish face. This border of whitish feathers begins above the bill and goes down to the chin, wrapping around the back of the eye. This white border on the white-faced ibis may be absent in spring and late summer, so it's wise to also check leg and eye color. If you look at a white-faced ibis's face more closely, you'll notice it has a red iris to go with its red face. At any season, a dark ibis with reddish facial skin and a red eye is a white-faced ibis. (I use a phonetic spelling of ibis—eye-bis—to remind myself of white-faced's most constant field mark.)

LEGS AND BILLS

Two other field marks that indicate a breeding-plumaged white-faced ibis are leg color and bill color. The legs of a white-faced are bright red during the breeding season, and the bill is distinctly gray. In comparison, the legs of a glossy ibis are rather dark and the bill is brown, not gray. Of course, these physical characters can be obscured by marsh grass or mud, so they are not always useful.

CAUTION!

I've seen many an eager birder try to turn a breeding-plumaged glossy ibis along the East Coast into a vagrant white-faced. This confusion is understandable, because in high breeding plumage the glossy ibis shows a light-colored outline to its facial skin similar to that of the white-faced. This outline is pale blue-gray, not white, and much less distinctive than the white-faced's. The glossy's white face outline is incomplete—it usually does not meet behind the eye. A closer look at the high-breeding glossy reveals the dark face, dark (not red) eyes, and brownish bill that distinguish it. The glossy's face and eyes have no reddish color at all. On a white-faced ibis, the face's white-feathered border is quite broad and wraps around the outside of the eye, isolating it and making it stand out a bit. On a glossy ibis, the eye is not as distinctive, being dark on a dark background, and not offset by a white border.

WHITE IBIS

White ibis is easy to identify in all plumages except for very young birds, which are not as wholly white as you might expect. Adult white ibises are bright ivory overall with small amounts of black at the tips of the wings, and a bright red bill and red legs. It is a rare day that an adult white ibis is misidentified. Juvenile white ibises, on the other hand, might give you a moment's pause. They do not look quite like any other ibis because they are mostly brown. If you do not live in the southeastern United States where these birds are a familiar sight, your first encounter might leave you confused. The chocolatey brown upperparts, streaky brown heads, white bellies, and light orange legs are a mere shadow of the adult bird to come.

A white ibis born in the spring will be mostly brown-bodied until early winter. By the following March, large patches of white begin to show, and the bird's molt into adult plumage is complete by its first birthday. Even during this confusing blotchy phase, the young white ibis still sports the white belly and orange bill of its species. Its beady light blue eye is also present in all plumages.

CONFUSING YOUNGSTERS, WINTER ADULTS, AND HYBRIDS

If you have the opportunity to go birding in the rice country of southern Louisiana in winter you will find many thousands of ibis, with all three species represented (though there will probably be fewer glossy ibises than white or white-faced). This is North America's best location for learning about our winter ibises. The really tough ibises to separate are the winter and immature white-faced and glossy ibises. They require study and good close views, and even then, it may be simply impossible to separate them. To muddy the waters even further, recent field studies indicate that these two species hybridize with some regularity; hybrids and aberrant individuals may be uncommon, but they shouldn't be altogether dismissed from consideration.

BY THE REDS OF THEIR EYES

By February, most young white-faced ibises begin to show their telltale red irises, but until that point the differences between them and glossies are subtle at best. Nonbreeding adult white-faced ibises retain the red eyes and red facial skin into the winter season, but they lose the white border around the face. The subtle pale blue-gray lines around the face of adult glossy ibises are reduced in the nonbreeding season, but the facial skin and eye remain dark. The field characters that separate these birds in winter, especially younger birds, are still being sorted out by the experts, but it is fair to say that you should not fret if you are puzzling over a winter ibis. You are not the only one to have this problem.

When you see an ibis, particularly a dark one, look it straight in the eyes. If you see a red iris, you'll know you have a white-faced ibis. If you see a dark iris, you might have a glossy ibis (though it might be a dull or young white-faced ibis, in which case you'll want to check for the glossy's breeding plumage, or settle for "ibis sp." in your field notes). Perhaps to make all of this easier to remember we ought to suggest changing the white-faced ibis's name to the "red-eyed ibis." It might not be easier to say, but it may be easier to remember. ✝

BASICS OF HAWK ID

Know your basic red-tail and the rest will come.

A VETERAN HAWK WATCHER ONCE ADVISED ME: "KNOW your red-tail and all the other buteos will fall into place." We were standing at a hawk-watch site, surrounded by birders searching the sky for migrating raptors. I managed not to ask my next question: "What's a buteo?" for fear of getting some incredulous looks. This was many, many years ago and I've since learned the definition of buteo (a large broad-winged soaring hawk belonging to the genus *Buteo*). However, my friend's comment has stuck with me and served me well in the ensuing years.

Unless you hang out at hawk migration hotspots and have the regular opportunity to see hundreds of raptors passing by overhead, identifying soaring hawks can be tricky. Hawk watchers use subtle clues such as shape, size, and flight style to identify distant specks most of us would pass off as floaters in our eyes. The ability to sort such subtle information into accurate identifications is the result of years of accumulated experience. Most of us will never get to that level of expertise, so we need some handy raptor identification tricks to help us.

BUTEOS IN GENERAL

Here's the beauty of the buteos. Whereas falcons or accipiters may soar, usually they seem to be in a hurry to get somewhere else, and our views of them can be quite abbreviated. Give a buteo a set of warm thermals, however, and it will hang around like a persistent houseguest, providing you great looks from several different angles. It's important to take advantage of these opportunities.

Most buteo identification is done on distant soaring birds and is based on wing shape and the patterns found on the underwing and tail. An adult red-tail may flash its red tail as it turns in the sunlight, but plumage variation is extensive among buteos. If you look closely, no two adults of the same species are exactly the same. Juvenile birds can look quite different from adults. (See Soaring Buteos on page 71 for more on identification of juvenile buteos.) The conditions under which you're watching a buteo are important, too. High winds and extreme weather conditions can make a soaring buteo reef in its wings for better control. On hot rising air, or thermals, a buteo may spread its flight feathers to the maximum so it looks more like a soaring vulture or eagle.

If your head is starting to swim, that's only natural. Don't be discouraged — there's a key to all of this.

THE RED-TAIL KEY

For the bird watcher trying to sort out the large soaring hawks, the red-tailed hawk holds the key.

The red-tail is the most frequently seen hawk all across North America. Drive along any highway and watch the roadside trees and power lines and you are bound to see one, if not several.

Red-tails are stocky-bodied, substantial-looking hawks. Most soaring red-tails appear light below and dark above and hold their wings in a slight dihedral (swept slightly upward from the body). The typical adult red-tail shows a light breast, a dark belly band, and a rusty red tail. But like other buteos, red-tails are highly variable and therefore potentially frustrating. On some birds the belly band is missing. Some lack the namesake red tail. Some are nearly all black, whereas other red-tails are so pale below that you'd swear the prairie sun had bleached all the color out of their feathers.

SO HOW DO YOU "KNOW YOUR RED-TAIL"?

There is one field mark that absolutely separates the red-tailed hawk from any other hawk in North America — the patagial bar. The hardest thing to learn about this field mark is its name. The patagial bar is the contrasting dark area on the leading edge of the underside of the wing, extending from the body to the "wrist" — slightly less than halfway out the wing. In nearly all ages, races, forms, and color morphs this dark patagial bar is present. On juvenile Harlan's red-tailed hawks and on the darkest of the dark-morph red-tails the patagial bar is slightly obscured by the dark wing linings, but the patagials are present and visible on most red-tails you'll encounter.

THE IDENTIFICATION FORMULA, THEN, GOES LIKE THIS:

> Soaring large buteo with dark patagial bars = red-tailed hawk

A second clue: backpack straps

Let's say your buteo is perched, not soaring, so our handy patagial bar clue is out the window. Now what? There's a second clue located on the bird's back, on the scapulars. A red-tail's back is almost all dark from the brownish head to the rusty tail. Slicing across the back are two converging lines of white speckled scapular feathers that form a large light V. Some birders refer to these as the "backpack straps." None of our other North American buteos consistently shows this field mark. Even juvenile red-tailed hawks (the ones that might be young enough to be wearing a backpack to school!) show this diagnostic white V. This can be really useful for first-year red-tails, which lack the familiar red tail.

SO REMEMBER THIS IDENTIFICATION FORMULA:

> Perched large buteo with white backpack straps = red-tailed hawk

A third clue: wing windows

There are times when you'll encounter a soaring buteo that's streaky and brownish underneath, lacks a red tail, and shows pale patches in the outer portions of the upper wings. These wing patches, sometimes called "wing windows," can cause confusion because several of our buteos have them — most typically, red-shouldered and rough-legged hawks and a number of immature raptors may show a hint of the wing windows. But these two species show other field marks that should rule them out. Many young golden eagles have bright white windows in the wings, but

red-tailed hawk
adult

their large size makes them fairly easy to peg as nonbuteos.

Don't let the absence of a red tail and the presence of the wing windows confuse you. Your bird may well be a first-year red-tailed hawk.

The streakiest, most nondescript young red-tailed hawk will still show many of the other characteristics of its species, most notably the dark patagial bars. The size and shape of the bird should be an indicator, and it shouldn't take too much imagination to see how the tail, lightly barred with brown, will soon turn rusty.

A FINAL THOUGHT

The plumage permutations of the red-tailed hawk rival the number of flavors in your neighborhood ice cream parlor. When confronted with an unfamiliar buteo, first ask yourself: "Is this or isn't this a red-tail?" Most of the time, the answer will probably be "Yes, it is." Work your way through these identification clues and you'll be able to answer your question quickly and correctly. ✦

SOARING BUTEOS

Six juvenile hawks, from broad-winged to ferruginous

SO . . . YOU'VE GOT YOUR RED-TAILED HAWK DOWN, right? Now it's time to go to work on some of the other buteos. We'll consider flying birds seen from below. The vast majority of buteos encountered are flying overhead, and flying hawks actually give us more to work with in almost all cases. We'll also consider juvenal plumages, which are generally more similar from species to species. Differentiating between the adults is, for the most part, easy by comparison.

We'll consider five *Buteo* species in addition to red-tailed hawk. From smallest to largest, they are broad-winged, red-shouldered, Swainson's, rough-legged, and ferruginous. Red-tailed hawk fits best between Swainson's and rough-legged. Although the Swainson's hawk's wingspan is slightly larger than that of the red-tailed, it's a lighter, slimmer bird overall. Beginning with broad-winged, let's examine each species, paying special attention to how it differs from our keystone, the red-tailed.

BROAD-WINGED HAWK

Broad-winged hawk, an engaging little buteo of forests, is saddled with a decidedly unhelpful name. Yes, its wings are broad for their length, but not strikingly more so than other buteos. Broad-winged hawks are seldom seen far from woodlands, except during their epic migrations, when they sometimes travel in flocks numbering in the thousands. When not in transit, they like to still-hunt from phone wires and similarly exposed perches along woodland edges, whether they're in New Hampshire or Panama.

If you do get a glimpse of a broad-winged hawk overhead, it's likely to strike you as small and compact, but with distinctly pointed wings. In full soar or level flight, the wings look evenly tapered. They narrow smoothly to the wingtips, which are held fairly tightly closed, without showing much space between the primaries. The tail is usually moderately fanned, adding to the overall neat, trim look.

When the same bird streams out of one thermal and sets its wings in search of another, its shape can change rather drastically. The tail often closes, making it look longer, and the wings pull back so their trailing edge is nearly straight, with the leading edge often thrust forward a bit at the elbows.

Whatever posture a young broad-winged takes, you are likely to notice that it is fairly evenly whitish below, without much in the way of obvious markings on the underparts. There are two markings you should look for, though. Nearly all broad-wingeds show a neat, dark border on the trailing edge of their underwings that is one of the best clues to their identity. It runs from the outermost primaries around the wing tips and along the trailing edge of the wings. It does not run along the leading edge of the wing. This dark outline can be seen on flying birds from a surprising distance, though it is less distinctive on young birds than on adults.

Juvenile broad-wingeds are variably marked with dark spotting or blotching underneath, especially along the sides of their chests. This often lends them a dark-cheeked, pale-throated look. Be aware, though, that some individuals may be heavily and evenly streaked on the belly, similar to juvenile red-shouldered hawk. This can be especially confusing in late spring and summer when young broad-wingeds (birds born the previous summer) are molting, and the primaries give the appearance of wing windows like the red-shouldered hawk's. These young broad-wingeds still have a dark trailing edge on the underside of the wings, but their tails are pale, with a few very narrow dark lines. Most of these tails have a single broad, dark band just short of the tip (a subterminal band).

RED-SHOULDERED HAWK

Juvenile red-shouldered hawks have a rather different tail pattern than young broad-wingeds, and this is probably the mark that varies least for differentiating between the two. On red-shouldered, the tail is dark brownish with a lot of narrow whitish lines crossing it (usually five),

Soaring Buteos

broad-winged hawk immature

red-shouldered hawk immature

red-tailed hawk immature

rough-legged hawk adult male (light morph)

Swainson's hawk immature

ferruginous hawk immature (light morph)

breaking it into narrow dark bands of even width. Seen from below and backlit, it may read as a pale tail crossed by five or so dark bands. In any case, it's quite different from broad-winged's tail, which is pale with a few very narrow dark lines, but with a single broad dark band just short of the tip, called a subterminal.

The tail of the red-shouldered is longish, which, combined with a rounded (not tapered) wingtip and a rather stiff, choppy flight style, makes it possible to briefly mistake it for a large accipiter. Eventually, though, the tail will fan out a bit, revealing the bird's true buteo identity.

In practice, identifying a flying red-shouldered is often a matter of waiting to see the windows. Many soaring buteos show a pale area in the primaries, but in red-shouldered hawks this area is unusually distinctive. Just inside from the dark, blackish wingtips is a narrow, contrasting panel of near translucence, which then merges with the pale but opaque underwing. The wing windows of other buteos do not exactly duplicate this distinctive slash of light.

Two more quick points. One, juvenile red-shouldered hawks are usually fairly evenly marked with brown streaking underneath, whereas broad-wingeds are typically pale with dark markings restricted to the sides of the chest, and red-tailed hawks show a white chest and dark belly. Two, in the isolated California population of red-shouldereds, juveniles usually show some of the reddish color on the body and wings displayed by all red-shouldered adults, making them easily recognizable.

BIG OPEN-COUNTRY BUTEOS

Our last three buteos are birds of open country that frequent marshes, farmland, plains, and prairie. Two, Swainson's and ferruginous, are essentially birds of the Great Plains and westward; the rough-legged hawk is found from coast to coast, though it tends to be patchy in its distribution.

Swainson's hawk is in many respects a western analog to broad-winged, sharing its habit of undertaking long-distance migrations to and from the Neotropics in large flocks. Classic light-morph juveniles also superficially resemble broad-wingeds in two other ways: a pale tail crossed with thin, indistinct dark bands including a dark subterminal band, and a tendency for the splotchy dark markings underneath to be concentrated around the lower cheeks and sides of the chest.

It's important not to overemphasize what are, in many respects, super-

Rough-legged Hawk	Swainson's Hawk	Ferruginous Hawk
TAIL	**WINGS**	**SIZE**
• **MOSTLY WHITE.** Rough-legs are well-marked overall. The white tail has an obvious dark subterminal band.	• **LONG.** Longer than a red-tail's. Held in a vulturelike dihedral. Two-toned, with flight feathers darker than wing linings.	• **HUGE.** Our largest buteo, almost eagle-sized. Appears pure white or very light-colored below in flight.

ficial similarities. Though they share some markings, broad-winged and Swainson's hawks are at least as different as a station wagon is from a minivan. Start with Swainson's big wingspan, which is usually an inch or two larger than even a red-tail's, and more than a foot longer than broad-winged's. Not only are Swainson's wings long, they're slim and pointed for a buteo, appropriate for an open-country bird that might commute between the Dakotas and Argentina. The ways in which they maneuver those long wings are distinctive, too. When soaring, the wings are held above the horizontal in a shallow dihedral, giving the Swainson's a vulturelike appearance in silhouette. In a glide, the wings assume a crinkled W shape, with the wrists thrust way forward and the tips swept far back.

In the majority of Swainson's hawks, the undersides of the flight feathers are quite a bit darker than the wing linings, giving them a distinctive two-toned effect when viewed from below. In some pale juveniles, however, the overall effect is closer to the look of the red-tailed hawk.

Let's consider sitting birds for just a moment. Swainson's hawk frequently perches for long periods on the ground, a habit rarely, if ever, seen in broad-winged, red-tailed, and red-shouldered hawks. It also likes hay bales, wire fences and fence posts, and other low perches. When perched, its long wings extend all the way to the tip of the tail, unique among the buteos discussed here, the rest of which have tails that protrude beyond the wingtips when at rest.

FERRUGINOUS HAWK

Another buteo often seen perched on the ground is the ferruginous hawk, which favors dry grasslands and similar open habitats of western North America. Our largest buteo, it brings to mind a big, ghostly red-tailed hawk. Like the Swainson's hawk, the ferruginous has very long wings with well-defined points at the tip, though its wings are broader and heavier than the Swainson's hawk's.

In flight, the juvenile ferruginous hawk gives the impression of being pure white below. The flight feathers, body, and tail are largely unmarked, save for some brown dots along the wing linings and clean blackish wrist "commas" where the wing linings meet the base of the primaries. There is no patagial bar, as there is on the red-tailed hawk, and there's no significant dark border to the trailing edges, either.

The wings are usually held in a shallow V, which allows inspection of the upper wing surface, unless the bird is high overhead. There is an excellent mark there — a pale panel of white in the primaries *entirely enclosed* by dark. The emphasis is needed, since pale juvenile red-tailed hawks often show a pale whitish panel in this area, too. But in red-tailed, the inner primaries are pale all the way to their tips, not tipped with dark as in ferruginous hawk.

If you have an old field guide on your shelf you might see ferruginous hawk listed as "ferruginous rough-legged hawk" and our final buteo, rough-legged hawk, listed as "northern rough-legged hawk."

That nomenclature highlights a structural similarity between the two: feathering that extends all the way down the tarsi (legs) to the toes, a sensible adaptation to the frigid conditions these birds endure for much of their lives.

But in spite of their feathery leggings, there is much that distinguishes these two. Ferruginous hawk has large feet, a large bill, and a long, crooked, yellow gape. Its head, also large, is very flat, with a nape that looks nearly square. It recalls an eagle, or a drill sergeant.

ROUGH-LEGGED HAWK

The rough-legged hawk is relatively small-billed and small-footed. Its fluffy, rounded head lends it a gentle, owlish look, especially in dark-eyed adults. Rough-legs also perch distinctively in the tops of trees, on branches that seem precariously small to support so large a bird. Another funny thing about rough-legged hawk is that the juveniles (and adult females) have distinctive dark markings on the wings and belly that make them easy to recognize by plumage alone. Therefore the bird depicted in our illustration is the more generic-looking adult male.

The first impression one gets from any rough-legged is that it's got a lot of markings. The flight feathers are bright and silvery with a heavy dark border. The wing linings are heavily spangled, even blotched. There are dark squares at the wrists; in adult males, these may be broken up a bit with pale markings. Most adult male rough-legs show a dark belly and bib, with a paler area on the breast.

The key mark, though, is the tail. It's mostly white, as in ferruginous, but it ends with a couple of thin dark lines and an absolutely huge blackish subterminal, kind of an amped-up version of the juvenile broad-winged hawk's tail.

As you work to expand your knowlege of buteos and other raptors, remember that hawk watching can be tough. Tough enough to make it very interesting indeed, as evidenced by the thousands of devotees who crowd raptor observation sites in spring and fall. Seeing hundreds (or even thousands) of broad-winged hawks or Swainson's hawks in a single day, interspersed with dozens of look-alikes in every conceivable plumage, is a crash course in becoming familiar with their identification. And there are experts all around you at a hawk-watch — you have only to ask. There's no faster way to learn. ✦

FALCONS

Size matters when identifying these feathered rockets.

WHAT IS IT ABOUT FALCONS? EVEN IN THE RAREFIED atmosphere inhabited by hawk watchers, falcons are special. Peregrine falcons have achieved a mythical status among birders, and merlins are not far behind. Even kestrels are given more attention than most other hawks, and people lose their minds over gyrfalcons.

Writers from Audubon to Peterson have had a go at explaining the allure of falcons. Virtually every adjective in the language has been appropriated for falcon literature. Even people who own hawks are called falconers rather than buteoers or accipiterers. The recognition that falcons are special goes back to a time when everyone watched birds yet no one was a bird watcher, at least in the sense we know now. It can all be summarized in a single sentence: Falcons are exciting!

Once we are past the mythology and the emotional response, we are back to the question of how we tell one falcon from another. Identifying falcons is like climbing a rickety ladder: you have to worry not only about the step you are on, but also the ones above and below.

North American falcons come in four sizes: small (kestrel), medium (merlin), large (peregrine and prairie), and WOW! (gyrfalcon). The identification challenges break out this way:

Kestrel versus merlin

Merlin versus peregrine and prairie

Peregrine versus prairie

Peregrine and prairie versus gyrfalcon

This means that the first step is to get into the right size category, or at least close enough to it so that you can eliminate some of the options. In most instances, sizing up a bird is not too difficult. For distant birds, or ones with the afterburners on (a typical state with falcons), the challenge is greater. If you do not get more than a passing look, a lot of birds will end up in your notes as "large falcon sp." or "medium falcon sp." Such categories are not something to fret about. Every bird watcher has need of them at times, even experienced hawk watchers. Some birds simply will not cooperate.

The size problem can be expanded: falcons, like most birds of prey, are sexually dimorphic by size. Females are larger than males, sometimes astoundingly so. The greatest difference is in peregrine falcons, but there are differences in all species. Overall, kestrels are smaller than merlins and merlins smaller than peregrines, but a large female kestrel and a small male merlin aren't that different, and the same is true for a large female merlin and a small male peregrine. Size is important because it gets you to the right grouping, but it does not always get you to the right species.

The considerations that follow are based on the assumption that you have gotten more than a two-second look at the bird — although the two-second look can be interpreted as a field mark for merlins in some cases, as we will see.

WHO, WHERE, AND WHEN

One of the pleasures of falcons is that you can see them almost anywhere in the regularly inhabited part of the continent, though some of them are unusual enough to make the heart speed up a bit. The basic cast of characters is as follows:

American kestrel: the smallest falcon, found continent-wide almost year-round. Also an uncommon to common migrant in many areas.

Merlin: the medium-sized falcon. Nests in the northern part of the continent and in small numbers in the mountainous West. Migrates across all areas, although most are seen at coastal hawk watches. Winters from southern Canada to south of the U.S.–Mexican border. Merlins are beginning to acclimate to city dwellings in the northern parts of their range.

Prairie falcon: one of the two large falcons. A western bird of mountainous areas and prairies, a close cousin and look-alike of the peregrine. They are largely resident, but some migrate south and a few wander eastward.

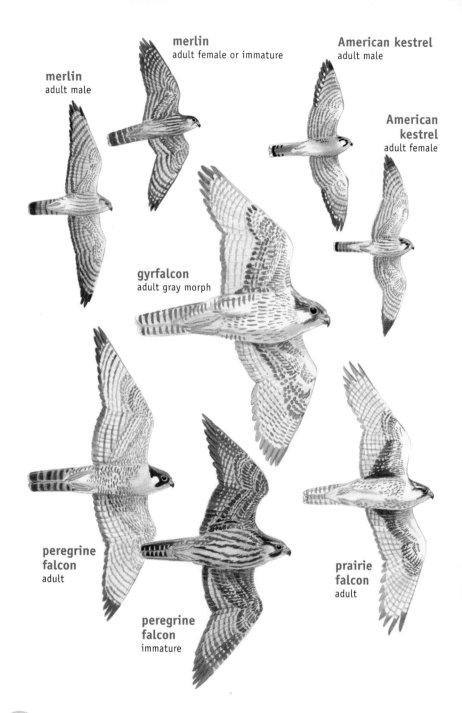

merlin
adult male

merlin
adult female or immature

American kestrel
adult male

American kestrel
adult female

gyrfalcon
adult gray morph

peregrine falcon
adult

peregrine falcon
immature

prairie falcon
adult

Peregrine falcon: the other, better known of the two large falcons. Once much rarer, now widely re-established in the East and West, still most numerous in the North. Many migrate long distances, moving to South and Central America for the winter, but some stay and can be found almost anywhere in winter.

Gyrfalcon: the WOW of falcons, a high-Arctic bird that moves south in small numbers most winters, making it to the northern tier of the United States. Reports south of that cause stampedes of birders.

The others: Aplomado falcons and several European birds that have been seen in North America a few times are not treated here. They are uncommon and the chances of seeing one are small.

THE GENERIC FALCON

Falcons are built for speed. They typically have long tails and long pointed wings, giving them a slim, aerodynamic look. They are often confused with accipiters, sharp-shinned hawk, Cooper's hawk, and northern goshawk. The accipiters also have long tails, and when they are in a downward glide with wings folded slightly back, the differences are not always obvious. Eventually the bird will pull up and the short broad wings of the accipiter will become obvious.

Contrary to popular belief, falcons soar like buteos and other hawks, especially on migration. Most people think of falcons (other than the wire-sitting American kestrel) as birds going past so fast you get whiplash trying to follow them. Although this is true for most falcons, many are missed because the observer assumes that any bird up high, drifting on the wind, is some other bird. Any time you see a high-flying hawk, check the wing and tail shape. Even when they spread their wings for maximum lift, falcons have long pointed wings and stand out from almost all other hawks.

When falcons are on the move, especially when flying low, they are harder to separate from the accipiters. One reason is that their wingbeats are so rapid that it is hard to see the wing shape, but that is actually a good clue. Accipiters can flap energetically, but rarely as quickly as falcons. They usually take a break every half-dozen or so flaps, something falcons do less frequently. If the bird is coming low and fast and the wings are really pumping, it is time to think falcon.

When perched, falcons look long and slim relative to their overall size; the profile is distinctive with practice. At close range, note that the wingtips on a sitting bird usually reach almost to the end of the tail. On accipiters, the most likely source of confusion, the wingtips fall well short of the tip of the tail.

THE SMALL FALCON PROBLEM

This challenge can be summarized as "I thought it was a kestrel but then I thought maybe it was a merlin." American kestrels are fairly common over most of their range, and many bird watchers spot one or two a day. Merlins, a sought-after bird, are much rarer in most areas. Trying to turn large female kestrels into merlins is a well-established form of entertainment among bird watchers.

There are two behavioral clues that help separate kestrels from merlins. If the bird is sitting on a wire, it is almost certainly a kestrel. Merlins can sit on wires, and there are records of it, but the behavior is so rare that if the bird is sitting on a wire and bobbing its tail, it is most likely a kestrel. Also, if the bird is hovering, it is a kestrel.

Identifying a well-seen sitting bird by plumage is fairly easy — any field guide will show you the characters. All ages and sexes of the kestrel show two dark mustache marks that aren't present on merlins; merlins are almost always much more heavily streaked below than kestrels are.

Birds in flight are tougher. The most important characters involve size, shape, flight, and overall color. Merlins in flight are noticeably darker than kestrels, especially on the underwing, which is helpful with birds overhead. Kestrels are fairly pale below, including the body and underwings. If the sun is behind the bird, the paler tail of the kestrel is usually evident, even when lighting does not make it possible to see the rusty color of the tail feathers. Another character that is often useful on kestrels overhead is the fine row of white spots along the trailing edge of the underwing. If you see them, it is a kestrel.

In flight down low, which is where merlins are far more frequently seen, the darker underwings are sometimes helpful, but are not always easy to see. Even when the underwings can't be seen, the overall darkness of merlins is a good clue. Less obviously distinguishing, but still helpful, is shape. The wings of a merlin are proportionately broader than those of a kestrel, especially the inner half, giving the bird a more robust, substantial look. Attitude is a highly subjective character and not useful unless you have had the opportunity to watch a lot of falcons, but those birders that have are continually struck by the sense that a low-flying merlin is a bird with a purpose. It seems to be intent, serious, a bird with someplace to go and little time for frivolity.

It is an article of faith at hawk watches that if a medium-sized falcon appears low over the trees or the dunes, popping up right in front of you, blasting past before anyone can even yell, it is almost certainly a merlin. This is not enough of a sighting for most of us to add the bird to our day list, but it is far from wrong. Another clue from the hawk watchers, especially those along the coast: if the bird won't detour 500 yards out of its way to dive-bomb a sitting hawk, it doesn't deserve to be a merlin. That may overstate the case, but it is undeniable that merlins are among the most pugnacious of hawks.

THE NEXT STEP UP THE LADDER — MERLIN VERSUS PEREGRINE AND PRAIRIE FALCONS

So, you've eliminated kestrel, which means the bird must be a merlin, right? Nope, now you have to eliminate the smaller versions of the larger falcons — peregrine and prairie.

If you are in the East, you can ignore the prairie problem and concentrate on peregrine. Peregrines are always larger, most obviously so. The smallest male peregrines are close enough in size to large female merlins, however, that caution is needed. The clearest structural difference is wing shape. Peregrines have proportionately longer wings than merlins, making them look slightly less chunky. Adults are paler than merlins overall, but the differences are not always striking, and young peregrines are as dark as any merlin.

There is no easy solution to this problem. If the bird is up high and soaring with spread tail and wings, it is more likely a peregrine. Sometimes, even on distant birds, you can see the strong mustache mark of the peregrine, a dead giveaway. Inevitably, some of the medium to large dark falcons will have to be treated as general falcon species.

In the West, prairie falcon gets added to the mix. The prairie falcon is a peregrine look-alike in size and shape, although the wings are slightly shorter and the birds on average are slightly smaller. The best character for prairie falcon is the overall paler color and the contrasting dark axillaries, the "wingpit." If you have a medium to large falcon with obvious dark areas on the underside of the wing next to the body, you have a prairie. On perched birds, the paleness of the prairie falcon is a good clue, and the small but distinct mustache mark is a clincher.

PRAIRIE VERSUS PEREGRINE

This is a problem confined almost entirely to the West, although a very few prairie falcons drift eastward in the fall. There are subtle differences in shape, but separating prairies and peregrines requires getting a decent look at the plumage.

On flying birds, the overall paleness of prairies is sometimes visible enough to be a good indicator, and the same dark axillaries and coverts that separate prairies from merlins will separate them from peregrines. In most cases, if the bird is seen only in flight, you have to see the wingpit to clinch the identification.

Sitting birds are almost as tough. The pale plumage of most prairie falcons is more easily seen on sitting birds, but beware of juvenile, heavily streaked, darker prairies. When all else fails, and assuming you can get close enough, check the head. Prairie falcons have narrow mustache stripes, nothing like those on peregrines. If you get even closer, check the area directly behind the eye. Both birds may show a short, thickish white stripe starting above and behind the eye, but only prairie falcons have white directly behind the eye. If you get that close, you might just want to ask the bird what it is — politely, of course.

WOW!

At the top of the ladder is the gyrfalcon, the biggest, baddest falcon on the block. They are extremely rare south of the Canadian border, even in the coldest winters, but there are records as far south as central California, Colorado, Texas, and Virginia. If you see a really, really big falcon in winter, anywhere from the central United States north, you have to stop and consider gyr. It won't happen often, but the fantasizing is fun.

The first clue to a gyrfalcon is size. They are big bulky birds, heavy chested, with shorter wings and tails than most other falcons. In flight, the broader, more rounded wings give a sense of power that is lacking in smaller falcons. Don't let the size fool you, though. Flat out, going low and on the tail of their prey, gyrfalcons are stunningly fast, eating up ground in great dollops.

Gyrfalcons come in several flavors, from vanilla to chocolate. White-morph birds are so pale and striking that it is hard to confuse them with anything except a snowy owl, although the owl's slow, generally floppy flight, very broad wings, and huge head make confusion merely momentary. White birds, which are typically adults, are very rarely seen south of the far north. The real problem is gray and dark (brown) birds. Gray birds, which includes most juveniles, are much paler than peregrine or even prairie falcons. They are also birds whose best field mark is the near absence of field marks. They tend to be almost unicolor, with no striking plumage characters. They have a narrow mustache stripe that is not always present or visible, and the crown tends to be paler than the rest of the head, but otherwise they are almost plain. In flight, many gyrfalcons show a two-toned underwing, with the primaries and secondaries (the trailing edge of the wing) paler than the rest.

Perched gray and dark-morph juveniles are more like peregrines, being darker overall and heavily streaked below. The best characters are the obvious bulk, the very thin mustache stripe, the lack of pattern on the head, and the shorter wings, which do not come close to the tip of the tail.

A bigger problem than peregrine or prairie in many areas is goshawk. Because gyrs have broader, shorter wings than other falcons, they are closer in shape to goshawks than other falcons are to accipiters. Adult goshawks are grayish and pale, increasing the similarity, and young goshawks are dark and heavily streaked, as are many young gyrs. Adult goshawks have a dark head with a bold white eye stripe. In flight they have uniformly pale underwings, not the two-toned effect of gyrs, and at all ages goshawks have much broader and more rounded wings.

Are you ready to identify confidently every falcon you see? Not even the most experienced hawk watchers make that claim, of course, and some birds will get away. Falcons are movers — many birds will show themselves for just a few seconds and be gone. But any bird watcher can become better at naming falcons, even those that just zip by. The trick is to remember the ladder and try to decide quickly which rung you are on and whether you want to go up or down. It isn't easy at first, but it is worth the effort, because almost any falcon can show up almost any-where. ✗

ACCIPITERS

No silver bullets

THE GOOD NEWS IS THAT YOU CAN LEARN TO PUT THE
PROPER NAME ON MOST OF THE ACCIPITERS YOU SEE.

THERE ARE NO SILVER BULLETS WHEN IT COMES TO hawk identification, not even for the bulletlike accipiters. Hawks, even when they are seen close up (which is fairly rare), are tough. There are two factors that make hawks a challenge: where you see them, and what you see.

Most of us see hawks under less-than-ideal circumstances. Either they seem several miles away straight up, or they are visible for about half a second as they dart through the woods, or they are flying directly away across a field, or they are perched along a highway watching us go by at warp speed. None of those situations is reminiscent of most of our bird watching experiences, which involve ducks swimming placidly on lakes, sparrows at feeders, or warblers in a tree.

Even when we do see them well, problems persist. Most hawks are symphonies in brown and white. There are no gaudy colors, few striking patterns. The field marks are subtle. Face it, hawks travel incognito.

So much for the bad news. The good news is that you can learn to put the proper name on most of the hawks you see. It only takes experience and a willingness to misidentify, or let go unnamed, a whole kettle of birds while you learn. When it comes to hawk identification, there is no substitute for doing it.

Two of the most widespread hawks in North America are the smaller accipiters, sharp-shinned and Cooper's hawks. They occur over almost the entire continent at one season or another, and they are regular visitors to backyards, although they don't come for the largesse of the homeowner, but to prey on the birds that are there. Accipiters are bird-hunting,

Cooper's hawk
adult male

Cooper's hawk
adult female

sharp-shinned hawk
adult male

sharp-shinned hawk
adult female

woodland hawks. There is a third member of the group, the northern goshawk. It is not included here because it is much rarer and much less frequently seen around human habitation. Away from some of the northern hawk watches, a goshawk is a show stopper.

GENERAL ACCIPITER IDENTIFICATION

Before deciding whether a bird is a sharp-shinned or a Cooper's (sharpie and Coop to most bird watchers), you need to decide that it is, in fact, an accipiter. That is not always easy; even experienced hawk watchers struggle with high-flying birds. The basic accipiter is relatively broad-winged, short-winged, and long-tailed. They are built for chasing other birds through the woods, and short wings are an advantage because they supply bursts of speed and allow maneuvering in tight places. The long tail is a rudder for steering and quick turns.

Accipiters can be seen flying overhead in migration, when they join kettles of other hawks or travel alone. They can also be seen darting through the woods, zipping past so quickly it is hard to tell what sort of bird they are. They are quite often seen hunting at feeders. If you have a hawk visiting your yard, especially if the area is wooded or there is a stand of trees nearby, it is almost certainly an accipiter. They are rarely seen over fields, they never hover, and they generally do not perch in the open. In fact, it is hard to see a perched accipiter unless it is in your yard.

Now that we have decided the bird is an accipiter — see, wasn't that easy? — we can tackle the problem of which kind. This is usually much harder than the initial problem, because sharpies and Coops are depressingly similar. They are, in most ways, large and small versions of the same bird, with subtle differences thrown in. To start, before getting into the subtleties, focus on two characters: size and shape.

SIZE AND SHAPE

Cooper's hawks are always larger than sharp-shinned hawks. In accipiters (as in all hawks) females are larger than males, and the difference can be dramatic. A big female Cooper's hawk positively dwarfs a puny male sharpie. This would be a great field mark if you ever saw them sitting side by side, but you won't. A small male sharpie is tiny when seen close up. The toughest challenge is female sharpies and male Coops, which are very similar in size. Size can still be a good clue, however. Try comparing the hawk to a bird you are more familiar with. A male sharp-shinned is about the size of a jay, a female sharpie is about half again the size of a jay, a male Coop is a little bigger than a female sharpie, and a female Coop is nearly the size of a red-shouldered hawk.

Size is reflected in prey preference. Sharpies at the feeder will favor sparrows and finches, usually topping out at jays for females, although even they may be a struggle. Coops favor larger birds — jays and up — and have a special fondness for mourning doves. If the hawk in your yard is taking doves, it is almost certainly a Cooper's, especially if it has no trouble dispatching them.

The other general clue is the shape — and in particular, the shape and size of the tail. Although often harder to judge, tail length can be even more useful than size, especially on high-flying birds. Cooper's hawks have longer tails than sharp-shinneds, both in real measurements and proportionately. This is very noticeable on female Coops, less so on males. On male Coops, however, tail length is so close to that of female sharpies that it is used by only the most experienced watchers, and even then with some risk.

TAIL SHAPE

Tail shape is a clue, although again, it doesn't work as well with male Cooper's. Field guides tend to home in on the rounded tail of Cooper's versus the squared-off tail of sharp-shinned. In fact, many female Cooper's hawks have visibly rounded tails that are most noticeable when the bird is soaring overhead. Tail shape is much harder to judge on sitting birds and birds seen flying low and fast or only briefly.

sharp-shinned hawk
immature male

Cooper's hawk
immature female

A WORD OF CAUTION is in order about tail shape in the fall when birds are in molt. When the outer tail feathers of a sharp-shinned hawk are not fully grown, the tail can appear slightly rounded. When the central tail feathers of a Cooper's hawk are not fully grown out, the tail can appear squared-off. Tail shape is a good indicator on some birds, but it should always be combined with other characters.

HEAD SIZE

SECOND CAUTION: Field guides note that on high-flying birds, the head of Cooper's sticks out past the bend of the wing, and the head of sharp-shinned does not. This is generally true, but it is often hard to judge, and many birders are confused by sharp-shinned hawks that have just chowed down. Immediately after eating, the crop, or throat, of a hawk is distended, resulting in the appearance of an enlarged head. Don't jump the gun on head size alone.

TAIL TIP

THIRD CAUTION: Field guides also point to the white tail tip on Cooper's hawk. Most Coops, especially in late fall and winter, when they are in fresh plumage, have a broader white tip on the tail than sharp-shinneds. This difference diminishes with wear and is less useful in the spring. It is also much easier to see from above than below, though the width of the white tip is visible from underneath in some circumstances. The rule is, if the bird seems to have a very broad white tip it is probably a Cooper's. If it seems to have a narrow tip, or no white at the end of the tail in the fall, it is probably a sharpie. In other seasons the white tail tip on the tail isn't much help.

It is time for the nitty-gritty, the head-to-head comparison of sharp-shinned and Cooper's hawks. To try to reflect the circumstances under which most of us see sharp-shinned and Cooper's hawks, we will deal with the birds in three sections: distant flying birds, perched (or sitting) birds, and close flying birds.

DISTANT FLYING BIRDS

These are birds seen overhead, usually in migration, at a hawk watch or from your yard. In most parts of North America you can go outdoors in spring or fall on a good flight day and have a reasonable chance of seeing either, or both. The advantage — and it is a considerable one — to going to a hawk watch is that you have other people to share your notes and frustrations with, and experts to jump in and tell you what they think the bird is.

The difficulty with distant hawks is that little dark specks do not have field marks in the sense we are used to: no wing bars, no streaks, no eye line. Field guides are only moderately successful at explaining the characters hawk watchers use to identify these birds, in part because the characters are subtle, and in part because the only real way to learn them is to go and stand next to someone who has already been through the training school. You can read and read, and look at pictures until you get itchy eyes, but when you want to learn how to identify flying hawks you go to a hawk watch.

Remembering what we said about size and shape, the rule of thumb is that Cooper's are the longest accipiter, and sharp-shinneds are the most compact. The longer tail and greater head projection of Cooper's make it seem longer than it is wide. The shorter tail and smaller head and proportionately longer wings make sharp-shinneds seem more compact and shaped more like a buteo, such as a broad-winged or red-tailed hawk.

SITTING BIRDS

These are the birds most of us see at the local park or in our yard, and struggle with. The experience gained at a hawk watch is only minimally useful in these circumstances, but because we often get a longer, more detailed look, these are also the birds we can learn to identify with some confidence.

When talking about seeing accipiters close up, we have to dive into the issues of age and sex, two words that, used together, bring a pleasant shudder of anticipatory horror to watchers of daytime television, but to bird watchers, mean an extra set of field marks to be confused by.

The differences in sex are almost entirely issues of size, which we have already discussed. Females are, in general, slightly duller in all plumages than males. There is a lot of overlap, though, and plumage is nearly useless in deciding whether the bird is male or female. Age is a different matter. Immature accipiters look very different from adults, and it can be helpful to know whether the bird is an adult or not.

ADULTS

Adult Cooper's and sharp-shinned hawks have slate blue backs and underparts heavily barred with rufous. Any difference in back and underpart color is too variable to be useful in telling the two apart. The best field mark on a sitting bird is the head. The crown, or the top of the head, of Cooper's hawk is generally dark blue, contrasting sharply with a paler nape. The crown of sharp-shinned may be slightly darker than the face, but there is no sharp contrast with the nape. From behind, the bird appears to be one color from the top of the head to the tail. Any time you see a sitting adult accipiter you should look first at the head. After that, you should check the tail for both length and the width of the white tip. Then check the thickness of the legs.

Leg thickness is one of those subtle back-up characters on adult accipiters that isn't diagnostic on its own, but makes for a useful comparison. It is a much more valuable field mark on young birds. Never pass up the chance to look at legs. The legs of sharp-shinned hawks are pencil-thin, giving the bird a slightly longer-legged look. The legs of Cooper's hawks are noticeably thicker, resulting in a slightly shorter-legged look. With a little practice, you will find that the difference is sometimes striking.

IMMATURES

Close up, immatures are much harder to tell apart, and if you are like most birders, you see more young birds than adults. It is not a conspiracy; in fall and winter there are more young birds than adults.

Immature birds of both species are brown on the back, with variable white mottling, and streaked with brown on the breast and belly. There are subtle differences between them, but there is also overlap in most characters, and multiple field marks are necessary for a confident identification.

Immature Cooper's and sharp-shinned hawks are never tougher to identify than when they are just sitting there letting you look at them. The best field mark is size, which was discussed earlier. A big bird is a female Coop, a small one is a male sharpie.

A second field mark, the streaking on the breast and underparts, is worth a close look. On most Cooper's hawks, the streaking on the breast is fairly fine and dark brown and doesn't extend very far onto the belly. On most sharp-shinneds the streaking is heavier, broader, with teardrop-shaped spots, and extends farther onto the belly; sometimes there is a reddish tinge to the streaking. The extreme variations are probably diagnostic, but don't ignore the other characters. If everything else points to Cooper's or sharp-shinned, the breast streaking alone should not be the deciding factor.

The third best field mark is the length and shape of the tail. Especially long-tailed birds are almost surely Coops. It is harder to gauge the shorter tail of sharpies, but on sitting birds the tail shape is a more useful character than it is on flying birds. Sharpies of all ages and sexes almost always show a notched tail when they are sitting. Sitting Cooper's hawks rarely show a notch in the tail.

The white tail tip can also be a help, at least until late fall. The wider white tip is even more visible on sitting Coops than on flying ones, although, as in all things related to accipiters, a caution is in order. On immature sharpies the last tail band is pale. It is not white, but it contrasts with the dark band above it, and in some light and at some angles it can appear to be a very broad white tip. Be certain you are looking at the tip of the tail rather than the last band, and consider the field mark no more than slightly indicative from mid-winter on.

On most sharp-shinneds the breast streaking is heavier, broader, with teardrop-shaped spots.

Here is where leg thickness becomes important. Even though it is subtle, and you need experience to judge it, leg thickness can be one of the more valuable characters for separating a young Cooper's from a young sharp-shinned. Surf the Internet or check your library for photographs of sitting accipiters to compare leg thickness. Once you become comfortable with the difference, it can be a useful character.

Now for the really subtle stuff, the characters where the words "usually," "probably," "overlap," and other hedges are needed.

Both immature sharpies and Cooper's have brown heads. Some Coops lack the pale eye stripe that almost all sharpies show. If the bird is noticeably plain-headed it is probably a Coop. Some Coops also show a slight rufous wash to the face that is absent in sharpies. The contrast between the crown and the nape is missing in young birds, but Cooper's will sometimes show a mottled crown, a mix of pale and darker feathers that is rare in sharpies.

The backs of both birds are brown, variously mottled with white. Some Coops are rather heavily mottled, and some sharpies show virtually no white mottling. A large number of Coops and sharpies are somewhere in the middle. This is another character that diminishes in usefulness as the season wears on.

CAUTION: Some field guides use undertail coverts as diagnostic for identifying accipiters. The undertail coverts are a key character in identifying goshawks: they do not help at all when separating sharp-shinned and Cooper's.

CLOSE FLYING BIRDS

These are birds seen barreling through the woods or dashing across the yard. They are usually close to eye level and moving at Mach One. All field marks except size and tail length are irrelevant on these birds, because the look you get is almost always brief and confused, and you waste the first half of it trying to decide if the bird is a hawk or not.

I wish I could say something helpful here, but I can't. The vast majority of hawks I can't identify are close-up, flying accipiters. Most of the birds identified under these circumstances represent a combination of guesswork, experience, and gut instinct about size and shape. Some of the identifications are unquestionably wrong. Once in a great while the bird will actually stop, perch in sight, or suddenly soar up above the trees, and you can check your call. After nearly thirty years of playing this game I am finally at the point where I am more often right than wrong, but I still blow some of them.

The best advice, assuming an unsatisfactory glimpse, is: keep trying, play the game as often as possible, jump in with a guess every time in case the bird does give you a chance to check up on yourself, and call most of the birds "accipiter sp." It's just for fun in the end.

CONFUSED? READY TO THROW IN THE TOWEL?

Take heart. In the beginning a lot of accipiters get away unidentified, but there are ways of telling them apart, and as time passes it gets easier. The trick is not to push it, not to insist on putting a name on every bird. Use every encounter as a learning experience. Enjoy the challenge. If every identification were easy, much of the pleasure would be gone from bird watching. ✦

EAGLES

Identifying bald eagles, young and old

LATE ONE DECEMBER I FOUND MYSELF AMONG A LOOSE aggregation of birders standing by a roadside in Bombay Hook National Wildlife Refuge in Delaware. To our north stretched a field, and somewhere in it there was supposed to be a northern lapwing, a handsome Eurasian shorebird that always makes news when it appears on our shores.

After a bit of waiting, we briefly saw the lapwing fly by on its odd, paddle-shaped wings. It landed out of view in a low spot, and all of the assembled birders headed out along the field edge in hope of a better look. As we walked along, a dark bird appeared in the distance and beat its way toward us.

Though far away, the bird was obviously large. Very large, maybe even huge. The long wings flapped with unmistakable power, quickly halving the bird's distance to us. A man and woman who were walking more or less beside me stopped nearby, and all three of us examined the oncoming bird, the lapwing momentarily forgotten.

Though the dark bird was flying quite low, the light was dim, and it was not easy to discern detail against the sky. But it was still apparent to me that we were looking at a juvenile bald eagle, and that if it continued on its present course, we were going to have a thrillingly close encounter with it.

That is exactly what happened. The eagle passed right over our heads, close enough that one might almost have felt the rush of air off its wings. I turned to my neighbors, wanting to somehow acknowledge the experience we had just been fortunate enough to share.

golden
eagle
juvenile

turkey
vulture

bald eagle
third-year "osprey head"

soaring birds

turkey vulture

golden eagle

bald eagle

bald eagle
juvenile

bald eagle
second year

bald eagle
adult

But instead of returning my contented gaze and wide smile, they were looking at each other with faces that betrayed puzzlement, not elation. Instantly, I knew that they were unsure of what the bird was — an unsettling emotional state in which I've spent far too much time myself.

Finally, the man spoke *sotto voce*, cocking an eyebrow at his companion, "TV . . . or BV?" She shrugged helplessly, saying nothing, and silently they headed on toward the spot where the lapwing had disappeared.

My heart didn't exactly sink, but it briefly took on a bit of water. These people had just had an eagle zoom right over them, but they hadn't fully enjoyed it because they were unable to recognize it as such. Instead they were trying to make their observations fit their mental image of turkey vulture or black vulture, and it wasn't working.

I considered telling them what they had missed, but many of you will know what stopped me — a feeling that I would only be making a small private humiliation both larger and public. I love to teach, but you have to pick your moments.

The story ends happily, though, as we all soon enjoyed wonderful views of the lapwing. I'd wager that the couple have completely forgotten the big dark bird that left them scratching their heads, but I have not. And so, picking my moment, I'd like to offer a few pointers on bald eagle identification.

To begin with, the two birders would have had no trouble had our eagle been an adult. Though a lot of birders struggle with identifications of all sorts, very few people hesitate to call an adult bald eagle just that, provided it was reasonably close.

But the very distinctiveness of mature bald eagles sets a trap into which far too many birders fall — the root problem that keeps so many birders from coming to really know bald eagles is that the adults are just so darn distinctive.

Most everyone, if asked how to identify a bald eagle, could at least stammer out a few words that, reduced to the simplest terms, might be stated as follows: "big + brown + white head + white tail = bald eagle." This white head–white tail algorithm is so firmly entrenched that you'll frequently see people trying to force other birds into it — great black-backed gull and osprey leap to mind.

The basic equation isn't false, but stopping there is a little like saying, "ham + eggs + white toast + black coffee = breakfast." Sure, that's a breakfast, perhaps you even think it's the ideal one, but wouldn't it be nice to have blueberry pancakes every now and again? How about some fresh-squeezed orange juice?

If you limit yourself to only the most basic field marks and recognizable plumages, you may not starve, but you'll be missing out on a lot of great stuff. Careful, though. Once you let go of the idea that all bald eagles have white heads and tails, you're going to go through a period of discomfort, when you'll suspect that nearly any big dark bird might fit into your newly expanded definition. You may at times feel that you no longer know what any bald eagle looks like. After all, when you begin to include all the possible plumages, you find that bald eagles may show dark heads with dark bellies, white heads with dark bellies, or dark heads with white bellies. Their tails can be dark, white, or some of each.

You may briefly flirt with the idea of abandoning birding in favor of something less complicated and more easily grasped — particle physics, for example. Such thoughts are just growing pains and will pass, leaving you with a richer, more nuanced understanding of the species.

PLUMAGE IN FOUR PARTS

Let's take a closer look at those plumages and divide them into four categories. Adult plumage, which everyone recognizes, is attained in the fourth year of a bald eagle's life and replaced by identical feathers from then on. Juvenal plumage, worn for a bird's first year, is characterized by a dark brown head and body, though near the end of this time, the belly may fade to a paler brown. Years two and three are probably the hardest to get a feel for, but painted in broad strokes, here's how it goes.

Remember that we are going from a dark-headed, dark-bellied bird in year one to a white-headed, dark-bellied bird in year four. In year two, the belly is mostly whitish flecked with brown, but the entire head and breast are still dark, giving the bird a hooded look. In year three, the head whitens and the belly darkens. Early on in this year, bald eagle bellies will be predominantly white with brown flecks, but the brown will win out, replacing most or all of the white. The face, crown, nape, and throat will go from mostly brown to mostly white.

As the head whitens there often remains a dark brown eye stripe. At first, this brown lends the bird a heavily masked Ninja or bandit look. Later on it can thin, creating a faux osprey face. Of course, you mostly see these facial details on perched birds.

If you do get a perched bird, or a low-flying one, you might also look for beak and eye color, which both go from dark to yellow as an eagle moves through its first four years.

THE TAIL'S DETAILS

You may be wondering why tails haven't been discussed yet. The reason is that they are quite variable and are often not a good indication of a bald eagle's age. They can be anywhere from dark with some whitish mottling (as they often are on juveniles) to pure white (as they typically are on adults). In between, the tail usually shows a white to whitish base, with a variably thick dark terminal band across the tip.

Some balds have tails that are very like those of a golden eagle in pattern, though not in length. Balds are always proportionately short-tailed and large-headed, whereas goldens have long tails and small heads. Tail length can be difficult to judge when birds are soaring with tails fanned; it's more apparent on a bird gliding by with its tail folded.

BALDS VERSUS GOLDENS

Speaking of golden eagles, I think birders generally overestimate the difficulty of telling them apart from balds, mainly because their common names both contain the e-word. In this case, "eagle" simply means "big raptor," because the two are not closely related in a taxonomic sense.

The previously mentioned differences in head and tail proportions are usually the best marks to use on distant flying birds. If you get a flying eagle close up, the first thing to look at are the axillaries — the feathers on the underside of the wings where they join the body — otherwise known as the "wingpits." I have never seen a bald eagle young enough to still have a brown head that didn't also have white or whitish axillaries. And I've never seen a golden eagle of any age that didn't have solidly dark wingpits.

Naturally, if you have an eagle-sized bird with dark wingpits and a white or whitish head, it will be a bald. But only if you are seeing the head color correctly. Occasionally a golden eagle at some distance may appear to be white-headed, especially if it has a lot of the gold feathers on the neck from which it takes its name.

Let's go back to the question of the lapwing field, "TV . . . or BV?"

Although it's true that many people confuse our two eagles with black and turkey vultures, the only pair to choose between is turkey vulture and golden eagle. Both have long-tailed, small-headed silhouettes, and they share a habit of soaring in a dihedral posture, with wings raised a bit above the flat horizontal. What you will not see either golden or bald eagles doing is teetering from side to side as turkey vultures so often do. Turkey vultures "rock." Black vultures have a short tail, but their small size and snappy, frequent flapping make them fairly unlike either eagle.

SHAPE

Especially when attempting to identify flying raptors, shape is among the very first things one should assess. Shape is important and useful on bald eagles, too, but there is a pitfall here.

One thing that's great about shape as a field mark is that it tends not to change much in birds, despite differences in age and sex, whereas plumages vary drastically. But many birds actually do change their shape somewhat as they move from juvenile to adult. With most small birds, and many large ones, these differences are slight. Raptors are an exception. Quite a few of them do alter their shape perceptibly over the first year or so of life, and bald eagles are a good species for demonstrating the phenomenon.

A juvenile bald eagle has wings that are considerably wider and blunter than those of an adult. Look at a good photograph or painting of a first-year bald eagle in flight, and you will see that it looks a bit like a flying door. The secondaries are quite long and the wingtips blunt. An adult bald eagle calls to mind something more like a flying board, perhaps a snowboard, though that last image overstates the roundness of the wingtips considerably. But it looks a good deal more aerodynamic and less hulking.

The tails of juveniles are also longer, especially in first-year birds. Balds still have those big heads that project well out past their wings, and even the longest-tailed bald looks stubbier than any golden.

If you happen to see a second-year bald eagle — the ones with mostly white bellies and dark bibbed heads — look carefully at the trailing edge of the wings; they will often appear ragged and uneven, as the longer secondaries of the first year are replaced by shorter ones. The tail may show a similar unevenness.

bald eagle
juvenile

If bald eagles are infrequently seen in your area, you can look for the shape difference between juvenile and adult red-tailed hawks. Like bald eagles, the young birds have longer tails than adults. The difference in the wings is reversed, though, with the juveniles having narrower wings than their elders.

Why would such differences in shape occur at all? One plausible explanation says that the shapes of juveniles give them more leeway for less skillful flying, whereas the adults have a more high-performance structure that allows for greater maneuverability but is harder to control.

I once heard a bird identification expert discussing how it felt to study identification. "At first, you think you've got it pretty well figured out," he said, "but then you look at it some more, and it starts to seem confusing again. Then you reach another place where you think that this time, you really understand it, until you suddenly realize that things are a lot more complicated than you ever suspected. And so on . . . "

Wherever you are in your study of bald eagles, I urge you to go out and punch through to that next level. Even if some of the progress you make is later revealed to be partially incorrect, you'll still be a better birder for it. ◢

BASICS OF SHOREBIRD ID

Here's a pep talk :

DON'T PANIC, YOU CAN DO THIS.

ARE SANDPIPERS AND THEIR FAR-TOO-NUMEROUS KIN really birds? The question arises because of the way many bird watchers view the little beasts. You see it all the time at pond edges and wet fields and sewage plants. Suddenly a small brown bird is spotted working along the water, and half the bird watchers immediately turn away, searching for sparrows and distant hawks. They feel defeated before they begin, and so they do not begin at all. Shorebirds are just too hard.

I am sympathetic. On one of my first bird watching forays away from home, I went to the great coastal impoundments of Delaware in early August, one of the shorebird gathering spots. I was well armed with ignorance and the standard field guides of the day. The guides had served me well as I struggled through my first encounters with warblers and sparrows, and I had no hint that they would fail me here. In fact, they didn't. My friend and I (he was no more experienced and no less confident) positively identified all the shorebirds we saw. In fact, we identified all the shorebirds, at least all of the ones that could possibly be found in coastal Delaware in the fall. A clean sweep. In one memorable flock of no more than twenty birds we found all the peeps: least, semipalmated, pectoral, western, white-rumped, dunlin, sanderling, and Baird's. We blew through the dowitchers, finding both species without effort. Shorebirds were a snap.

I have no idea how many species of small brown shorebirds we actually saw that day, although I am fairly certain there were some leasts and

S H O R E B I R D S

least sandpiper
fresh breeding
adult plumage
(also called alternate,
nuptial, or summer plumage)

least sandpiper
fresh nonbreeding
plumage (also called
basic, nonnuptial, or
winter plumage)

least sandpiper
fresh juvenal plumage
(juvenile)

a few semipalmateds. I base that on twenty years of returning to the coast and rarely failing to find both of these in the fall — not on the belief that we correctly identified any birds that day.

WHY ARE SHOREBIRDS SO DIFFICULT?

To start with, shorebirds are not as hard to identify as most people think. Granted, they are not spring male warblers, but their reputation is not entirely deserved. The widely held view that they are difficult to identify accurately stems from a number of problems.

THE PROBLEMS

1. **FIELD GUIDES.** Most field guides don't have enough space to explain all the difficulties. Many field guide authors assume that if you are taken with shorebirds, you will acquire one of the specialty books.

2. **VIEWING.** It is hard to get close to shorebirds. Viewing shorebirds, at least the small ones, almost always requires a spotting scope. A lot of shorebird watching takes place in the late summer and fall, when heat shimmer and mosquitoes make favored sites a challenge even for intrepid observers.

3. **TERMINOLOGY.** Shorebird identification is often couched in unfamiliar terms. Words like "tertials" and "scapulars" and "primary extension" pop up with distressing frequency.

4. **PLUMAGES.** This is the bugaboo. To correctly identify many shorebirds you need to know what plumage they are in. Most observers despair over simply remembering the field marks. Being told that they change, depending on the age of the bird, is just too much.

THE GOOD NEWS

None of this is as difficult as it seems. All the problems can be solved — just take them one at a time. It is, in fact, fairly easy to learn most of what you need to know to identify shorebirds. You may not be able to identify every distant brown speck, but you can put a name on a lot of birds that you might otherwise ignore.

THE SOLUTIONS

1. FIELD GUIDES. Some are better than others, and more is better than fewer. Check out the field guides on the market, choose the one that best suits your needs, and refer to it often. With this guide, and any others you carry as backup, you can identify most of the shorebirds you see. The more involved and dedicated you become, the more likely it is that you will want to acquire a specialty shorebird guide.

2. VIEWING. It is possible to see shorebirds up close and in good light. Many allow fairly close approach, especially where habitat is limited, such as at smaller mud flats and ponds. Start with the birds you can see well. The point here is not to learn to casually throw a name on the minute brown speck a half-mile away doing the dance of the seven veils behind a shimmering curtain of rising heat. That comes only after you've been hooked for a while.

3. TERMINOLOGY. Every field guide has a drawing labeled "parts of a bird." Most bird watchers glance at it once, see dozens of names and parts, and flip right past it. Go back and study it for a minute. The impression that learning the parts of a bird is equivalent to learning Mandarin is wrong. You already know almost all the terms. Once you eliminate words like "head," "breast," "wing," "eye line," "bill," and "leg," there are only a half-dozen terms that may be new. Once you reduce the problem, terminology is eliminated as a roadblock, and mastering terminology is half the battle in any endeavor.

4. PLUMAGES. Okay, now we're down to it. Shorebirds are not as easy as warblers, but they are not the grayish brown morass most folks assume. There are, and we can cheerfully ignore the occasional exception, only three plumages to deal with: adults in breeding plumage, adults in winter plumage, and juveniles. These are the same three plumages you have already learned, without panicking or even thinking about it, for warblers! Adult spring, adult fall, and youngsters. The old familiars.

Field guides use a variety of terms to describe these three basic plumages. Some employ the user-friendly version: "breeding," "non-breeding," and "juvenile" (or "juvenal," depending on the nitpickiness of the author, meaning the first set of feathers or the plumage a bird has when it leaves the nest). Some adopt, with adequate justification, more technical

Quick Shorebird Terms

PEEP: A bird watcher's term for the small, generally brownish shorebirds in the genus *Calidris*, including least, semipalmated, western, white-rumped, and Baird's sandpipers.

TRANSITIONAL PLUMAGE: Many shorebirds in the fall are in the process of molting from summer to winter plumage, and this is their transitional plumage.

SCAPULARS: Shoulders. The scapulars are the feathers that cover a bird's shoulder area when it is sitting.

SCALLOPED EDGES: On many shorebirds in fresh juvenal plumage the feathers on the upperparts (back and wings on a sitting bird) are dark, but they have pale fringes or edges. The pale edges contrasting with the dark centers of the feathers make the bird look scalloped.

TERTIALS: On a sitting shorebird the tertials are the feathers that overlie the primaries. That is, if you look at the back end of the bird, the last group of feathers you see are the tips of the primaries, which sit on top of the tail. Just past the primaries is a set of largish feathers that usually are differently patterned than the primaries or the rest of the upperparts. They are the tertials. Check the "parts of a bird" diagram in the front of any field guide for a drawing that shows where the primaries and tertials are located.

terms: "alternate" (for breeding), "basic" (for nonbreeding), "juvenal" (for juvenile). Or "nuptial" (breeding), "nonnuptial" (nonbreeding), "juvenile." Some prefer seasonal versions: "summer" (breeding), "winter" (nonbreeding), "juvenile." Note that "juvenile" is fairly consistent, although in extreme cases you may run across variations such as "first basic." The lack of consistent terminology is frustrating, but there is no simple way around it. Pick the guide of your choice and learn its system. Some bird watchers solve the problem by laying out five or six guides and making a chart. It's not a bad trick. By the time you've finished, you won't need a chart anymore.

THE PLUMAGE TRICK

It may not be absolutely necessary to know the age of the shorebird you are looking at, but it certainly helps in many cases. It doesn't matter with avocets and oystercatchers and most yellowlegs, because there is either no chance of confusion or there are easily observed field marks that don't change with age. We are concerned here only with the birds in which knowing the age makes identification easier, including the small sandpipers, the dowitchers, some plovers, and a few other, less frequently seen groups. To identify these birds, you need to start with age, but there are shortcuts that make it easier than it sounds.

The first shortcut is season, which is the reason that it makes sense to start your journey into shorebirds in the spring. Almost all the shorebirds you see in the spring are adults in breeding plumage, just like warblers. A few may still be acquiring breeding plumage, and a few may still be in winter plumage, but the vast majority of birds will be in breeding plumage. All that is required (not to make it sound too easy) is to figure out the field marks, just as you would for any other bird. The problem comes in the late summer and fall when shorebirds are headed south. Then you add juveniles to the mix; and adults, depending on the timing and the species, can be in either breeding or nonbreeding plumage (and sometimes in between, but that's easy to recognize).

QUICK AND DIRTY
AGING OF FALL SHOREBIRDS

To illustrate the generic differences in the ages of shorebirds, let's use the least sandpiper as an example. I have chosen this species because it occurs in every part of the country, is a regular visitor to pond edges and other wet habitats, and is often easy to approach.

Least sandpipers are small brown shorebirds, compact and even dumpy looking. Field guides tend to focus on the fact that they have yellow legs, which is true and does separate them from most similar species. Anyone who has looked at shorebirds, however, knows that leg color can be a difficult thing to see. At a distance, or in bad light, or when the bird is wading in water or has mud on its legs, it is less useful. Besides, we aren't looking for single field marks; we are trying to determine the age of the bird.

In spring, least sandpipers are quite brown, with some pale fringes and edges on the back and wing feathers, and strong streaking on the throat. Spring is easy.

In fall it is possible to see all three plumages of least sandpiper in one small flock. Some of the adults are still in breeding plumage, although it tends to be a bit worn and somewhat duller than it is earlier in the season. There may also be adults that have largely acquired their winter plumage. They are very plain, gray-brown on the upperparts with a gray-brown wash on the throat. In this crowd juveniles really stand out. Juveniles are the brightest of the group. They are usually redder on the upperparts, with bright white edges on most of the feathers, making them looked scalloped or fringed. They usually have bold white stripes running down the back; the throat is streaked and dusky.

What is important is not the details (those are in the guides), but the pattern that is repeated in most shorebirds. In most species, juveniles are brighter above, more heavily marked with white and red, and more spangled. They tend to be plainer below. Adults in breeding plumage are similar to juveniles, but are visibly duller above and more heavily marked below. Adults in winter plumage are almost always clearly duller than either juveniles or breeding adults. In most species they are plain above, with little or no spotting or color, and equally plain below.

What is important is the pattern that is repeated in most shorebirds.

Once you learn the basic distinctions, you are ready to recognize the age of most of the shorebirds you see. Now the problem is reduced to the same challenge you have with any bird: fitting the field marks to the bird. It is not a snap, but the biggest hurdle has been cleared, and now the guides begin to make sense. 🐦

YELLOWLEGS

The shorebirds every bird watcher is likely to see

ONE OF THE SHOREBIRDS ALMOST EVERY BIRD WATCHER comes across at one time or another is the yellowlegs. Yellowlegs occur throughout most of North America during most seasons of the year, and they are the birds most likely to be spotted at the edge of a farm pond, wet field, lake shore, or in a drainage ditch. They pop up almost anywhere there's water, and they are the most widely distributed inland shorebirds.

Naturally, there are two yellowlegs. They are shorebirds, after all. Learning to tell them apart is one of the first steps in tackling the larger problem of shorebirds in general. With practice it even turns out to be reasonably simple. Mastering the yellowlegs can provide you with the confidence to consider harder groups.

When identifying yellowlegs, the key characters, in descending order of importance, are size, bill size and shape, plumage, and calls. Most of the time you can solve the identification problem with just the first two, and sometimes only one of them is necessary.

SIZE

As the names imply, there is a size difference between greater and lesser yellowlegs. It may seem obvious, but since we are talking about shorebirds it pays to be precise. The greater yellowlegs is, on average, 20 percent larger than lesser yellowlegs. Twenty percent may not sound like much, but it is considerable, and the difference is often striking. When they are seen together it is a snap to tell the two apart; greaters tower over their smaller cousins. Watching them side by side, one wonders why it is ever difficult to identify a yellowlegs.

The problem is that we often see single yellowlegs, or groups of three to five birds, all apparently the same size. Single birds seen without the benefit of comparison are trickier, and angle, distance, and the depth of the water the bird is standing in can confuse even experienced observers. When looking at a single yellowlegs, size is at best a good clue, but it should not be considered diagnostic on its own.

It is not always necessary to see the two yellowlegs species together to make a size comparison, however. Two other birds often seen with yellowlegs are killdeer and spotted sandpipers (not shown here). Both are widely distributed, common inland birds that share many of the same habitats with yellowlegs in migration, and they may be helpful when making comparisons to try to estimate a yellowlegs' relative size.

The body of lesser yellowlegs is about the same size as killdeer or spotted sandpiper; the legs of the lesser are visibly longer than those of these other species, as is the neck. Greater yellowlegs are distinctly larger than either killdeer or spotted sandpiper, not only towering over them, but looking much bulkier as well. Greater yellowlegs are closer to dowitchers in size than to spotted sandpipers and killdeer.

BILL

When size alone won't resolve the issue, look closely at the bill. The bills of greater yellowlegs are not only larger than the bills of lessers (which one might expect), they are proportionately larger. With a little practice it is usually easy to tell the difference between the two. The bill of a greater yellowlegs is visibly longer than the length of the head, about one-and-a-half times as long. (The length of the head is the distance, in a straight line, from the base of the bill to the rear of the crown.) The bill of lesser yellowlegs is about the same size as the length of the head. To get an idea of how this looks, check out the accompanying illustrations of the two on page III, in your field guides, or on the Internet and do a quick calculation using the edge of a piece of paper. Once you have actually measured the birds, the difference is easier to see.

The bills are also different structurally. Greater yellowlegs has a thicker, heavier bill, especially at the base. The bill of lesser is finer, thinner,

solitary
sandpiper
in flight

greater
yellowlegs
in flight

solitary
sandpiper

lesser
yellowlegs
breeding adult

lesser
yellowlegs
fall juvenile

greater
yellowlegs
fall juvenile

greater
yellowlegs
breeding adult

and appears more pointed. This difference, while subtler than size, can also be made useful with practice.

It is an article of faith that the bill of the greater yellowlegs is distinctive because it curves upward slightly. In profile, when the bird is still, this is true, and in a few cases it can be fairly obvious, even at a distance, but the upturn is subtle. Just because the bill of a particular bird does not appear to curve up does not mean it is automatically a lesser. This is a field mark that is best used as a positive: when you see a slight upcurve to the bill, it is a greater. When you don't, it is time to look at other field marks.

The other bill character that can be useful is color. The bills of lesser yellowlegs are all-black at all seasons. The bills of greater yellowlegs in fall and winter are two-toned, black on the outer half and dark gray on the inner half. The difference between dark gray and black may not be dramatic, but it is often surprisingly easy to see in the field. Any bird with a two-toned bill is a greater. Any bird with an all-black bill could be either one — especially in the spring, when the bills of greaters tend to be all dark.

PLUMAGE

If all else fails, or if you want added confirmation of your identification, it is time to look at plumage. The very thought of shorebird plumages sends many people into a sort of ornithological nervous breakdown. Relax. We are going to do the short version, in part because the differences between the two species of yellowlegs tend to be consistent in all seasons, and in part because the differences between ages, sexes, and seasons are not as great in yellowlegs as in many shorebirds. Besides, most of the subtler plumage variations just don't help much with species identification.

In spring, both yellowlegs are blackish brown and spotted with white above, and whitish with variable bars and streaks below. Both are streaked and spotted with blackish or dark gray on the throat and upper breast. The greater has fairly heavy dark bars on the flanks, which the lesser lacks.

In fall, adults of both species are gray above and mostly white below. The most distinctive plumage difference at this season is that lessers are plainer above, with little or no spotting on the crown and back; greaters are usually distinctly spotted with white. The differences are not always great, however, and bill size and color, very visible at this time of year, are more useful.

Not all yellowlegs seen in the fall are adults. Many are young birds, in the dreaded juvenal plumage. ("Juvenal" is the term meaning the plumage of juvenile birds.) In the case of yellowlegs, juvenal plumage is no reason to panic. Juveniles look like adults, except that they are more obviously streaked on the throat and are a warmer brownish gray above. On lessers this shows as diffuse dull gray streaks that often look like a grayish wash at a distance. On greaters, the streaking is darker and more distinct, and there is usually some barring on the flanks, which is absent on lessers of all flavors.

Greater yellowlegs have a thicker, heavier bill, especially at the base.

VOICE

Sometimes a yellowlegs resists all attempts to identify it to species, and it becomes necessary to settle for just saying, "I saw a yellowlegs." Often this happens because the bird decides to vacate the premises at the precise moment you're ready to give it a thorough going-over. Watching the bird fly away is not going to help much. Greater and lesser yellowlegs are essentially indistinguishable in flight — gray above, mostly white below, with a white rump and mostly white tail. There isn't really a dime's worth of difference between the two.

Luckily, flying yellowlegs are notably noisy beasts. They call when they take off, when they land, when they are thinking about taking off, when something annoys them, and when they are flying overhead. About the only time yellowlegs are consistently silent is when they are eating and while they're asleep.

This means, of course, that the very next yellowlegs you see will fly off silently, but hang in there. Most yellowlegs will call at some point when you are watching them.

The calls of the two are distinctive, but learning to tell them apart with confidence requires practice, and it is well worth the trouble to listen to bird tapes to get a better feel for the differences.

The typical call of greater is louder and more strident than lesser's, which is not only soft, but almost mellow. A loud, startling, brassy, "Here I am! I am a yellowlegs!" call means it is a greater. A softer, shorter, more tentative call usually means it is a lesser — or a less assertive greater.

The number and pattern of the notes are also a clue (though not completely diagnostic) to which species is talking. The call of greater is three to five loud, descending notes, most often written as *whew whew whew*. The call of lesser is usually two or three notes, most often transcribed as *tu-tu-tu*. While clearly heard birds can be identified with confidence, distant birds are often impossible to categorize. Both yellowlegs give a single short sharp note while on the ground (perhaps an alarm call) and the differences between the two are very slight.

BEHAVIOR

There are also some subtle behavioral differences you can watch for. Lesser yellowlegs tend to be more common on smaller ponds and on lake shores that are heavily wooded or have vegetation growing right up to the edge. Lessers also tend to be more social, occurring in slightly tighter groups, both in flight and when feeding. Lessers often move quickly forward through the water, sweeping their bills back and forth like tiny avocets. So do greaters, though it appears to be rarer. Greaters also tend to feed in slightly deeper water than lessers. None of these differences is perfectly consistent or diagnostic, but if you watch a lot of yellowlegs you will notice that they hold true more often than not.

OTHER SPECIES

There are three birds that may be confused with yellowlegs. Each is distinctive in its own way, and it should be possible to eliminate each without too much effort. The most common source of confusion is solitary sandpiper, another inland freshwater shorebird with a wide distribution. Solitary sandpipers live up to their name, being found rarely in groups. They prefer streams, wooded swamps, and small sewage ponds, and tend to shun the open mud flats the yellowlegs like. It is possible to see them together at times, however, and those times are good opportunities for comparing them.

The solitary sandpiper is a slender, shorter-necked, shorter-legged bird, smaller than a lesser yellowlegs. The bill is shorter and proportionately thicker than the bill of lesser, and the legs are greenish rather than yellow. Leg color, when seen well, is a good way of separating the two. Keep in mind, though, that the legs of solitary sandpipers can look quite yellowish

fall juvenile

fall juvenile

Greater Yellowlegs

SIZE
- **LARGE.** Notably larger than lesser. Much larger than killdeer or spotted sandpiper.

BILL
- **LONG,** at least 1½ times length of head.
- Slightly upcurved.
- Two-toned, gray at base, black at tip, except in spring.

PLUMAGE
- More heavily marked below than lesser, often with heavy bars on flanks.

CALL
- **LOUD,** ringing, three to five notes.

Lesser Yellowlegs

SIZE
- **MEDIUM.** Notably smaller than greater. Body about same size as killdeer and spotted sandpiper.

BILL
- **MEDIUM,** same length as head.
- Straight, not upcurved.
- All-black at all seasons.

PLUMAGE
- Less heavily marked below at all seasons, does not show heavy barring on flanks.

CALL
- **SOFTER,** more mellow, shorter than in greater.

in some lights or when they are wet. This impression usually disappears if you keep watching the bird. In addition, solitary sandpipers are more finely spotted on the back and more delicate-looking overall than lessers. The plainer head and face set off the solitary sandpiper's striking white eye-ring, which usually stands out at any distance, unlike the eye-ring of the lesser.

In flight, solitary sandpipers show a dark rump and tail with white, barred edges, very different from the white tail and rump of yellowlegs. In addition, the solitary's underwings are very dark, unlike the pale underwings of the yellowlegs. This can be especially helpful, as solitary sandpipers have a habit of holding their wings up above their back for a second or two after landing.

In the fall, Wilson's phalaropes may also look like lesser yellowlegs. They are yellow-legged, gray above and white below, and have a white rump. But winter Wilson's are very plain birds that show little contrast, being much paler above and below than yellowlegs. They are also smaller, much shorter-necked and shorter-legged, and have a very thin, needlelike bill.

Stilt sandpipers can also look like yellowlegs, because they have green-ish yellow legs and are larger than most shorebirds. Stilt sandpipers are more likely to be mistaken for dowitchers, though. They are chunky and short-necked, and the long bill droops at the tip. They also feed in a sewing-machine fashion, probing the mud like dowitchers. (See page 125 for more on stilt sandpipers.)

Tackling shorebirds means starting with one small group at a time, and there is no better place to start than with yellowlegs.

PLOVERS

Sifting through the "ringed" plovers

THE FOUR WIDELY DISTRIBUTED SPECIES OF SMALL plovers in North America that show a single breast-band might well be called "shorebirds with training wheels." In delightful contrast to the majority of shorebirds, whose often difficult identification has brought many a birder to the edge of tears, these little birds are crisply patterned and, at least in the case of breeding adults, quite easily sorted out.

These four plovers, the semipalmated, piping, snowy, and Wilson's, can be collectively referred to as "ringed plovers." However, there is another small plover species, *Charadrius hiaticula*, known in North America as the common ringed plover and in the Old World as the ringed plover. This species, which breeds sparingly on Canada's Baffin Island and is a rare but regular vagrant to certain outposts in Alaska, will not be covered here. It is so similar in appearance to the semipalmated plover that only those with a good deal of field experience should attempt its identification even in the limited area where it is known to occur.

Another plover with breast-bands, the killdeer, doesn't really fit in our group. Its large size, terrestrial habitat, distinctive voice, and bright rufous rump and uppertail put it in a class by itself. Besides, it has two black rings, not one.

One thing that unites our ringed plovers and makes them popular, even with shorebird-phobic birders, is that they're cute. Watching them scurry over the sand like little wind-up toys brings a smile to even the

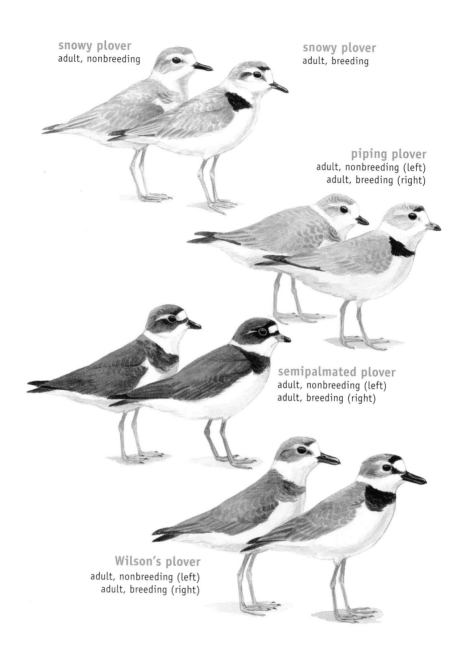

snowy plover
adult, nonbreeding

snowy plover
adult, breeding

piping plover
adult, nonbreeding (left)
adult, breeding (right)

semipalmated plover
adult, nonbreeding (left)
adult, breeding (right)

Wilson's plover
adult, nonbreeding (left)
adult, breeding (right)

most jaded among us. But their cuteness derives from some special environmental adaptations and can give us some insight into their evolution.

For starters, they have short bills. In comparison, think of a dowitcher, a curlew, or even a dunlin, which is perhaps closer to the archetypal shorebird. Their long bills are useful for probing the mud, and though godwits, for example, can be spectacular, they aren't cute. Many of these shorebirds also have beady eyes, or at least small ones. Most plovers, on the other hand, and especially the ringed group, have quite large eyes. And big eyes are always considered cute, whether on babies, puppies, velvet paintings, troll dolls, or birds.

Big eyes and short bills not only make the ringed plovers cute, but superbly suit them to spotting their prey visually, then deftly picking it from the sand or mud. When they see something edible, their ridiculously fast gait carries them to it in seconds, without need of flight. This feeding style contrasts sharply with the methodical dowitchers, who probe the depths with their long sensitive bills, slowly working their way across a flat.

One other "cute" behavior to watch for is foot-stirring. You'll often see a plover reach out one leg, then actually stir the surface of the mud with its toes. This apparently causes small worms and other arthropods to come to the surface, or to at least wriggle, so the plover can spot and grab them. Semipalmated plovers seem especially prone to this behavior, probably because they like a bit wetter substrate than other plovers.

Be careful: gaining confidence with the ringed plovers has been known to lead people to look at other shorebirds.

You will most likely encounter one of our four ringed plover species on an ocean beach, lake or river shore, or mud flat. In many areas geography aids the identification. To make things interesting, though, let's say you're birding somewhere along the Gulf of Mexico, perhaps at Fort Myers Beach in Florida or at Bolivar Flats in Texas, where any or all of the four may be found. Let us further imagine that it is spring — April or May. At that time of year, the plovers should be adults in breeding plumage, which makes identifying them fairly straightforward. Get their leg color and one or two other marks and you've got them.

Not many shorebirds permit this sort of thumbs-up/thumbs-down treatment, but the ringed plovers do. They offer an accessible way into the often confusing world of shorebird identification. Of course, we're simplifying things a bit, but it's a reasonable place to start. Let's take a look at the characters in the chart below and make sure we've got our terms straight.

BACK COLOR

A common convention is to divide the ringed plovers into two groups: those whose upperparts are a medium to dark brown, not unlike wet sand, and those that are colored like dry sand — pale gray-white or very light tan — above. Semipalmated and Wilson's plovers have backs and wings that are definitely in the first category, and the plumages of piping and snowy plovers fall into the second. Another character that breaks down into the same groups is the size and shape of the ring. In the first group, semipalmated and Wilson's plovers exhibit complete, fairly wide breast-bands. In the second, piping and snowy plovers show only thin or incomplete ones. The snowy plover is often described as having "collar buttons," because its ring is generally restricted to two elongated dark patches on the sides of the neck.

Ringed Plover Quick Reference Chart

	"bright" legs	"dull" legs
"wet sand" back: complete ring	semipalmated	Wilson's
"dry sand" back: broken/thin ring	piping	snowy

CAUTION:
Valid only for adults in breeding plumage

LEG COLOR

With our quartet of plovers broken into two groups, we need another character that will bring us to the species level. Leg color serves nicely if we define it broadly. "Bright" means somewhere in the orange to yellow-orange range. "Dull" means anything from black to a dull pinkish color. Presto — our pairs are split. Our first group, those with backs the color of wet sand, break into the bright-orange-legged semipalmated and the dull-pink-legged Wilson's. The second group, those with backs the color of dry sand, break into the bright-orange-yellow-legged piping and the dull-black-legged snowy plover. If you're still feeling lost, check out the chart on page 120.

You may be content with this much — a relatively easy, straightforward rule that allows you to confidently and correctly name most of the ringed plovers you see. Sooner or later, though, you may want to identify one of these birds in the nine or so months of the year that are not breeding season, or you might encounter an individual bird that seems to defy categorization.

BILL SHAPE

Fear not. There is another character that will allow you to identify any ringed plover in any season if you take time to learn it: bill shape. Of course, the details of bill shape are often harder to discern than things like back color, but most of the time these birds will allow fairly close approach. Be wary, though, of getting close to nesting areas. You might easily distract the parents from looking after their eggs or young, which might then fall prey to a sharp-eyed gull or crow. Even worse, you might step on a chick or an egg, which are exquisitely camouflaged.

We'll begin with the easiest bills and work our way up in difficulty. The Wilson's plover has, for its size, a real honker of a bill, longer and thicker by far than any other ringed plover. The bill is always black, too. So the Wilson's turns out to be easy. At the other end of the thickness continuum is the snowy plover, which has a thin, rather long bill, at least in plover terms. The snowy's bill is also always all-black. You might think of the snowy as having a bill like a warbler — fine and straight, like a nice pair of surgical forceps.

That leaves us with piping and semipalmated plovers, whose bills might be compared with those of vireos. They are somewhat thick and stubby relative to the snowy, but still diminutive next to the Wilson's. Of the two, the piping's bill shape is more distinctive — it always looks chunky or swollen, with the upper and lower edges of the bill appearing almost curved. I say almost because they are actually straight, but the thickness at the bill's base and through much of its length creates an impression of roundness. The effect is heightened by the abrupt way the bill ends, quickly coming to a point that looks almost blunt.

Semipalmated plovers might have the least remarkable bill shape of the four species, but this is just another way of saying that they are the ones most of us see most often, and thus they become the standard against which we judge the others. The bill on the semipalmated starts with a medium-thick base and tapers fairly evenly along its length before coming to a fine point.

BILL COLOR

Note that you will see some birds of all four species, especially in winter, that have all-black bills. The snowy and Wilson's plovers always have black bills. The semipalmated and piping often show at least some orange at the bill base and have extensive orange in the bill during breeding season. So the presence of orange on the bill indicates that you have either a semipalmated or a piping plover.

I mention color (which most eyes go to first) after shape because shape is really what will get you through in the clinches. It takes a certain amount of discipline to look past the bright orange bills and legs of spring, but your efforts will be rewarded on a steamy summer day when your friends are thrown by a proliferation of juveniles and adults, many of them in molt. Knowing the details of bill shape allows you to divine the true identity of these birds almost magically.

Don't forget that even as good a mark as bill shape should always be buttressed with the consideration of other field marks, especially if you think you've found something unusual. A bird may appear to you to have a bill shape perfect for a piping plover, but if it has a dark brown back and a wide black chest band, you might want to take another look.

Go out in spring when the adult birds are easiest to identify, and then spend time really watching known-identity birds. Even if you have only one plover species available to you, you can learn that one's characters inside out and be a big step ahead when you visit the ranges of other birds or when a vagrant graces your patch.

But be careful: gaining confidence with the ringed plovers has been known to lead people to look at other shorebirds. Before you know it, you may be out there with people you formerly thought of as at least mildly insane, endlessly sifting through distant flocks of nearly identical birds. You have been warned.

snowy plover
adult, breeding

piping plover
adult, breeding

semipalmated plover
adult, breeding

Wilson's plover
adult, breeding

MEDIUM PROBING SHOREBIRDS

Willet, stilt sandpiper, and the dowitchers

KENN KAUFMAN POINTS OUT IN HIS *FIELD GUIDE TO Advanced Birding* that, but for differences in size and shape, there would be identification problems for shorebird species as different as willet and least sandpiper, or dunlin and Hudsonian godwit. In their winter plumage, most species are simply gray or brown above and whitish below, with no field marks to steer you in the right direction. Size, shape, and behavior are the key components to shorebird identification.

In this chapter we'll outline the identification challenges posed by four similar species, which we call the medium-sized probing shorebirds: willet, short-billed dowitcher, long-billed dowitcher, and stilt sandpiper.

THE DOWITCHER CAVEAT

First, a caveat: we do not discuss the dowitchers separately. Separating long-billed dowitcher from short-billed dowitcher is one of the single most difficult identification problems in North America. The two were considered the same species until an ornithological paper was published in 1950 describing the differences between the two, and even today, experts must struggle to identify silent dowitchers in nonbreeding plumage.

For our purposes we will give one oversimplified tip for telling the two species apart: listen to the call. The short-billed dowitcher gives a mellow *tu-tu-tu*, almost always in a rapid succession of three or more notes. Long-billeds give a high-pitched *keek*, usually singly, but sometimes in rapid fire.

long-billed
dowitcher
breeding plumage

stilt sandpiper
breeding plumage

stilt sandpiper
adult, nonbreeding

willet
breeding plumage

stilt sandpiper
nonbreeding

short-billed
dowitcher
nonbreeding

short-billed
dowitcher
first winter

long-billed
dowitcher
first winter

willet
adult, nonbreeding

The two calls differ entirely in quality and should not be confused with each other once you have heard them. To delve more deeply into the dowitchers would take another ten pages of discussion of molt, subtle feather differences, and general impressions of size and shape. From here on, we'll simply refer to the two species collectively as dowitchers.

SHAPE, SHAPE, SHAPE

Shape is the most important characteristic for shorebird identification. It takes experience to judge shape relative to other shorebirds, but it is a good idea to have a sense for the shape of the birds before discussing them further.

The dowitchers are chunky, even dumpy, short-legged shorebirds that look low-slung. A feeding dowitcher, with its short legs and long bill, shows a flat-backed posture. The back is nearly horizontal while the dowitcher probes with its sewing-machine motion. A dowitcher's leg length is about as long as its bill length. They typically look fairly short-necked (almost wrestlerlike) but may stretch their necks when alert.

The stilt sandpiper looks much like a dowitcher in shape and size (and

Feeding styles of probing shorebirds

stilt sandpipers
tip forward when probing for food

dowitchers
the back is nearly horizontal when the bird is probing for food

feeding style — more on that in a moment) but is longer-legged, longer-necked, and slimmer overall. The bill of a stilt sandpiper is distinctly shorter than its legs. When a stilt sandpiper feeds, it tips forward noticeably (because of the longer legs and shorter bill), so that the back angles down toward the head, and the wingtips and tail point upward.

The willet is a monster compared to dowitchers and stilt sandpipers, and when these species are seen side by side, the difference is obvious. Willets are chunky, long-necked, and especially long-legged birds. Because its legs are about twice as long as its bill, a feeding willet tips over more than a stilt sandpiper, with its tail well up in the air.

BILL SHAPE

The single most important aspect of shape, and the single most important shorebird field mark overall, is the shape of the bill. Bill shape is very useful for sorting out the larger shorebirds and can be used even for distant birds or birds observed under poor light conditions.

Categorizing shorebirds by their bill shape is a matter of asking a few questions. Is the bill downcurved (like a curlew, whimbrel, or dunlin),

Bill shapes of probing shorebirds

stilt sandpiper
a thin bill that
droops at the tip

**short-billed
dowitcher**
a long, straight bill

willet
a heavy, straight,
chisel-like bill

upturned (like a marbled godwit), or straight (like a Wilson's snipe, Wilson's phalarope, or dowitcher)? Is the bill longer than the head (like a dowitcher, greater yellowlegs, or godwit) or shorter than the head (like a least sandpiper, surfbird, or plover)? Is it thick-based (like a willet or a surfbird) or extra-thin (like Wilson's phalarope or lesser yellowlegs)?

In our group of medium-sized probing shorebirds, bill shape is distinctive for each species. Dowitchers have long straight bills with essentially no downturn (though there may be a very slight downturn in the longest-billed birds). Dowitcher bills are narrow at the base and are roughly the same thickness throughout their length. The bills measure at about 2 to 2^1/$_2$ times the length of the head.

Don't be fooled by dowitcher bills, though. While long-billed and short-billed dowitchers do have average bill length differences, there is an overlap. Thus, even birds in the hand are not always safely identified by the length of the bill. In almost all shorebirds, females have longer bills than males (this helps them feed on different foods at different depths on the same mud flat), so a small difference in bill length, or even curvature, does not necessarily mean a different species. This applies to peeps and curlews and other shorebird species, as well as our probing shorebirds.

Stilt sandpipers, in contrast to the dowitchers, have shorter, thinner bills that droop distinctly at the tip, as though the end got too hot and started melting. The downcurve is most obvious at the tip of the bill, unlike the bills of dunlin and curlew sandpipers, which curve throughout their entire length.

Willets have fairly long, thick bills that do not noticeably taper throughout their length. The base of the willet's bill is thick, and the tip often appears chisel-like. On a side note, there are two willet subspecies that differ in bill length; western birds are longer-billed than eastern ones.

PATTERN IN FLIGHT

Sometimes it is a blessing when the bird decides to fly away. "Darn right," you are probably thinking. "That way I can give up before I start pulling my hair out." Sorry, you're not getting off the hook that easily. A shorebird's plumage pattern, shown in flight, can actually help solve a mystery bird's identification.

The willet is our most distinctive shorebird in flight. While a winter-plumage willet standing on the ground looks all-gray, in flight its wings are largely black with a wide white stripe down the center. The tail is whitish or pale gray. The overall effect this plumage creates is a flashing pattern of white, black, and gray that is hard to miss under any conditions.

Dowitchers in flight are distinctive too, with an obvious wedge of white that extends in a point up the center of the back. Their tails are whitish with narrow black bars, and the rump is whitish with even narrower bars. No similar shorebird shares the white wedge up the back, so seeing a dowitcher in flight really helps identify it, provided you can see the bird's back. Otherwise, dowitchers look fairly even-colored above, with only a very faint wing stripe.

Stilt sandpipers also offer clues to their identity when in flight. They appear fairly even-colored above with mostly dark wings and back, and a narrow white wing stripe. The stilt sandpiper's tail is dark in the center with white edges, and it has a contrasting white rump. Only a few shorebird species have dark tails and white rumps: stilt sandpiper, white-rumped sandpiper, and curlew sandpiper. Other species with white rumps (for example, yellowlegs and red knot) have whitish or grayish (not dark) tails.

LEG COLOR

One of the first things to check when identifying shorebirds is leg color. It helps when comparing least and western sandpipers; when picking out yellowlegs and rare ruffs; and when you encounter a ruddy turnstone out of its stunning breeding plumage. Leg color helps out with our probing shorebirds, too.

Dowitchers and stilt sandpipers both have dull olive-greenish legs, though the legs of stilt sandpipers are slightly yellower, and those of the dowitchers are greener. Willets have dull gray or bluish gray legs without any greenish tones whatsoever. So, blue or gray legs equals willet, while greenish or greenish yellow legs equals dowitcher or stilt sandpiper.

WINTER PLUMAGE

Winter plumage for these species is a mix of gray above and white below. However, there are some subtle and some not-so-subtle differences. Winter willets are gray-backed with a fairly extensive grayish wash on the foreneck and upper chest. There are no bars or spots on the flanks or elsewhere on the underparts. And the willet's face is plain, too, without a prominent supercilium (eyebrow). As a result, they appear to be plain gray overall.

Winter dowitchers, in contrast, have brownish gray upperparts that contrast sharply with their white bellies. Faint grayish barring along the sides extends onto the flanks. The underparts are mostly white, but the chest and throat are grayish, creating a two-toned look below. The face is clearly marked. A pale supercilium contrasts against a dark cheek and crown, giving the winter-plumaged dowitchers a capped appearance.

Stilt sandpipers in winter show an evenly gray back, several degrees paler than winter dowitchers. The chest is streaked along the sides with a fine gray wash. Though the stilt sandpiper has a pale supercilium, it lacks the dowitchers's capped appearance. On the flanks, the stilt sandpiper is clean and unmarked in winter plumage, like the willet. Winter dowitchers always show barring on the flanks. This flank-barring, or lack thereof, can be helpful when you encounter a single winter-plumaged bird (especially if its bill is not visible).

BREEDING PLUMAGE

In breeding plumage, which is held primarily from April through August, these species present different opportunities for confusion. Breeding-plumage dowitchers are the most uniquely patterned. They are bright orange or brick red below, and the upperparts are dark brownish with some fine cinnamon edging. Over the course of the spring and summer, wear affects the plumage, and the birds become progressively duller. Eventually, they become patchy-looking, and isolated areas of bright orange stand out against the otherwise gray plumage. The barring on the flanks of dowitchers is prominent throughout the breeding season.

The stilt sandpiper looks entirely different in breeding plumage than it does in nonbreeding plumage. In breeding plumage, the stilt sandpiper is dark overall, with a dark back and dense dark barring on a gray chest. The eye line remains prominent, and in high breeding plumage, the cheek and cap turn rusty. The flanks and belly become heavily barred with black, which is perhaps the most distinctive characteristic. Breeding stilt sandpiper flanks are much more heavily marked than those of breeding-plumage dowitchers. This flank-barring alone is one of the best ways to identify the "stilt sand" in breeding plumage.

Of all these probing shorebirds, willets have the least dramatic color change from nonbreeding to breeding plumage. In high breeding plumage, the willet appears to be a gray bird that went to the salon and had lots of fine brown streaks added to its feathers. These streaks are most visible on the bird's breast and belly. It is worth noting that willets in the western portions of North America are vastly paler birds, with pale gray backs and light brown markings on the chest. Eastern bird watchers might be confused momentarily by this western willet, but if it flies or calls it will reveal its true identity. The barring on the willet's flanks may be as thick and pronounced as it is on the stilt sandpiper, but the rufous cheek and cap and the decurved bill of the stilt sandpiper are absent. Telling them apart shouldn't be too difficult.

CALLS

Calls are always useful when identifying shorebirds, but few birders take the time to learn more than a few of them. Dowitcher calls, you may remember, are *tu-tu-tu* for short-billed, and a high *keek* for long-billed.

Willets say *willet*, more or less. Actually, on the breeding grounds the willet call is a lengthy *pill-will-will-et . . . . . pill-will-will-et*. During the winter their calls have the same gull-like quality but are shortened to *wee-ill* or *wheee-ahhh*, or simply *will*.

The stilt sandpiper is not as vocal as the other two species and only rarely calls when flushed. It gives a low, hoarse *querf* when startled.

BEHAVIOR

The rapid "sewing-machine" motion of feeding dowitchers is a well-known and reliable behavioral field mark. Dowitchers, when they are not sleeping, running, or flying, seem to be constantly stitching. As they stitch they slowly walk forward. Other species that regularly probe mud flats (dunlin, for example) do not employ the same consistent, regular motion.

Stilt sandpipers employ a similar feeding method, which is especially confusing when a stilt sandpiper mixes in with dowitchers and all the birds seem to be stitching with the same enthusiasm. However, the stilt sandpiper is prone to picking at the surface occasionally (dowitchers practically never do) and also tends to stitch for shorter periods, bringing its head up more often. Another useful behavioral clue is that the longer-legged stilt sandpipers often forage in deeper water than the dowitchers do. In a mixed flock, the birds in deeper water are often the stilt sandpipers.

Willets, by contrast, pick at the surface while walking along. They almost never seem to have more than the tip of their bill in the mud, so that the feeding behavior is more yellowlegs-like than dowitcher-like. (For a discussion of the yellowlegs, see page 109.)

RANGE AND HABITAT

In the lower forty-eight states, the willet is a common breeder on inland prairie marshes, marshes in mountain parks, and eastern tidal marshes. A vocal shorebird in these regions is most likely to be a willet. Dowitchers or stilt sandpipers breed in the Far North and are not present inland until mid- to late summer. Sitting on high perches is a behavior of shorebirds in breeding habitat; migrant shorebirds never would. It is safe to bet that if you see a dowitcher in Colorado sitting on a fencepost and calling, it is probably a willet.

In winter and during the spring and fall migrations, though, the three species could be almost anywhere, and they overlap broadly in habitat. Dowitchers and willets can be found in almost any setting, although east of the Mississippi, the willet is very rare inland while dowitchers are regular. Stilt sandpipers, however, are unlikely to be found in tidal settings. Stilts prefer freshwater marshes, fresh pond edges, or sewage plants, and mostly eschew coastal areas and tidal mud flats. I have never seen stilt sandpipers on the ocean beach, while the other species are regular there. Habitat won't help you much with these species, since they all prefer mud flats, but if you think you have a stilt sandpiper on the coast, be sure to double-check your identification. West of Colorado, the stilt sandpiper is rare, and the most regular location for it is California's Salton Sea, though a loner could turn up as a rarity almost anywhere. Be sure to let local birders know if you do find one in the West.

OTHER POTENTIALLY CONFUSING SPECIES

Dowitchers have such long bills that it's tough to confuse them with species other than willet and stilt sandpiper. Wilson's snipe, with its long, probing bill, differs considerably in color pattern. Snipe are very heavily marked on the back, with warm buff and cinnamon striping and scalloping. Winter-plumaged dowitchers are grayer and more monotone than snipe ever get, so their dullness is actually distinctive. Snipe, being cryptically colored, are also much harder to see than dowitchers.

The stilt sandpiper is a "missing link" type of bird, with nothing that resembles it closely, but several birds that might resemble it in the right set of circumstances. The bill shape and head shape resemble both dunlin and the very rare curlew sandpiper. Both of these species have black legs but very different breeding plumages, though in winter they are similar. Dunlins show a dark stripe down the rump in flight, but curlew sandpiper's white rump is similar to stilt's. Stilt sandpipers are longer-legged than both of these species and show a more "tipped-up" feeding profile. Leg color is a very useful field mark here — both dunlin and curlew sandpipers have black legs; the stilt sandpiper's are yellow.

Willet can be easily confused with yellowlegs by the unwary. Leg color (yellow in yellowlegs) and flight pattern (yellowlegs have no wing pattern at all) will simplify the task. But birds standing in deeper water, or farther away, can be tough. The willet has a thicker bill, and the paler gray plumage shows less contrast between the upperparts and underparts. Yellowlegs are very dark gray or brown on the back in winter, but willets look only slightly darker above than below.

Another species similar to willet is Hudsonian godwit. A good look in flight will distinguish the willet — although Hudsonian godwit has a white wing stripe, it is narrow, and the wings look nothing like the bold black and white wings of the willet. Hudsonian godwit does have a striking pattern of black and white, but it is on the tail.

A FINAL WORD

Any of these medium, probing shorebird species should be identifiable based on their feeding behavior, size, and shape. Take your time, practice on cooperative birds, and you'll soon be ready to sort out a few dowitchers. ✦

BASICS OF GULL ID

Navigating gull identification

USING RING-BILLED AND HERRING GULLS

NO GROUP OF BIRDS FILLS BIRD WATCHERS WITH AS much dread as gulls. They are the Gordian knot of avian identification challenges, a black hole into which hope and sanity are sucked, never to be seen again. Dedicated gull watchers, that tight little band of larophiles, are viewed with the same wariness we usually reserve for people on street corners waving signs proclaiming doom and screaming at passersby — definitely high on the "let's avoid" list.

This chapter is not intended to convert you into one of those obsessives who spend their days on winter landfills muttering about alternate molts of lesser secondary coverts (and if you understand that last part, stop reading now — it's too late for you). A passion for gull arcana is a rare disease, and no one can be dragged to it unwillingly. But you do not have to dedicate a lifetime to the study of plumages and soft parts to readily identify most of the gulls you see.

Many bird watchers, justifiably put off by discussions of the extremes of gull identification, have prematurely thrown in the towel on gulls. The fact is that the identification of most gulls is no harder than the identification of most sparrows or warblers. You can learn to confidently put names on almost all the gulls you see without memorizing reams of dense technical literature (or crawling around landfills in winter). In fact, all you need is the same field guide you use for warblers and sparrows.

There is a shortcut to gull identification. After reading a few hundred words, you'll learn a different way to look at gulls. You can master this if you are willing to clear your mind and start from scratch.

THREE KEY POINTS

FIRST, rare gulls are rare. That may seem overly obvious to state here, but it's an important fact that often gets overlooked; no one talks about the common gulls. At bird club meetings or on the bird alert reports, no one says they saw a flock of ring-billed gulls. They say they saw a third basic hybrid backcross intergrade whosis with aberrant soft part colors. What they probably saw was a ring-billed gull, but gulls tend to inspire this sort of thing, generally among the addicts. The truth is, 99 percent of all the gulls you see are the ones you expect to see. If you pull into the local fast food restaurant parking lot and see a bunch of gulls waiting for vagrant French fries, they are almost certainly all ring-billed gulls, no matter what they look like. Remember, rare gulls are as rare as rare sparrows.

SECOND, gulls are variable. Not all herring gulls look alike, no matter what age they are. Don't let this unnerve you. A certain amount of variation is a fact of life with gulls, but it doesn't affect identification in most cases. Concentrate on the big similarities, not the small differences. If you do, you can identify most of the gulls you see — better yet, you can identify them correctly.

THIRD (and most important, because this is the area where you can make a breakthrough), gulls have a bewildering variety of plumages related to age. It is possible to look at a flock of herring gulls and see what looks like dozens of species, all recognizably different from one another. This is the factor that makes most people head for easy groups, like sparrows. The reason it may seem impossible to tell one gull from another is that field guides don't always have the space necessary to tell you that it is possible to sort them out by learning to recognize the age of the bird you are looking at. If that sentence is making you consider flipping the pages to another chapter, don't. There is a shortcut to learning how to discern age, and it's one any bird watcher can master.

ring-billed gull
first winter

ring-billed gull
second winter

ring-billed gull
third winter (adult)

herring gull
first winter

herring gull
second winter

herring gull
third winter

herring gull
fourth winter (adult)

THE SHORTCUT

There are two things you need to learn about gulls to become competent and confident in your identification.

ONE: There are only three basic kinds of gulls — little ones, medium-sized ones, and big ones. Ignore the pages and pages of gull pictures in your field guide and focus on that fact. There are a dozen or so big gulls, and half that many little and medium ones, but it doesn't matter. We are only interested in the three sizes.

The small gulls, such as Bonaparte's and little and black-headed, take two years to get to adult plumage. They present few identification challenges, because young birds look fairly similar to adults, and field guides do a good job of explaining them. We don't need to talk about them here because most bird watchers don't have a lot of trouble sorting out small gulls.

The medium-sized gulls, such as ring-billed, mew, laughing, and Franklin's, take three years to get to adult plumage. They're a little trickier than the small gulls, but the field guides are still reasonably good at presenting these birds.

The big gulls drive bird watchers nuts. They include the commonest of the four-year gulls: herring, great black-backed, California, and western, as well as less common big gulls that for sanity's sake, we won't get into here. They take four years to get to adult plumage, and there is at least one recognizable plumage for each year. (Actually, there are two plumages for each year, but the difference between winter and summer is not large.) So how do we sort through this bewildering array of plumages? By moving on to the second part of the shortcut.

TWO: Gulls start out brown and end up gray or black and white.

Once you know the age of the bird, the identification becomes much easier — not always dead simple, but much easier. Once you memorize this sequence (and if you can remember phone numbers, PINs, and Social Security numbers, you can do this), everything seems easy. Young gulls of the four-year persuasion (the big ones) are mostly brown in their first year. In their second year, they are brown with a little gray or black. In their third year, they are predominantly grayish black and white with a little brown. After that they look like adults. It is a logical sequence and it is the key to understanding big gulls. It breaks down like this:

THE BASIC SEQUENCE OF
Age-Related Plumage

FIRST YEAR: brown
SECOND YEAR: mostly brown
THIRD YEAR: mostly adult
FOURTH YEAR: adult

In fact, looking at this sequence, it becomes obvious that the only gulls you really need to learn to identify are the young ones and the adults, because second-year birds are similar to first year, and third-year birds are similar to adults. The best thing about gulls is that no matter what the age, the most important field marks — size, shape, overall color, and bill size — do not change. Field guides often emphasize leg color, eye color, bill color, and the number of white spots on the ends of the wings. All these marks can be useful at times, but they are less important than overall shape, size, and general color, at least to start. You can identify 95 percent of all the gulls you'll ever see without bothering with eye or leg color. Besides, these characters vary, both with age and among individuals, and it is this variation that seduces the gull fanatics. It is for advanced study, so leave it for when you get hooked.

A FOUR-YEAR GULL
(HERRING GULL)

Let's look at the sequence using the most widespread of the large gulls, the herring gull, as an example.

Young birds, the ones in their first year, are brown above and below. The amount of brown below varies slightly, with some birds being paler on the head or breast, but there are no gray feathers. The rump and tail are dull brown, and the tail ends in a broad black band. As the winter wears on, the feathers fade a little, but there is still no gray. This is the important factor: first-year herring gulls have no gray.

In their second year, herring gulls acquire gray feathers in the center of the back, the same color as adults have. Otherwise they look like first-year birds, though they are usually paler below and on the head. The key is that second-year herring gulls have gray (i.e., adult) feathers only on the center of the back.

The big change happens between the second and third years. By their third year, herring gulls are mostly gray above and white below, just like adults. However, there are still some brown feathers mixed in on the upperparts, and sometimes they have a little bit of a tailband left over. They also don't usually have the adults' full yellow bill with the red spot. The key is that they look like adults, almost.

By the fourth year, and for as many as twenty years after that, they look like adults, gray above and white below.

Once you get the basic sequence in your head for herring gull, most of the four-year birds become easy. It also lets you sort through the mass quickly to spot the odd bird. Great black-backed gulls are bigger and darker than herrings. California gulls are smaller and a little darker. The white-winged gulls, such as Iceland and glaucous, are almost white in all plumages. Thayer's is impossible (not really, but they do require extra study and access to a good guide). The point here, again, is not to provide field marks for all these birds, but to make it easy to recognize what age the bird is. When it comes to gulls, the age is the starting point.

A THREE-YEAR GULL
(RING-BILLED GULL)

The same basic sequence occurs in three-year gulls such as ring-billed and mew. Because the sequence has to be crammed into only three years, the patterns are slightly different, but they are even easier to learn.

First-year ring-billeds are gray on the back and shoulders; variously brownish on the wings and underparts; and they have brown tailbands.

Second-year birds look like adults, but they usually have a few brown feathers on the back or wings and sometimes show a little bit of the first-years' tailband.

Adults are gray and black above and white below.

In the case of the three-year gulls with hoods (Franklin's and laughing), the sequence is similar. They get blacker above and whiter below as the years pass. Most good field guides show these species well.

If you can keep the basic age distinctions in your head, gull identification becomes no harder than fall warblers or sparrows or shorebirds. In fact, I think they are easier than shorebirds because they are bigger, they are easier to get close to (keep those French fries handy), and there are far fewer of them.

The best way to sort out the gull problem is to go to the local beach or

> *Looking at the sequence, it becomes obvious that the only gulls you need to learn to ID are the young ones and the adults.*

lake (or fast food joint parking lot) and look at a flock of the common local species. Don't try to find a rarity, because odds are against there being one. Just get comfortable looking at them and putting an age on each bird. Then look at birds of different ages and notice how similar they are once you ignore obvious differences in color. After one or two trips, you'll be amazed at how much simpler the whole process seems.

Understanding the basic sequence of age-related plumage won't result in putting a name on every single gull. But it will make it fairly simple to put a name on most of the gulls you see. If you happen to get addicted to gulls now that you've got a good start, there are great guides that go into excruciating detail about all the subtleties and anomalies. The best of the best is Peter Grant's *Gulls: A Guide to Identification*, a wonderful book for the fully committed gull watcher. Who knows, in a few years you may be the one at the local bird club meeting talking about third basic hybrid backcross intergrade whatevers. ⤙

HOODED GULLS

How to know the hooded gulls,
EVEN WHEN THEY GO "BALD" IN THE WINTER

IDENTIFYING GULLS IS NOT LIKE IDENTIFYING CARDINALS or great blue herons. Those birds we see and know, and we don't even have to think about what they are. They're nice and easy, with pretty colors and good sets of distinctive features that make them fast and familiar friends. With gulls, this is less often the case. We see them gliding by overhead, or scattered across a beach or parking lot. Some of them look pretty ratty and we don't even want to know what it is they're eating, so we often shelve them for other pursuits. Some gulls are easier to identify than others, and the smaller ones with black heads are among the easiest to learn. They are the "hooded gulls" because, while they have white heads for much of the year, their spring breeding plumage sports a crisp, handsome black hood.

The hooded gulls include not only Bonaparte's gull, laughing gull, and Franklin's gull, but also little gull, black-headed gull, and Sabine's gull. The little gull and black-headed gull are actually Eurasian species that have established a regular presence in North America, but are still generally scarce. Sabine's gull is an Arctic breeder that migrates and winters at sea, mostly far offshore, but it, the little gull, and black-headed gull can show up just about anywhere. The other three species — Bonaparte's gull, laughing gull, and Franklin's gull — are found more commonly across larger parts of North America. Sometimes they are seen in big concentrations, though not usually together — they tend to stick to their own species.

We will focus on these three species because they are the most frequently encountered of the bunch. Most of them are easily separated from one another, but if you aren't familiar with all three, they can pose an identification challenge. Franklin's gulls and laughing gulls are the most similar, while Bonaparte's gull is quite different from either one and is more likely to be confused with black-headed gull or little gull.

DISTRIBUTION

Bonaparte's, laughing, and Franklin's gulls can initially be separated by their ranges and habits. If you are offshore either coast watching a flock of small gulls feeding closely together, then they are probably Bonaparte's. If you are driving through the prairie pothole region of North Dakota in June and you see a hooded gull, the odds are it's a Franklin's. If you are in Florida in winter and find yourself watching several hooded-type gulls sitting on the beach, you can be reasonably sure they are laughing gulls.

Bonaparte's gull is common along both the Pacific and Atlantic coasts in winter and is found in significant numbers on the Great Lakes and along the Mississippi River valley. During spring and fall migration, this species may be encountered on almost any body of water in North America. It is unusual among North American gulls, because it nests in trees, building its nest as high as twenty feet above ground in spruces in the boreal forests of Canada and Alaska.

The laughing gull is a coastal species that only rarely strays inland. It is common on the East Coast from south Texas north through North Carolina in winter and farther north to the Canadian Maritimes during the summer breeding season. It also breeds in the Gulf of California, though it rarely strays north from there. Laughing gull is primarily an eastern species, breeding by the thousands in colonies in salt marshes and other coastal areas.

Franklin's gull is a highly migratory species, much more so than either the laughing or Bonaparte's. It breeds on lakes and ponds in the prairies of central Canada and the United States, and then leaves North America altogether for points farther south, spending the winter along the western coast of South America. This bird is primarily a central flyway

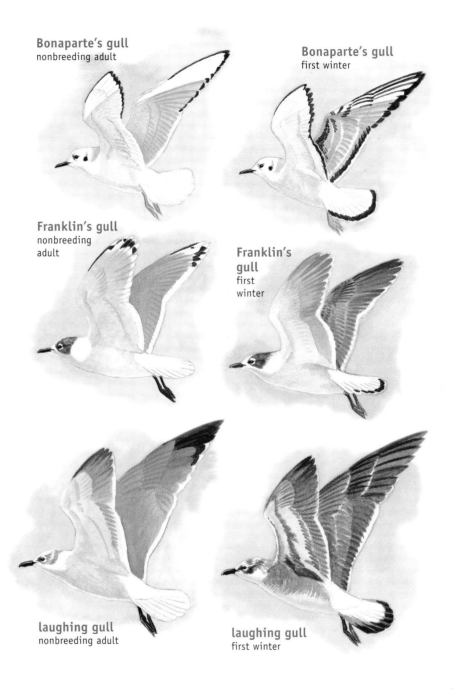

Bonaparte's gull
nonbreeding adult

Bonaparte's gull
first winter

Franklin's gull
nonbreeding
adult

**Franklin's
gull**
first
winter

laughing gull
nonbreeding adult

laughing gull
first winter

species. However, in the process of traveling between the two continents, it has turned up in just about every state and province in North America.

SIZE DIFFERENCES

Bonaparte's gulls are the most distinctive of the three hooded gulls. (They fall into the "small gull" group — see page 137.) Everything about them is dainty and compact, right down to their fine, straight bills. Compared with laughing gulls and Franklin's gulls, Bonaparte's gulls are small — only about two-thirds the size of a laughing gull.

Laughing gulls are the largest of the three hooded gulls discussed here, with rather long wings and a longish, drooping bill. These characters lend it a more slender, elongated look than its close cousin, the Franklin's gull. (Both laughing and Franklin's are "medium gulls"— see page 137.) The laughing gull's habits are almost stereotypically gull-like. They loaf around beaches, seldom far from saltwater, and often mix with other coastal gull and tern species. Their laughing call is one of the quintessential sounds of eastern summer beaches.

All the hooded gulls start out as brown juveniles and end up as black, white, and gray adults

Franklin's gulls are a little more compact, about four-fifths the size of a laughing gull. They have shorter, and slightly more rounded wings and shorter, straighter bills than laughing gulls.

AGE AND SEASONALITY

Identifying a gull becomes simpler if we can age it and determine which plumage it is in. Each of these hooded gulls requires at least two years to reach adult plumage. It's not important that you remember the age/plumage sequence for each gull species — your field guides will illustrate these for you, and there's a good overview on page 136. But remember this: all the hooded gulls start out as brown juveniles and end up as black and white or gray and white adults.

Adults of these three species in breeding plumage are easily recognized by their complete black hoods. They are crisply marked overall in this plumage; their white underparts may even take on a rosy pink color (especially in Franklin's gull). The bill color of Franklin's and laughing gulls changes from black to a deep red during the breeding season.

HOODS AS HAIR

In winter, adults mostly lose their complete breeding season hoods. The white foreheads that remain make the winter adults look like they've lost their hair. Bonaparte's gulls go the "baldest," retaining just a dark ear spot. Franklin's gulls keep the most "hair"; this strong suggestion of its summer hood is an excellent field mark for this species in all plumages and ages. Winter adult laughing gulls show just a wash of gray streaks from fall through spring—in fall it looks as if they've gone gray, and by spring have completely lost their hair.

BONING UP ON "BONIES"

Size, structure, and plumage pattern set "Bonies" apart from laughing and Franklin's. Bonaparte's gulls are small-bodied, small-headed, small-billed birds in comparison. The Bonaparte's gull's pale gray mantle, combined with its white underparts and the relatively small amount of black in the wings, gives it an overall pale appearance. White primaries, narrowly tipped in black, give a twinkling flash as they fly. Laughing and Franklin's gulls both have a dark, rather than pale, gray mantle in all ages and plumages. In flight, the Bonaparte's gull looks more ternlike than gull-like — its calls even sound like those of terns. This buoyant flight style and the Bonaparte's gull's slender, pointed wings are obvious identification clues even on birds viewed at a long distance. Most birders will tell you that Bonies have a grace about them — especially in flight — that the other two hooded gull species lack.

A close look at a Bonaparte's gull reveals a thin, straight bill that is all-black, though some first-winter birds may have a pale base to the bill. At all ages and at all seasons this gull's legs are light pink in color. This is an excellent clue to consider as you scan a flock of standing Bonies: anything with orange or red legs is something different! Keep in mind, though, that Bonies form tight flocks when feeding at sea or on inland lakes, and their flocks tend to be more homogenous (containing only Bonaparte's gulls) than the other gulls'.

Immature (first-winter) Bonaparte's gulls show a more distinctive upperwing pattern than the other common hooded gulls do. Most noticeably, these young birds show a clean white tail with a black terminal band. In this plumage they are confused more often with black-headed gulls than with laughing or Franklin's.

FOUR LESS-COMMON HOODED POSSIBILITIES

The black-headed gull is bigger in every way than a Bonaparte's gull. This rather rare visitor from Europe is seen with some regularity, mixed in with large winter gull concentrations in harbors and bays along the Atlantic Coast. Look for the black-headed gull's orange bill and legs (in first-winter birds) or deep red bill and legs (on winter adults). The black-headed gull in winter often looks as if it is wearing headphones, as opposed to the mere ear dots of the Bonaparte's gull. Picking one out of a flock of winter Bonaparte's gulls is simply a matter of looking for one that's bigger than the rest.

On the other end of the often-confused-with-Bonaparte's-gull spectrum is the little gull, named for its diminutive size. The little gull is a winter vagrant to the Mid-Atlantic coast, where it is usually found in the company of Bonaparte's gulls. Its tiny size and bill, all-dark underwing, and white wingtips are diagnostic. But if you are lucky enough to see a little gull, it's sure to be the bird's diminutive size that first catches your eye.

Birders should keep in mind that black-legged kittiwakes, though larger, can appear similar to Bonaparte's gulls, especially at a distance. Immature kittiwakes, however, have a dark neck collar and a distinctive bold M pattern on the upper wings. Adult kittiwakes lack a significant dark hood and always show a yellow bill.

Along the Pacific Coast, the Sabine's gull might cause momentary confusion with a Bonaparte's gull. These species are similar in size, but the Sabine's sports a boldly patterned upperwing of black, white, and brown in juvenile or first-winter birds, and black, white, and gray upperwings in adults. Adult Sabine's gulls have a black bill with a yellow tip, which is considered diagnostic. Though the Sabine's gull is mostly pelagic (it spends the nonbreeding seasons at sea), as a vagrant it is often found in the company of Bonies.

FRANKLIN'S VERSUS LAUGHING

Franklin's and laughing gulls are confusingly similar in appearance in breeding plumage. They both have rather dark, slate gray mantles and black wingtips, but the wing pattern differs between the two. If you can see the pattern of either the underwing or upperwing moderately well, you should be able to differentiate between these two species.

WINGTIPS

Laughing gulls in all plumages show almost entirely dark wingtips both above and below, with virtually no white visible. Franklin's gulls in adult plumage have black bars on the wingtips, but there is substantial white inside that black bar and the tips of the primaries are also white. So while laughing gulls appear to have solid black wingtips, Franklin's gulls' wingtips are more patterned.

TAILS

First-winter birds of these two species show different tail patterns. Young Franklin's gulls have a narrow and incomplete tail band; it covers only the middle tail feathers, and doesn't extend all the way to the outer feathers. Young laughing gulls, in contrast, have a complete broad black tail band from edge to edge. This black tail band disappears by the time laughing gulls reach their second-winter plumage.

HOODS

In immature and nonbreeding plumages, Franklin's gulls always have extensive hoods, covering most of the back half of the head. These hoods have more clearly defined edges than the hoods of winter laughing gulls. This makes the Franklin's white nape much more visible in all seasons. Laughing gulls are more diffusely patterned on the head and have an overall paler head in winter, when their napes are messy and gray.

BILLS

Picking an odd laughing gull out of a flock of Franklin's gulls (or vice versa) is made slightly easier when you compare their bills. Laughing gull bills are longer, thicker, and appear to droop slightly at the end. Franklin's gulls have smaller, straight bills.

MOLT EARLY, MOLT OFTEN

Perhaps because they cover such long distances in their migration, Franklin's gulls have evolved an unusual trait among gulls — they undergo a complete molt twice a year. Most gulls molt only their body and head feathers in the early spring prior to breeding, and then molt all their feathers (including wings and tail) after breeding, during the late summer and early fall. By mid- to late summer these gulls look really ratty and worn (especially in the wings and tail) because these feathers have endured a year's worth of hard use. Franklin's gulls, having replaced all their feathers more recently, always look fairly fresh no matter what plumage they are in.

A FINAL WORD

These three hooded gulls — Bonaparte's gull, laughing gull, and Franklin's gull — though superficially similar, are really quite distinct from one another. Range and behavior, or some combination of the two, will be a good aid in determining the likely candidates for your area. Understanding a bird's size and proportions will also help you make a proper identification.

There are times when laughing gulls and Franklin's gulls may be especially difficult to separate, but close inspection will reveal a number of differences in their structure (body and bill), head pattern, and wing pattern. If you have a flock of hooded gulls to pick through, take your time and look them over carefully. Consider any anomalies in size, structure, wing pattern, and head pattern. Bonaparte's, Franklin's, and laughing gull flocks sometimes hold other, less-common hooded gulls, and unearthing something unusual is a rare, but treasured, thrill. ➥

MEDIUM-SIZED TERNS

Commonly encountered and commonly misidentified

SEABIRDS PRESENT A DIFFERENT SUITE OF IDENTIFICATION challenges than songbirds do. Many warblers, vireos, and even sparrows are easily named if they momentarily come down from the treetops or pop up from the weeds and briars to give us a decent look at them. Most of these species have many, many field marks with which we can work.

Waterbirds may be better as a group about staying out in the open, but their identification is often not as simple. You might have a group of small sandpipers virtually at your feet, yet be unable to identify them to species.

There's a sameness in the plumage and structure of many gulls, terns, and other shorebirds that makes them hard to know. The four medium-sized *Sterna* terns of North America are a classic example. All of them are basically white to pale gray, with limited black or blackish markings on the head and in the wings.

However, their similarity to each other does not mean that if you see one, you can pick a name out of a hat and have a one-in-four chance of being correct. Two of our medium terns, Arctic and roseate, are much less common than the other two. Though Arctic terns do pop up at inland locations once in a great while, they are mostly coastal or marine. Roseates are even more restricted in range and habitat, occurring only at widely scattered locales along the Atlantic coast.

The other pair of species, Forster's and common terns, are much more common and widespread. Getting to know these two — or even just one if that's all there is in your region — is really the best chance you have of correctly recognizing any vagrants you may happen upon, or of quickly coming to terms with the terns you see when you travel.

It's tempting to start with common tern as the base model, then describe Forster's and other species in relation to it. This is the usual approach, perhaps because the name "common" leads us to expect that it is the ordinary, prototypical tern. In fact the entire population of the common tern departs from Canada and from the mainland portions of the United States in late fall to spend the winter months in Central and South America. We're going to start with Forster's, though, because over many parts of the continent it is the most abundant, frequently encountered tern species.

FORSTER'S TERN

The single most useful field mark for identifying adult Forster's tern is its silvery white upperwing highlights. Forster's tern is the "frosted" tern — think of frosted as in 1970's hairstyles, only subtler. It can take a few seconds of watching, and at least reasonably favorable light for you to pick up the contrast of bright silvery primaries against the pale gray of much of the rest of the wing. Once you see it, though, it's obvious and quite different from the basically smooth, even dorsal color presented by our other terns.

Almost all Forster's terns show this frosting, the only exceptions being just-fledged juveniles and some extremely worn late summer–early winter birds. But both of these show the second most useful field mark: the dark eye patch. Except for spring or early summer adults in perfect breeding (or "alternate") plumage, all Forster's terns show sizeable black patches around their eyes, giving them a sort of raccoonlike or Lone Ranger look.

Nearly everyone describes the unique head pattern of the Forster's tern as being a black mask. But remember that all our terns have black around the eyes. The real difference is that in the Forster's, the black does not meet across the nape, leaving us with that memorable mask. But before you start lobbying the American Ornithologists' Union to change Forster's tern to "white-naped tern," remember that the gull-billed tern also has a white nape, though the amount of dark around the eyes in that species is usually much smaller and less well demarcated, and the overall effect is quite different. Perhaps the nomenclature committee would entertain a motion for "black-eared tern."

common tern
adult, breeding

common tern
adult, nonbreeding

Forster's tern
adult, breeding

Forster's tern
adult, nonbreeding

Forster's tern
adult, breeding

common tern
adult, breeding

CONSIDER THE BILL

How would you go about identifying a sitting Forster's tern in high breeding plumage — when it has a full black cap and you're not sure if the wings are frosted? There are a number of features to examine, starting with the bill.

In the Forster's tern, the bill is proportionately long and large (and longer than the common's bill), though still within a range that would be termed medium. In breeding season, it's black-tipped like the common tern's, but the orange base is paler than the common tern's darker orange-red. Of course, both these terns have black bills most of the year, but if they are colored up, use the color clue.

Tail length can also help — the Forster's is proportionately long-tailed. When sitting, adults' outer tail feathers usually project noticeably beyond the wingtips. In common terns the tail tips typically fall short of the wings.

COMMON TERN

Let's consider the common tern more directly. There is an exremely useful field mark for it, and as in the Forster's, it has to do with the upperwing pattern. In most common terns most of the year, there is a dark wedge or spike that runs from the "fingertips" (the tips of the outer primaries) toward the "wrist." It's not extensive, running less than half the width of the wing at its widest, and much less than that as you get toward the wingtip. But once you've seen it, you'll be amazed how well you can pick it up even at a distance.

WINGS DOWN UNDER

While you're looking at the upperwing pattern of terns, you also ought to get in the habit of looking at the undersides. It can be hard to differentiate between the two at first, but persist. Keep watching, and notice the differences. Many birders seem to assume that what's above will be duplicated below, which leads to confusion and imprecision. It is incredibly helpful to realize that when a bird raises and lowers its wings, we see a different side of the feathers, and in most of the wing, different feathers entirely.

So what will you see under the wings of common terns? Mostly white. But there is also a rather thick blackish line formed by dark tips on the outer primaries, and the dark outer edge on the wing. On Forster's terns you'll see a kind of pale echo of this pattern. Rarer species, such as Arctic and roseate terns, have even less dark below. But it isn't necessary to try to tackle them all at once. Learn one or two terns extremely well, and you'll quickly recognize a vagrant as being different, and you'll even have a big leg up on how.

PIECES OF THE PUZZLE

Some veteran tern watchers believe that the best field mark for the common tern is the carpal bar, which is most obvious on sitting birds. This bar is a dark line that runs along the top edge of the shoulder. Most common terns except adults in breeding plumage have it; no Forster's does. You can see this bar in flight, too, but it doesn't catch your eye to quite the same extent as the marks on the underwing.

In breeding plumage, the common tern is not white-bodied as it is the rest of the year, and as Forster's always is. Instead, the underparts are distinctly gray, only a bit paler than the back. The lower face, or cheek, is white, and stands out rather starkly between the black cap and gray throat and neck. This white cheek pattern is even more prominent on the Arctic tern.

Also watch the tail pattern, which is easier to do when the birds are in the air. The common has a basically white tail with thin gray outer margins, giving it a dark-edged look. Forster's has a gray-white tail, but the outer edges are white, the subtle opposite of common's.

Be sure to check the leg length on sitting or resting birds. Forster's terns are noticeably leggier and stand tall on bright orange legs. The common tern's red-orange legs are shorter, giving the bird a stumpy look. And the less-common Arctic tern's blood red legs are the shortest of all.

There are a goodly number of other things to notice about terns, and you'll want to discover some of them on your own and with the help of the increasing number of excellent references that are available. Now you should have enough of a framework to quickly identify most common and Forster's terns you see, most of the time. And even if you get stumped now and again, there are few birds more immaculate and graceful to see than terns, whatever their species. ➤

LARGE CRESTED TERNS

Combing through the "balding" beauties

AS BIRDS GO, TERNS ARE CONSPICUOUS. THEY SIT AT the edge of the shore, on docks, and on sandbars; at the beach they press up against each other in flocks and dot the sand like salt and pepper. They're often in the company of gulls, and maybe this is part of the reason we so often overlook them. They keep mixed company.

What really limits tern identification most is time and distance. Often we see them only as they fly by, which allows us precious little time to note any field marks. Further complicating matters is the fact that these birds are often discovered at some distance; combine distance with some heat haze, and a bird may become so blurred that simply identifying it as a tern is an accomplishment. Some species are easier to identify than others, and the larger crested species are easier than most. Knowing these big crested terns makes tackling the smaller terns easier.

The large crested terns that we find in North America include the Caspian tern, royal tern, elegant tern, and Sandwich tern. For the most part, these birds are easily separated. There are times when Caspian tern and royal tern might be confused, and other times when royal tern and elegant tern are difficult to separate, but with practice and a few helpful tips you should be able to identify almost any crested tern you encounter.

DISTRIBUTION AND RANGE

Terns are birds of the coasts and beaches. The exception is the Caspian tern, which is found over much of interior North America and is no stranger to freshwater areas. If you see a large tern inland, odds are it's a Caspian tern. The other three, though, are seldom found far from saltwater. The elegant tern is a bird of the Pacific coast; the Sandwich tern is found along the Atlantic and Gulf coasts. Royal terns are found on all three coasts, but are less common on the Pacific, where they are regular only in southern California. When you first encounter a large crested tern, consider your location and consult your field guide's range maps, and your options should be narrowed considerably.

SIZE

Getting an idea of a particular bird's size also helps to narrow the possibilities. The Caspian tern is the largest tern in the world. It is bigger than a ring-billed gull and dwarfs smaller gulls like Bonaparte's. The Caspian tern is a bruiser. Next largest is the royal tern, followed by the elegant. The Sandwich tern is the smallest in this group, but is still noticeably larger than a Forster's or a common tern. Tern flocks often consist of two or more species, so size comparison is often possible and always useful. The more you look at these birds, the more you can use them as references for each other. Assessing the size of a lone bird is more challenging, but it is unusual to encounter a solitary tern, and even then it may still be possible to judge the bird's size given a little time.

BILL

After size, the next most significant character of our crested terns is bill shape. The Caspian tern has a thick, stout, deeply red bill. The bill colors of all the terns may fade slightly after the breeding season and bill color can be hard to judge, but the Caspian's bill is almost always red, with perhaps a slight orange hue. The royal tern has a moderately thick, daggerlike orange bill, but it is not nearly as thick as the Caspian's. At times, the royal tern's orange bill may have a reddish tint, but it is always more orange than red. The elegant tern's bill color is similar to royal tern's, but differs structurally. The elegant tern has a long slender bill that is quite fine at the tip, which is often rather pale. The bill is slightly decurved, giving it a drooping look. The Sandwich tern is the only one of the bunch with a dark bill. It is a black, fairly straight and thin bill of moderate length, with a pale yellow or whitish tip.

Nonbreeding adult terns

royal tern

elegant tern

Sandwich tern

Caspian tern

ADULTS

All of these crested terns exhibit a similar overall pattern as adults. Their pale bodies are white below and grayer above, with some black in the wingtips and a variable amount of black on the head. They acquire distinctive satiny black caps for the breeding season, but in winter all but the Caspian tern have white foreheads — like the receding hairline on a middle-aged man. All of our large crested terns show black legs as adults.

Caspian terns differ from the other species by showing extensive black on the underside of the wingtips and a mostly black cap throughout the year. The cap is rich and completely black during breeding season, but the color becomes more diffuse during the winter. The other three species show extensively white foreheads surrounded by black in non-breeding plumage. The period during which they acquire this pattern differs from species to species. While elegant and Sandwich terns are on the same schedule (they start "balding" by August), royal terns begin to show their white foreheads much earlier, sometimes beginning in mid-June. This is helpful to remember during the summer when you are trying to distinguish between a royal tern and an elegant tern. If it's early July, and you've got a biggish, white-foreheaded tern with a receding black cap, chances are it's a royal.

Also at all seasons, note that the elegant tern shows a shaggier mane than the royal tern does. The elegant's crest is fuller and longer, and during the nonbreeding season, the black on its head is a little more extensive, usually encompassing the eye. The royal tern's eye, on the other hand, is usually isolated in white in nonbreeding plumage. Adult Sandwich terns are whiter overall than the other species, often approaching a cool, milky ivory, while the other crested terns show darker degrees of a gray cast to the upperparts.

YOUNG BIRDS

Larger crested terns require two to three years to reach adult plumage. Juveniles are frequently tinged with buff or gray-brown above, and their backs look slightly scaly on close inspection. From a distance, they appear to be more patterned above than they do in adult plumage. The bill on juveniles is not as richly colored and looks washed out, and the black caps are just shadows of what they will become. Juvenile terns are more compressed in size and shape than adults, with slightly shorter bills. For the most part, however, the same characters you use to separate the adults are useful for identifying birds in juvenal plumage.

SHAPE

Among the terns, the differences in shape may seem subtle, but they are useful. The Caspian tern's structure is very different from the others. It is a broad, stocky bird with a big head, thick bill, and broad wing base and has a proportionately short tail. It is almost more gull-like than ternlike.

Royal terns, though still quite heavy, are not nearly as robust as Caspian terns, and they appear rather long-tailed and more elongated overall. The elegant tern is slender, with a long thin bill and a rather narrow wing base. Sandwich terns are similar in overall shape to elegant terns but are smaller and have shorter, straighter bills.

VOICE

Before we see a tern, we are often alerted to its presence by its calls. Terns are vocal birds; voice is a great way to detect them and identify them. Caspian terns have a distinctively loud, rasping call. Royal terns give a rolling, abrupt *keeirup* in flight. Sandwich and elegant terns are closely related and have occasionally hybridized, and they give rather similar, loud *kreerik* calls. The call of a Sandwich tern is a little higher-pitched and more abrupt than that of an elegant tern. In each species, juveniles have weaker, thinner calls than the adults.

FLIGHT STYLE

There are some behavioral clues that can aid identification, but they may seem subtle at first; among them is flight style. Caspian terns have a rather slow, steady wingbeat that lends the species a tough, majestic air. Royal terns move faster on average than Caspian terns and have a determined, more urgent flight, with stronger wingbeats. The elegant tern is also a strong flier but is lighter on the wing than the royal tern and appears more buoyant. Sandwich terns are smaller and more acrobatic, with quicker, jerkier wingbeats than the other, larger terns.

CANDIDATES FOR CONFUSION

Among terns, the larger crested species are probably the easiest to identify. The royal tern may require more study than the others, because in size and structure it can be confused with either a Caspian tern or an elegant tern. Its orange-red, medium-sized bill and its head pattern are distinctive enough to make identifying a royal tern a fairly simple task most of the time. A Caspian tern could be mistaken for a gull rather than a tern, so look carefully at its bill and head shape and pay attention to its general comportment.

The smaller, medium-sized terns like common and Forster's terns may vaguely approximate a Sandwich tern in appearance, but the Sandwich is always larger, paler, and has a longer, pale-tipped bill. While flying terns vocalize often, some birds streak past silently, and they may have to go unnamed. Such are the struggles of even expert birders. ➤

CUCKOOS

Going cuckoo

OVER YELLOW-BILLED, BLACK-BILLED,
AND EVEN MANGROVE

THE PROBLEM WITH PUTTING THE RIGHT NAME ON A cuckoo is not that they look alike (which they do) but that nine out of ten times we get a terrible look at the bird. They are usually seen for just a few seconds, hidden in the foliage where the light is bad; part of the bird always seems to be covered by a maddeningly placed leaf or branch. They are shadows living in a world of shadow, and we identify far more cuckoos by call than by plumage.

I can't get you better looks at cuckoos. That takes patience and luck. What I can do is describe the field marks you should be looking for, so that you can use your few seconds to focus in on the characters needed to tell you which species you're lookiing at. The trick is not to waste time trying to remember every field mark, but to instantly home in on a few key characters. If you get a decent look, even a short one, you should not have too much trouble identifying a cuckoo.

THE GENERIC CUCKOO

The first step is to realize that you are looking at a cuckoo. The recognition is not always automatic, because they are rarely in the open so we don't see many.

Cuckoos are medium-sized birds that look long and slim, an impression emphasized by the long tail. They are a soft gray-brown above and whitish to slightly buffy below. The muted colors and lack of strong con-

CUCKOOS

trasts are clues — a bird sitting in shade, as cuckoos almost always are, is nearly colorless. The bill is medium long and slightly decurved. If you are looking at the front of the bird, the alternating patches of black and white on the long tail are diagnostic for cuckoos everywhere — except in the extreme Southwest, where the pattern is shared by the gaudy and unmistakable trogons.

Cuckoos are notoriously difficult to identify in flight, which is frustrating because often the first look we get is when the bird flushes from a clump of leaves right in front of us. Telling which cuckoo it is may not be possible, but a flying cuckoo is distinctively a cuckoo. Note the seemingly languid, loose flight; slow wingbeats; longish wings; and the strikingly long tail. There are few birds that look like a cuckoo in flight or have a tail so long in proportion, and almost none of them is found in dense vegetation. The most common mistake bird watchers make in those circumstances is to call a briefly seen cuckoo a sharp-shinned hawk. If the look you have is that bad and brief, you have no chance of getting the bird to the species level.

THE CANDIDATES

There are three regularly occurring cuckoos in North America. The yellow-billed and black-billed are widespread birds that breed across the eastern two-thirds of the United States and into southern Canada. The yellow-billed is a rare and declining breeder throughout the West; it breeds south to the Gulf Coast and into Mexico. The black-billed is slightly more northern, breeding into southern Canada in the prairie provinces but not in the Gulf Coast states or in the West. Both species winter well south of our borders.

The third candidate, the mangrove cuckoo, is resident in the southern half of the Florida peninsula, confined, as the name suggests, to mangrove thickets.

Two Old World/Eurasian cuckoo species (the common cuckoo and the oriental cuckoo) have been recorded as vagrants in western Alaska and will not be covered here. In addition, there are several members of the cuckoo family that are also not covered. Both the smooth-billed and the groove-billed ani are actually cuckoos. So (to the surprise of many) is the roadrunner, the only member of the family that almost anyone can identify, including nonbirders in fast-moving cars.

Cuckoo identification is a spring through fall challenge, although fall

black-billed cuckoos

yellow-billed cuckoos

mangrove cuckoos

migrants are rarely seen because they are rarely vocal. Finding a yellow-billed or a black-billed cuckoo in North America in winter is almost as unlikely as finding an ivory-billed woodpecker.

A CAUTION ON RANGE

Field guide range maps for yellow-billed and black-billed cuckoos are accurate but don't tell the whole story. Within the range of each species, there is an amazing amount of variation in abundance from year to year. In any given locality, they may be common one year and scarce the next. Breeding abundance is dependent on the availability of caterpillars, especially tent caterpillars. When caterpillar populations are low, cuckoos are generally scarce. This variation in abundance can be seen even during the course of one year. Birds arriving in the spring may be fairly vocal, but by midsummer they might be hard to find; they may have moved on in search of areas with more food. The result is that cuckoos are rarely evenly distributed within their breeding range. If you don't find cuckoos this year, wait until next.

SEPARATING YELLOW-BILLED AND BLACK-BILLED

Sitting birds are generally alike: whitish below, gray-brown above, with long tails patterned in light and dark. The key features, the ones you should check quickly, are the color of the bill, the color and pattern of the underside of the tail, and the eye-ring. Secondary field marks include bill size and the color of the primaries.

Bill color. Bill color is the most striking feature, and the difference between species is obvious even in low light. Yellow-billeds (hence the name) have an almost entirely bright yellow bill with a dark upper ridge. The same pattern appears on young birds as well, although on birds just out of the nest the yellow area is grayish and the pattern is similar to that of black-billed. The all-dark bill lasts only a short time, however; it is rare to see a yellow-billed without a yellow bill.

Black-billeds are named for their all-dark bill, although it is not uniformly black. The basal two-thirds of the lower mandible is dark gray. The difference between that and the rest of the bill, which is black, is evident only in good light and at fairly close range. If you get a good look at the bill you should have no difficulty identifying either bird, with the possible exception of very young yellow-billeds. For those you can use other field marks, which are discussed below.

Tail. The tail is the second part of the bird to look at, depending on how much of the bird you can see and what direction it is facing. The key is the tail's underside, so it is useful only on birds facing you. The underside of the tail of adult yellow-billed cuckoos is a bold statement in black and white and is immediately diagnostic when compared with any age of black-billed. The white spots on the tails of yellow-billed are so large that it sometimes looks as if there is more white than black. The underside of the tail on black-billed is much less striking, with small white spots on a brownish background. The effect is of a dark tail with thin white bars across it.

Eye-ring. The difference in eye-ring color between adult yellow-billeds and black-billeds is striking and usually easy to see, although if you get a good enough look to determine eye-ring color you have undoubtedly seen enough of the bill and tail to identify the bird. You should check the eye-ring when you get the chance, however, because it is diagnostic, and seeing it should edge your certainty up from 98 to 99 percent.

Yellow-billeds have a bright ring of yellow skin around the eye (sometimes referred to as the orbital ring). It is not always easy to see, but even in low light, when exact colors may be hard to discern, it looks pale. (The eye-ring of adult black-billeds never looks pale; see below.) The pale effect is enhanced slightly by a small patch of black feathers around the eye of yellow-billed.

Adult black-billeds have a deep red eye-ring. The intensity of the color can make it surprisingly easy to see, even though it does not contrast much in tone from the gray-brown feathers surrounding the eye.

Young of both species lack the eye-ring color of adults and instead have grayish to greenish eye-rings. They should be identified using the other characters described above. If you don't see any obvious color in the eye-ring, don't assume you are looking at an immature bird. Some adult yellow-billed cuckoos have grayish eye-rings. Bad lighting and distance can conspire to keep you from seeing eye-ring color.

Bill shape. Bill shape can be a useful clue but requires experience with both species. You should take every opportunity to study the bill shape of cuckoos, but it is a field mark you will rarely have to fall back on. The difference, which can be subtle, depending on the angle you have, is that yellow-billeds have a thicker, heavier bill than black-billeds. It looks almost stout. Black-billeds have a slender, finer bill.

Primary colors. The color of the primary feathers can be hard to see on sitting birds and is likely to be useful only when birds are facing directly away from you and other field marks are hidden. The primaries are the long wing feathers that lie over the rump on sitting birds. The primaries of the yellow-billed cuckoo are bright rufous, whereas those of the black-billed have no rufous, or only a tiny hint of it. If you can see obvious rufous in the primaries, you are looking at a yellow-billed. If you don't, you may be looking at a black-billed — but you can't be certain because the rufous is not always easy to see and contrasts little with the brownish feathers of the upperparts. Unless you get superb views in excellent light, don't put much faith in the absence of rufous in the wing of a sitting cuckoo.

Underparts. In general, black-billed cuckoos have duskier whitish underparts than yellow-billeds do. Think off-white to the yellow-billed's white. If you're anywhere except south Florida (we'll get to that below) and you see a buffy throat and undertail coverts on a cuckoo, it is a young black-billed.

The key features, the ones you should check quickly, are the color of the bill, the color and pattern of the underside of the tail, and the eye-ring.

Flying birds. On flying birds, there is only one area to look at: the upperside or underside (depending on your angle) of the outer wing — the primaries.

The rufous that is so hard to see in the primaries of a sitting yellow-billed is usually strikingly obvious on a flying bird. The whole outer half of the wing is bright rufous, and even in low light with a brief view, it almost always jumps out at you. No other cuckoo has extensively rufous primaries, and if you see it you've got your bird.

It would be wonderful if the absence of rufous were quite as diagnos-

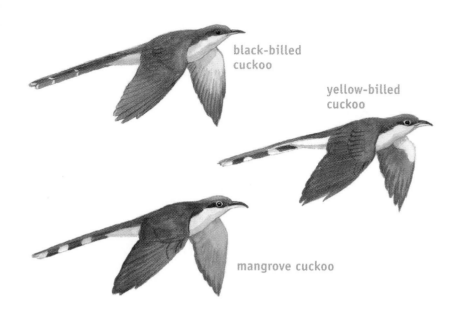

black-billed cuckoo

yellow-billed cuckoo

mangrove cuckoo

tic, but naturally it isn't. Absence is rarely as good as presence when it comes to field marks. Despite the fact that the rufous on the yellow-billed almost always shows, at some angles and in some light it doesn't. Before deciding that the lack of rufous means the bird was a black-billed, you have to be positive that you would have seen it if it were there. Absolute certainty in such situations is frustratingly hard to come by.

The apparent absence of rufous is, oddly, not as useful in identifying black-billeds as seeing just a tinge of rufous at the end of the wing. Black-billeds can have a small patch of rufous right at the end of the primaries. If you see a small patch of rufous at the tip of the wing you know you are looking at a black-billed, because if you could see that you would surely have seen the more extensive rufous of a yellow-billed.

Another character that can be useful as a clue on flying birds is the pattern of the tail, but, except in rare instances, it is helpful only on birds flying directly away. The large white spots on the underside of the tail of the yellow-billed translate into usually obvious white spots on the sides of the tail in flight. If you see large white spots on the sides of the tail, it is a yellow-billed. Not seeing them means essentially nothing. Black-billeds can occasionally show a few small white spots. If you don't see spots it could be because the light was bad, the angle was bad, or the tail was folded.

THE MANGROVE CUCKOO

In the southern half of the Florida peninsula we have a third cuckoo to contend with, the mangrove. We'll do only basic field marks because the area is limited and the bird uncommon.

There is really only one other cuckoo present here for most of the year — the yellow-billed. Black-billeds are rare in south Florida at any season, although a few have been reported in migration.

Mangrove cuckoos are most like yellow-billeds, especially in bill color and tail pattern. The same characters that distinguish yellow-billed from black-billed will eliminate black-billed when you are looking at a mangrove.

Separating mangrove from yellow-billed takes only a little more work. The key is that in all plumages, mangrove has an obviously pale to medium buffy wash across the entire underparts. Although young black-billeds can have buffy below, it is confined to the throat and vent and does not cover the whole underside the way it does on the mangrove cuckoo.

The bold black and white pattern on the underside of the tail is essentially identical on yellow-billeds and mangroves and eliminates black-billeds. There is a slight difference in the mangrove's bill — the upper mandible is all-dark and the lower is all-yellow. On the yellow-billed, the yellow on the bill includes a good portion of the upper mandible.

Another character that separates a yellow-billed from a mangrove is the mangrove's "mask." This dark feathering around the eye is much more extensive than on the yellow-billed, going from the base of the bill to the rear of the crown. It is much more obvious than the small dark patch of the yellow-billed.

Mangrove cuckoos lack the rufous in the primaries of yellow-billeds, which can be useful (with the appropriate cautions) on flying birds. Both above and below, flying mangroves look more like black-billeds, except for the sometimes obvious white spots at the edge of the tail.

Mangroves also have the yellow eye-ring of yellow-billeds. The bill is even thicker and more robust than that of the yellow-billed. Subtleties aside, the key field marks are the buffy underparts and the black mask.

VOICE

Voice is a critical component of cuckoo identification. It matters more than in many species comparisons because we hear ten cuckoos (at least) for every one we see, and because cuckoos, especially the yellow-billed, have a much larger repertoire than most bird watchers realize. Many yellow-billeds are misidentified because they have given an unfamiliar vocalization and are thus assumed to be black-billeds (which are often assumed to be rarer, even where they are not). There are differences between the vocalizations of the two, and they are diagnostic, but familiarity with the calls is immensely helpful.

Yellow-billed. The most widely known of yellow-billed cuckoo vocalizations is a long series of notes in two parts. It starts with a slightly hoarse, hard, crisp series of *cu-cu-cu* notes, ranging in length from only two or three notes to more than a dozen. The speed and length of the series vary, and it is the tone and quality of the notes that is important. The second part, and the one that makes it distinctive, is a series of slightly deeper, two-noted calls — *cudowl cudowl cudowl* — also variable in length, but typically slowing down with longer and longer pauses between notes. It often sounds as if it just peters out.

Another fairly common vocalization is a deep *cown* note given in a slow series with long pauses between notes. As many others have noted, it sounds almost as if the notes were being swallowed.

A less common call is a series of hard *cuk* notes, usually given rapidly.

The call that most frequently causes confusion with black-billed is a fairly slow, spaced series of *cu* notes, usually slowing down, and once again seeming to peter out.

Black-billed. The most common vocalization of the black-billed cuckoo is a fairly distinctive series of *cu* notes, often fairly long, all on one pitch. These are often given in triplets: *cu-cu-cu, cu-cu-cu*. The key is the very even pacing and the tone of the notes, which is hollow and clear, not like the harder tone in the notes of a yellow-billed giving a similar call.

The black-billed also gives a series of *cudowl* notes similar to yellow-billed, but clearer, in a slightly higher pitch, and usually more rapid. If the series peters out into a slowing series of *cu* notes, it is almost certainly a black-billed.

Mangrove. Mangrove cuckoo vocalizations are quite different from both the yellow-billed's and the black-billed's. They are harsh, slightly nasal, and grating. The most common is a lengthy series of *awn* notes, usually speeding up slightly, with the final notes somewhat drawn out.

It is extremely hard to learn to separate cuckoos by call based on written descriptions, because their calls are variable, and it is often the tone and quality of the notes that is important. Written descriptions of calls can help only when combined with actually listening to the calls. Fortunately they are available on a number of tapes and compact discs; it is worth acquiring several. Many cuckoos can be confidently identified by voice if you have spent some time with the tapes first. They are not as confusing as tortured efforts to describe them would sometimes lead you to believe.

With practice, you should be able to quickly and confidently identify almost every cuckoo you see, even if you get only the typical fleeting glance. The key is remembering what to look at — tail and bill on sitting birds, wings on flying birds — so you can focus on these characters immediately. You aren't likely to see a lot of cuckoos, despite the fact that they are fairly common, but you ought to put a name on as many of them as you can. ✕

OWLS

Wisdom on IDing long-eared, short-eared, and barn owls

FOR MOST BIRD WATCHERS THE BIGGEST PROBLEM IN identifying owls is finding one. Owls are nocturnal. Humans are diurnal, and when we are out at night, we can't even see well enough to avoid walking into trees.

If you are lucky or persistent enough to see an owl, you can usually identify it if you get a decent look. In some parts of the Southwest there are a bewildering number of small owls; in the Pacific Northwest, barred and spotted owls now overlap. But for the most part, owls sort themselves out easily into small, medium, and large, with only one or two species to choose from in each category. There is one widespread group that can cause trouble, though, especially when they are seen in flight.

THE TRIO

Short-eared, long-eared, and barn owls are all medium-sized birds that hunt over grassy fields and marshes and are most likely to be seen at dusk, just when field marks begin to fade from view. They have similar flight styles, hunt the same habitats, and are at least superficially similar in plumage. But even when the conditions are less than perfect, observers can confidently identify the three. Once you have gotten past my favorite stage in the process, which is looking up and saying: "Wow, it's an owl! Cool," the trick is to focus on a few key characters.

RANGE

In broad terms, short-eared owls are the most northerly ranging of the three, long-eareds the most middling, and barn owls the most southerly. In winter, all three occur over large portions of the United States.

Short-eared owls breed across Alaska and northern Canada south to the center of the United States in the West, and to New England and the eastern Great Lakes in the East. They do occasionally breed farther south, but only sporadically. They winter from southern Canada through the southern United States, except for the most southerly states, where they are rare. A separate race, which may be a separate species, breeds in the southern Florida Keys.

The first step in owl identification is finding one.

Long-eared owls breed from central Canada south to the United States–Mexico border in the West and through New England and irregularly south through the Appalachians to North Carolina in the East. Breeding birds are extremely hard to find, and the range may be larger. They winter from the northern United States south, except in the Southeast, where they are rare.

Barn owls breed throughout much of the United States, but they are rare in northern states and in the higher mountains. They winter throughout much of the breeding range.

From the U.S.–Canada border south, throughout the United States (except for the Southeast), an observer could find any of the three in winter or during migration. It is even possible to spot them outside their "normal" range, because we know little about the actual range limits for these birds.

THE CHALLENGES

Perched birds are reasonably easy to identify, and a reference to any field guide will give you all the information you need. There are only a couple

barn owl
adults

short-eared owl
adults

long-eared owl
adults

of small cautions necessary. The long-eared owl's long ear tufts can sometimes confuse observers into thinking they are looking at a great horned owl. The long-eared's slender appearance and smaller size should resolve the problem.

The palest barn owls, which are almost pure white below, are sometimes mistaken for snowy owls. The small size, the orange or yellowish and gray upperparts, and the heart-shaped face of the barn owl set it apart from the snowy.

Their daytime habitats are good clues, but should not be considered diagnostic. Short-eared owls most frequently roost on the ground in thick cover. Long-eareds prefer to roost in thickets and dense pines. Barn owls prefer more structured cavities, such as abandoned buildings. Overlap is common, however. Long-eareds roost on the ground at times, short-eareds in small pines, and barns will roost almost anywhere. The differences are real, but they are based only on averages. You can make an educated guess based on where you find the bird, but you need to confirm your guess by checking the field marks.

Flying birds are even trickier. All three owls hunt over open fields and marshes, and they have similar flight styles. The best time to catch one is within a half-hour of sunset. In general, the later and darker it is, the better your chance of finding a long-eared owl. They tend to be more strictly nocturnal than the other two. To increase the odds of finding any one of the three, pick the right spots. Not all fields are equal; the most important factor is that the ground should not have been plowed for at least three years. Regular plowing eliminates the small mammals that these owls feed on. Abandoned strip mines, prairies, marshes, and old fields are your best bets.

OWLS IN FLIGHT

These three owls are most frequently seen in flight and in fading light, so the field marks used for perched birds are rarely helpful. The orange facial disks of the long-eared owl are usually invisible in dim light, and the birds lower their ear tufts in flight, giving them the same profile as the other two. The barn owl's heart-shaped face, so obvious on perched birds, is hard to see on flying birds. Other characters are more helpful.

The key to the barn owl is the overall uniform, pale color of most birds. Except for the snowy, the barn owl is the palest of the North American owls. Many barns owls appear almost pure white below when they are in flight. Even birds with buffy breasts and bellies are quite white on the underside of the wings, resulting in an overall pale look. Some short-eared owls (primarily adult males) may also look fairly pale below, but they always have dark tips to the underside of the wings, a dark comma at the wrists, and a darker head and throat than barn owls.

The upperparts of a flying barn owl are a dead giveaway, and it is hard to see the underside of a flying bird without noticing the upper side as well. The buff and pale gray feathers on the back and wings give the bird a paler look than other owls, but in low light, degrees of paleness can be hard to judge. More important is the uniformity of the look. The birds may look slightly darker on the back, but the rest of the upperparts are basically a single color.

The conventional wisdom is that long-eared owls do not start hunting until it's almost dark and that any bird seen out when the sun is still up, or it's light enough to see, is a short-eared.

Both long-eared and short-eared owls have darker wings and obvious contrasting dark and light patches on the outer part of the wings. The high-contrast wing patterns of these two owls quickly eliminate the barn owl from contention. If it is light enough to tell that it's a bird, it is light enough to see the patches.

Flight style is not diagnostic, but it can be helpful. Both long-eared and short-eared owls jerk slightly, and flutter when flying. Their wingbeats are quick and irregular and almost snap. Barn owls are more regular fliers, with steadier, more rhythmic, flowing wingbeats. Use flight style as an indicator, but not as a diagnostic field mark.

A much more vexing problem is distinguishing flying long-eared from flying short-eared owls. The two have nearly identical wing patterns, and the overall color and flight styles are very similar. To separate the two with confidence, you need to look closely at the wingtips and the pattern of the underparts.

The easiest character to see is usually the pattern of the underparts. Long-eared owls have heavily streaked underparts. It is usually not possible to see the streaks on a flying bird, but they make long-eareds in flight look uniformly dark below. The only contrast is the pale area under the tail.

Short-eared owls vary from white to buffy below, and they are streaked only on the throat and upper breast. As a result, flying birds look decidedly two-toned below, paler on the breast and belly, and darker on the throat. The two-toned look is slightly muted on birds with a buffy wash across the breast and belly, but it is still visible. Telling the difference is easy once you've learned what it is.

Although the wing patterns of the two species are nearly identical, there is a slight difference in the pattern of the wingtips that is often useful and easy to see. Both have wingtips that are darker than the rest of the wing. On the short-eared owl, the color is concentrated so that it looks like the bird has solid black wingtips, whether they're seen from above or below. The distinction is emphasized because the pale patch on the inner wing is paler and less orange on short-eareds, resulting in greater contrast. If the bird has obvious dark tips to the wings, it is almost certainly a short-eared owl. The dark on the wingtips of long-eared owls is interrupted with paler, usually orangish, patches. The result is a patch that contrasts slightly with the rest of the wing, but doesn't look like a solid black wingtip.

Conventional wisdom holds that long-eareds do not start hunting until it is almost dark, and that any bird seen out when the sun is still up, or when it is light enough to see, is a short-eared. As a general rule, this seems to be true, but it would be a mistake to assume that all birds seen before dark are short-eareds. The majority might be, but because of the similarities between the two, many long-eareds may be overlooked or not carefully examined, and passed off as short-eareds — look closely at each bird to make certain. Using these field marks, it will be fairly simple to confirm your identification, and you might surprise yourself — and the local bird watching community — by discovering that the bird is a long-eared.

Voice clues are rarely helpful with these three. Long-eareds are notorious for their silence, even in the breeding season. During more than thirty years of looking I have seen a lot of long-eared owls, including birds at the nest, and on only two occasions have I heard them make a sound. Short-eareds are not much noisier, but they do call; their short, sharp barking notes, similar to a small dog, are distinctive.

The most vocal of the three is easily the barn owl. Even in winter they will give their characteristic hissing screech as they hunt low over a field or a marsh. What makes it distinctive is that it is a fairly long call and ends abruptly, as if it were being bitten off. It is a slightly high-pitched, raspy *sssssssssssssssssssshhpp*.

One of the underappreciated pleasures of winter bird watching is standing by a weedy field or marsh on a crisp evening watching the sun go down. Most nights you will see nothing more than a late northern harrier or a few blackbirds and crows going to roost, but one out of ten or twenty nights there will suddenly be an owl floating softly across the horizon, and those nights make all the others worthwhile. Keep in mind these few simple field marks, and you will have the pleasure of not only seeing an owl, but also of knowing which kind it is. It doesn't get any better than that. ◄

HAIRY AND DOWNY WOODPECKERS

One easy way to distinguish

THESE TWO WOODPECKERS IS TO REMEMBER, "DOWNY IS DINKY, AND HAIRY IS HUGE."

SOMETIMES, WHILE TRYING TO DECIDE IF A WOODPECKER is a hairy or a downy, I am reminded of Mark Twain's oft-quoted line: "Quitting smoking is easy. I've done it hundreds of times." My variation on this is: telling downy from hairy woodpecker is easy. I've done it hundreds of times.

Most bird watchers have trouble keeping the distinctions between the two separate because they just don't see enough hairy woodpeckers. In most parts of the continent, downies outnumber hairies at least eight to one, and in backyards the difference is often twice that. In general, hairies prefer older, more extensive woodlands, and those are less common where there are houses.

In winter, however, woodpeckers travel over a fairly large area during their daily feeding rounds, and almost anyone can have the good fortune to see a hairy at the feeder once in a while. More often, we encounter them when we are out birding — which is when we suddenly realize that we don't precisely remember how to tell them apart.

Field guides tend to focus on two field marks: the size of the bill and the presence or absence of black bars on the outer tail feathers. Both are reliable characters, but one requires experience and the other is useful only if you have a very good look. Before getting into those field marks, it is best to start with overall size.

Whenever I find myself looking at a woodpecker and trying to decide if it is big enough to be a hairy, it isn't. When a real hairy woodpecker

WOODPECKERS

shows up, the difference is obvious. The problem is just not seeing many hairy woodpeckers, and anyone can be fooled at first.

Hairy woodpeckers are not twice as big as downies, although when seen together, they often appear that way. Hairy woodpeckers are generally 9 to 9½ inches long, towering over the typical 6½- to 7-inch downy. A difference of 2 to 2½ inches may not seem like much, but it is significant when tacked onto a bird only 7 inches long, representing about a 30 percent increase in size.

If you are trying to decide whether a woodpecker is a hairy or a downy without using field marks — purely on the basis of size alone — it is probably a downy.

Sometimes, however, size is not that easy to assess. For one thing, birds perched up high, or five trees away, all look the same size. For another, woodpeckers have the endearing (or frustrating, depending on your point of view) habit of always being on the wrong side of the tree. If you look at a woodpecker and the size has not told you immediately whether it is a hairy or a downy, try looking at the bill.

Bill size: Hairy woodpeckers have woodpecker bills, big, chisel-like appendages that are obviously designed for hacking away dead wood and bark. Field guides like to point out that the bill of a hairy woodpecker is just as long as the head is wide from front to back. For me the difference in bill size is obvious because downy woodpeckers have absurdly small bills, bills that look like they couldn't make a decent dent in a twig, much less a tree. Once you have seen both birds well, the difference in bill sizes is even more striking than the difference in body size.

Tail feathers: When all else fails, it is time to check the outer tail feathers. Actually, if you are close enough to see the outer tail feathers, the differences in bill and body size should be so obvious that other characters are irrelevant. The enthusiasm for the tail-feather field mark in field guides and among some bird watchers grows out of the fact that, plumage-wise, there just is no other way to tell them apart. These are the nearly ultimate look-alike birds in plumage, and because some watchers are uneasy about using subjective criteria such as size, they want a clean, diagnostic plumage feature to boost their confidence in their identification.

On both hairy and downy woodpeckers, the outer two or three tail feathers are white. On the downy, the white feathers have a few black bars crossing them, and on the hairy the outer tail feathers are plain white.

hairy woodpecker
male

downy woodpecker
male

Birds are about half actual size, but in the
correct proportion to one another

While the character is diagnostic, it is also hard to see. If a bird has not fanned its tail slightly, the black bars on the downy may not be visible. If you see black bars you can be confident it is a downy. If you don't, double-check the other characters. The similarities in plumage apply to all ages and sexes, so the differences between male and female or adult and juvenal plumages won't help you determine which species is involved.

Voice: The other useful character for separating the two is voice, though it takes some experience to use it with confidence, especially the rattle call. Both hairy and downy woodpeckers have two primary vocalizations. One is a short, sharp *pik* call, and the other is a longer rattle, a rolling series of notes. As befits the bigger bird, the *pik* note of hairy woodpecker is louder, sharper, and more penetrating than the *pik* call of downy, which is soft and almost diffident. The hairy's call is also squeakier, sounding more like *peek*. A note of caution is in order. The *pik* note of a downy can be noticeably louder and sharper when the bird is agitated, as when involved in a territorial dispute or mobbing an owl.

The differences in the rattle call are the same. The hairy's call is a loud, ringing series of notes all on the same pitch, emphatic and obvious. The call of downy is a softer rattle, less sharp and less strident and it usually

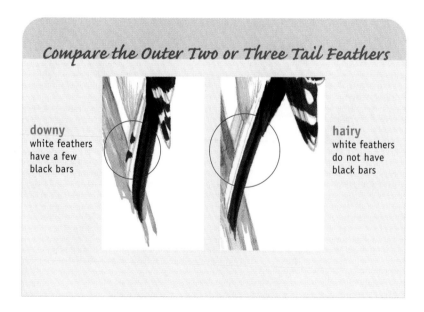

Compare the Outer Two or Three Tail Feathers

downy
white feathers
have a few
black bars

hairy
white feathers
do not have
black bars

descends in pitch. Until you are familiar with the calls, they are best treated as good clues rather than diagnostic characters. If the bird sounds loud and the call is sharp, it may well be a hairy. However, some of the best and most experienced bird watchers admit that they occasionally get fooled.

Behavior: Other general clues can be used to separate the two. In my experience, hairy woodpeckers are far less social than downies. Downy woodpeckers are often part of loose feeding flocks of chickadees, titmice, and nuthatches in the winter; it is much rarer to find a hairy traveling in such company. In addition, you sometimes see three or four downies in a group in winter; at any time except breeding season, even two hairies is a fair-sized flock.

As befits the difference in size, there are differences in feeding behavior. Downies often forage on smaller limbs and even on twigs or thick weed stems, whereas hairies prefer feeding on thicker limbs and thicker tree trunks. It is not impossible to find a hairy woodpecker on a small dead branch, but odds are better of finding a downy. In winter I have found a lot of downy woodpeckers in cut-over corn fields, tapping softly away on dried stalks, probing for insects. I have never seen a hairy woodpecker doing that. Hairies also tend to be shyer and less likely to come close to the observer. Downies can be quite curious at times and often respond readily to *pishing*, which rarely attracts hairies.

Learning to tell a downy from a hairy woodpecker quickly and reliably is mostly a matter of experience. The more of each bird you see, the easier it will become, and eventually you will be tossing a name out without a second thought. Unless, like me, you go too long without seeing a hairy, in which case the memory might need a little kick. ⎰

FLYCATCHERS

Whatever you do, don't fear the flycatcher!

ASK NEW BIRDERS WHICH GROUPS OF BIRDS ARE THE most difficult to identify, and most will cite sparrows or raptors; a few will mention gulls, or maybe shorebirds. But quiz them a year or two down the road and a new family heads the most-dreaded list: flycatchers.

Why the lag? Why don't flycatchers start out at the top of the heap? I think it happens for several reasons. First, flycatchers are so diverse that it can be difficult to conceptualize them as being part of a larger whole. It's not easy to appreciate, for example, the affinities shared by the scissor-tailed flycatcher and the Acadian.

Second, there's the nomenclature problem. Pewees, phoebes, kingbirds, kiskadees, tyrannulets — they're all flycatchers, but few beginners are aware of it.

Once birders do draw that line around the flycatchers, many of them despair of ever making any headway with them. There are just too many, and they are too hard to remember — they seem paralyzingly, drearily nondescript and uniform.

This despair results in part from the fact that field guides need to be both comprehensive and concise. Every species is covered, from the ubiquitous to the arcane, and they all get approximately equal coverage. There's often an emphasis on the really tough problems, to give birders an idea of the pitfalls in identifying flycatchers. This can sometimes leave you with the impression that flycatcher identification is more difficult than it actually turns out to be in the field.

What I propose to offer here might be thought of as Flycatchers 201. I'll assume you've got a good start on the easy ones, and that you're not yet ready to dive into the hair-splitting of divining Pacific-slope from cordilleran from yellow-bellied. But you might be familiar with the tightness in the stomach that grips a birder whose binoculars have just landed on a little brown-green blob, one that may have wing bars or eye-rings or both, but which certainly is a flycatcher. What do you do now?

A good first measure is to not panic. Take a deep breath. Yes, this bird may leave before you get it nailed down to species. Worse, it may not leave, and you might still never feel certain of what it is. Don't sweat it — every birder encounters birds they can't name, and real expertise is gained only after thousands of such incidents.

Instead of diving right in and worrying about precisely which species a flycatcher is, it may be more productive to start by assigning it to a genus instead, and then gradually expand into specific identification. There are three genera that we'll use as examples: *Sayornis*, the phoebes; *Contopus*, the wood-pewees and olive-sided flycatcher; and the ultimate confusing North American flycatcher group, the *Empidonax*.

PHOEBES

Phoebes almost don't make the list of real stumpers because they're familiar and fairly distinctive. The two western *Sayornis* species have either unique color (the coffee- and caramel-toned Say's) or pattern (the strikingly two-toned black). It's the eastern phoebe that really belongs in our group of potentially confusing flycatchers. Lacking streaks, spots, bright colors, or even the classic flycatcher accoutrements of eye-rings and wing bars, they are paragons of plainness.

Thankfully, they have a "tell" — a physical gesture that nearly always gives them away. In fact, in the minds of many birders, eastern phoebes are all but synonymous with their habit of tail dipping. They also frequent habitats that are easy to observe: watercourses, wood edges, and open country.

The plainness of the eastern phoebe's plumage, coupled with its behavior and habitat preferences, will usually see you home safely. A caution, though. Eastern phoebes are often misidentified in the fall, usually by birders who don't realize that phoebes are actually at their most color-

least flycatcher

willow/alder
(Traill's)
flycatcher

eastern
wood-pewee

olive-sided
flycatcher

eastern
phoebe
immature/fall
plumage

ful then. For example, birders along the East Coast frequently mistake bright eastern phoebes, which show a good deal of yellow on the belly, for western kingbirds. Fall phoebes can also show slight wing bars, making them confusingly similar to pewees.

Fall plumage. Many of us think that birds wear their brightest, freshest feathers in spring, and that is partially true. A male scarlet tanager coming north to breed in spring molts from dull olive-yellow to the feathery fireworks that we all know and love. But it's actually in the fall that the vast majority of songbirds molt all their feathers — body, wings, and tail — and are thus truly at their freshest. The tanager's new fall feathers are relatively muted in color — especially in comparison to its breeding plumage. But in a drab species like eastern phoebe, which doesn't molt at all in spring, the autumnal makeover can produce a bird that is brighter, crisper, and more colorful than many of us expect.

WOOD-PEWEES

If the eastern phoebe is the plainest of our flycatchers, the wood-pewees are only incrementally less so (eastern and western wood-pewees are, for our purposes, identical and are treated together). They do add wing bars to the mix, as well as a more peaked, crested head shape. But their lack of an obvious behavioral trait such as tail wagging, coupled with a penchant for wooded habitats where viewing conditions are difficult, makes them in many ways the most anonymous of our flycatcher groups.

Pewees can be thought of as phoebes slimmed down for racing. They are slender, small-headed, and long-winged. Their motions are lightning quick, and they have a habit of fluttering briefly upon alighting — perhaps because their feet are almost ridiculously small for their body. Note that the wood-pewees' tails are a bit shorter than the phoebes', an impression that is magnified by the length of their wingtips.

Wingtips. Birders have a technical term for talking about wingtip shape: "primary extension." It is mentioned whenever the subject of flycatchers is broached. When you look at the folded wing of a bird, you'll usually see the pointed wingtip feathers — the primaries — projecting beyond the more rectangular secondary feathers, which stack like a deck of cards above or on top of the wingtip. If the primaries jut well beyond the secondaries, the bird is said to have a long primary extension; if they're just barely visible, the primary extension is short.

Remember that this is a proportional measure, not an absolute one, so we're talking about easily assessed overall shape — not, in most cases, difficult judgments of a few millimeters. In general, you'll find long pointed wings (and thus long primary extensions) on birds that do a great deal of flying, especially in open country. More sedentary forest species tend to have shorter, rounded wings.

The olive-sided flycatcher, the regal cousin of the wood-pewees, demonstrates this principle nicely. A fairly long-distance migrant, it commutes between the northern boggy boreal forest and the tropics and tends to forage high, sallying up from snags and treetops. The degree of its primary extension is obvious; the long pointed wingtips jut downward and make the moderate-length tail look short in comparison. A large head, a long and heavy bill, and upright carriage combine to give this species a beefy, charismatic air.

Though it's garbed in the same dark olive tones as the pewees and phoebes, the olive-sided flycatcher has clean, bright contrast between its gray-olive vest and its white throat and belly. You should also look for two squarish white tufts of feathers on either side of the rump, near the inner secondaries. Though not always visible, they are a good clincher. Across much of the lower forty-eight states, the olive-sided flycatcher is a welcome, if uncommon, sight on spring and fall migration. If you're lucky, you'll hear it order: *Quick! Three beers!*

EMPIDONAX

Our final confusing flycatcher genus is *Empidonax*, a name that can inspire fear in even stout-hearted birders. True, there are some really difficult species pairs and trios within the empids, but remember: don't panic. We're just taking baby steps for now.

The *Empidonax* divide fairly neatly into two informal subgroups. The members of the first group are on the large-headed, short-tailed side; members of the second show smaller heads and longer tails, closer in proportion to the wood-pewees.

We can take the least flycatcher as our archetype of the first (big head and short tail) group. Compared with the wood-pewees and phoebes, it is compact, with a large rounded head, puffy chest and belly, short tail, and short primary extension. Though plain green-brown in color, it has prominent, contrasty wing bars and a bold whitish eye-ring. Overall, it's cute, at least in flycatcher terms.

For an example from the second (small head and long tail) group, we can resurrect the "Traill's" flycatcher, which was long ago split into two distinct species: alder flycatcher and willow flycatcher. This split was based largely on range and voice — like the two wood-pewees, they form a single visual unit; and we'll treat them as such. Their flat, slightly crested head shape, longer tail length, and more prominent primary extension all resemble the *Contopus* pewees. The willow, especially, often shows almost no eye-ring. But you won't often find either "Traill's" flycatcher choosing perches as high and in the open as the wood-pewees tend to. In fact, it's fair to say that all our empids gravitate toward perches that are somewhat secluded, often staying low in brush or toward the interiors of trees. Although they may come to woodland edges, they just don't seem to have quite the love of exposed situations shown by many of their brethren.

Empidonax: a name that can inspire fear in even stout-hearted birders. Relax. We're just taking baby steps for now.

Habitat. Habitat is often one of the best clues to the specific identity of an *Empidonax*. Willow flycatchers are rarely found far from wetlands dominated by (surprise) willows, and alder flycatchers associate heavily with their namesake shrub, too. Least flycatchers prefer open forests and wood edges.

Other things to consider when looking at empids, and indeed, at any flycatcher, are the shape of the bill and the pattern of the lower mandible. Ideally, you'd want to be underneath a flycatcher, looking straight up at it, to make this assessment, but the birds only seldom cooperate.

Westerners have an advantage here — many of the empids from the Rocky Mountains westward have fairly distinctive bill shapes and differ obviously in the amount of dark color toward the tip of the lower mandible. Easterners have to contend with a batch of more similar types; most show entirely yellow-orange lower mandibles and fairly broad, somewhat convex sides, a bit like a pumpkin seed. But even in the East, the more elongated shape of a "Traill's" bill is perceptibly different from the stubbier aspect of a least's.

Voice. Finally, it is hearing the snappy *chebek*! of the least flycatcher, the sneezy *FITZ-bew*! of the willow flycatcher, or the alder flycatcher's rolling, congested *free-beer* that will really give you confidence in their identity. In fact, even the birds themselves probably use voice more than appearance to identify each other. It's important to use voice as a check on your visual hypotheses.

As your ability to confidently distinguish broad groups of flycatchers increases, you'll naturally start noticing and retaining more information about each bird you see. A sighting that would have set you to tearing out your hair in frustration a year or two ago will instead present a pleasant challenge to your observational skills.

Yes, you can get bogged down worrying about the fringes of flycatcher identification. Many birders do, so much so that they never really make any headway with the group. But that's a little like saying that you can't lift five pounds because you can't lift five hundred. It's largely through careful repetition, building on your base, that you'll make strides toward true understanding. ❧

SHRIKES

Northern and loggerhead shrikes: don't mock the problem.

IDENTIFYING SHRIKES IS REALLY TWO DIFFERENT TASKS, each of which requires a different set of skills. It is analogous in some ways to the problem faced by good professional baseball players. Catching and throwing a baseball requires a specific set of skills; hitting one entails an entirely different set. Only the best players (and would that there were more of those on the teams I root for) have both sets of skills.

The first task is to separate shrikes from mockingbirds; the second is to separate the shrikes from each other. Failing to solve the first problem precludes getting a shot at the second. Many shrikes are overlooked because observers take a quick glance and pass the bird off as "just another mocker." The reverse also happens: the observer, having concluded that the mocker is really a shrike, is driven crazy trying to distinguish between the two shrike species, vainly searching for subtle field marks that aren't there.

The first step to mastering shrikes is making certain that you do — or don't — have a shrike in your sights. (I'll anticipate a question here: I have no idea why shrikes and mockingbirds look so much alike. There are a number of theories, running from the technical "convergent evolution" to "luck of the draw." One or more of them may be right.)

Let's start by examining a few facts about mockingbirds and our two shrike species. All these birds are colored in tones of black, white, and gray. Our goal is to make identifying them more "black-and-white" and less "gray."

WHEN AND WHERE

Both mockingbirds and loggerhead shrikes are fairly widespread in summer, occurring over much of the United States. Loggerhead shrikes (which are declining rapidly in many areas) are usually found in the Southeast, Midwest, and West, from southern Canada south. They are generally resident, but birds in the Midwest and West usually pull out for the winter and head south to the southern Great Plains and the southern tier states. Mockingbirds breed almost to the Canadian border in the East, but nowhere near as far north in the West, where they usually breed from the central Great Plains, central Utah, and northern California south. Wanderers are occasionally found all the way to southern Canada in the West. They are also largely resident, although the northernmost breeding populations usually go at least a little farther south in winter.

Northern shrikes are a different story entirely. They breed in Alaska and far northern Canada and are not an identification issue from mid-spring through late fall. They do move south in winter; the numbers vary greatly from year to year. They regularly reach Pennsylvania, the Great Lakes region, the central Great Plains, northern Arizona, and central California. In years when large numbers are moving, individuals (almost always youngsters) can be found farther south. Basically, in the warmer half of the year the problem is separating loggerhead shrike from northern mockingbird. In the colder half, all three birds need to be considered in most areas.

DISTINGUISHING SHRIKES FROM MOCKINGBIRDS

The keys to telling a mockingbird from a shrike, in roughly the order they are useful in the field, are shape, behavior, and plumage.

SHAPE

The reason to start with shape is that most of the confusion centers around distant birds. The closer you are, the easier it is to tell them apart. Mockingbirds are slender, long-tailed, thin-billed, small-headed birds. Shrikes, by comparison, are bull-headed, a look enhanced by the short, thick bill and proportionately short tail and thick body. A somewhat less

northern
mockingbird

loggerhead
shrike
immature

loggerhead
shrike
adult

northern
shrike
adult

northern shrike
immature

useful difference is the mockingbird's longer legs. Shrikes, like many songbirds, seem almost legless, especially when perched on a wire. Mockingbirds often appear a little leggy; if the bird seems to be sitting clear of the perch, it is probably a mocker. The legs of mockingbirds are not always visible, however, so it is not safe to assume that any bird that looks short-legged is a shrike.

BEHAVIOR

Beyond the basic look—long and slender in mockingbirds and chunky in shrikes—behavior is also a clue. Both mockingbirds and shrikes (especially loggerheads) sit on telephone wires. A shrike on a wire appears to be a patient bird. Shrikes hunt from wires and will often sit still for several minutes, hunched over and looking down. Mockingbirds, which also occasionally hunt from wires, are more likely to use the perch as a lookout. They tend to be more active, twitching and shifting, looking about, and often calling or singing. The difference is more subjective than a plumage mark but still valid no matter where the bird is. Even perched in hedgerows or on small trees, mockingbirds are in general active birds, staying in one place for shorter periods of time, wings and tail flicking, body turning. Shrikes tend to be still, moving only to fly from one perch to another or to swoop to the ground after prey.

Of course, any bird sitting on the corner of a house singing or hunting on a short grass lawn with its wings half raised is a mocker. It is also safe to assume that if the bird in question spends a lot of time harassing other birds, especially those too big to catch and eat (such as crows and jays), or actively dive-bombing people or cats, it's a mockingbird.

These clues can let you make a quick identification on some individuals, but on many others the only real solution is to get a decent look at the bird.

PLUMAGE

Shrikes and mockingbirds are always distinguishable by plumage despite the fact that they are superficially similar. Both are basically gray and white, with a dark tail and wings with white patches in the outer parts. Shrikes are overall more contrasty birds than mockers, with whiter underparts and noticeably blacker wings. There is one field mark that set-

tles the question immediately — the mask. Shrikes have a strong black mask that goes from the front of the eye to the rear of the face, and it can be seen at considerable distances in good light. Mockers do have a darkish area around the eye, but it never matches the mask of a shrike.

Many of the northern shrikes seen in southern Canada and the United States in winter are juveniles (hatched that spring) and they usually have moderate to heavy brown barring across the breast and belly. The presence of barring does not automatically tell you which shrike it is (see below), but it definitely eliminates the mockingbird. Juvenile mockingbirds are not barred below, but spotted, and the markings are lost shortly after the young birds leave the nest.

TELLING THE SHRIKES APART

This is the heart of the problem. In winter, from southern Canada to at least the central United States, and a bit farther south in the West, if you see a shrike, you have to decide which one it is. A few birds can be real troublemakers, but with a decent look and close attention to detail, most are straightforward. The three things to focus on are overall color, belly, and bill.

OVERALL COLOR

During their southerly migration, you are more likely to spot adult northern shrikes the farther north you are. Additionally, the farther north you are, the less likely you are to find a loggerhead.

Juvenile northern shrikes are decidedly brownish birds. The back is washed with brown and the barring on the underparts is also brown and fairly heavy. The mask is not as dark and does not contrast quite as strikingly as it does on adult northerns or on most loggerhead shrikes. The face pattern is still much more distinct than it is on mockingbirds. Birds in juvenal plumage are usually seen only in the fall. By winter the brownish tones are mostly gone, although the barring on the breast and belly still has a brownish tint and there is usually some brown on the face. Any shrike with strong brown tones is a northern. That does not mean that any shrike without obvious brown tones is a loggerhead; some northerns look paler, with little or no brown barring.

CHECK THE BELLY

If the bird is not obviously brown, look at the underparts. All northern shrikes have barring on the breast and belly, but on adults and on young birds late in the winter, it is fine, grayish, and harder to see at a distance or in poor light. It is there, however, and if you can see barring on the underparts the bird is a northern shrike.

Probably pointless caution: juvenile loggerhead shrikes are barred below, although the barring does not extend to the belly and such birds are also barred on the back and wings. The caution is probably pointless because this plumage is not held long, and the chances of a loggerhead shrike still having visible barring by the time northerns arrive is very small. The 99 percent reliable rule of thumb is, if the bird is barred in summer it is a loggerhead; if it is barred in winter it is a northern.

There are other clues besides the barring on the underparts. Young northern shrikes have, as noted above, more brownish and thus less-contrasting face masks than loggerheads. The mask is also relatively small and is barely visible, or not visible at all in the area in front of the eye. On loggerheads, the mask continues from the eye to the bill, and the area over the bill is also black, which is never true on northern shrikes.

Many field guides have focused on the differences in the mask. I suspect that they have done so in an effort to provide a single diagnostic field mark, something most bird watchers fervently seek. In general the shrikes' mask differences break out like this: loggerheads have a mask that is broad and black and surrounds the eyes. The mask of the northern does not fully enclose the eyes, and it is generally lighter black and thinner, especially in front of the eyes.

THE BILL

Bill shape can be a reliable, if subtle, field mark. Northern shrikes have a bill that is both longer and more obviously hooked than the loggerhead's shorter, stubbier bill. Relative bill size can be difficult to judge on a lone bird. The same is true for bill color. The difference is hard to see and is not clearly diagnostic. Young northern shrikes usually have an extensive pale area at the base of the lower mandible. It is true that if at least half of the lower mandible is pale, the bird is almost certainly a northern. But this mark is not easy to see, even in good conditions, and as the winter

Comparing adult shrikes' masks and bills

loggerhead
shrike

northern
shrike

wears on, the mark becomes increasingly less useful as the pale area becomes smaller with the approach of spring.

TELLING ADULT SHRIKES APART

Some of the northern shrikes that come farther south are adults, and they are a greater challenge. The differences between adult northerns and adult loggerheads are subtle and usually require a close look at the bird to see — and some of them are subjective.

The diagnostic character is the underparts. The breast and belly of adult northern shrikes are finely but distinctly barred with pale gray. Adult loggerhead shrikes are plain-breasted and plain-bellied. The catch is that if you see the barring, you know it is a northern. If you don't see any barring, you have to decide if you are just too far away, or if the light is bad, or if this is an adult northern that has almost no barring on the underparts. Move on to the other field marks that we've already outlined: the size of the bill and the width and blackness of the mask. Two other fairly subtle clues may be present on the shrike's face and if they are, the bird is a northern. Many adult northerns show a thin white line outlining the lower half of the eye — almost like white mascara. Pale lores (between the bill and the eye) are another good clue pointing to an adult northern. Viewing the bird from several angles is key to picking up these subtleties.

There are other, more subjective characters that can help. Northern shrikes are about 10 percent larger than loggerheads. The difference is not great and requires having seen each species a few times, but on occasion the largest northerns can seem decidedly big. In general, adult northerns are visibly paler on the back than loggerheads. The gray is almost silvery on many northerns, increasing the contrast with the wings. Many adult northerns look almost black and white, unlike the clear gray, black, and white of loggerheads. The difference is accentuated —especially in flight but sometimes on sitting birds—by the obvious white rump on northerns. Unfortunately, the fact that the bird has a white rump is not diagnostic. Loggerhead shrikes come in a confusing and controversial number of subspecies, some of them with white rumps and some with dark gray rumps. If the bird has a gray rump it is a loggerhead; if it has a white rump it could be either.

There are also some subtle behavior differences that can provide a clue to the identity of the bird, although they are not diagnostic. If the bird is sitting on the top of a small tree or shrub and the tail is bobbing, it is more likely to be a northern than a loggerhead. Northern shrikes hunt from the tops of small trees more often than loggerheads, but both may do so, and northerns also hunt low and in shrubs. The tail pumping is probably a better clue. Northerns, unlike loggerheads, seem to be persistent tail pumpers when they are perched and northerns may hover more when hunting than loggerheads do. Remember, these are clues, not diagnostic field marks.

Almost all shrikes can be identified with confidence if you get a decent view of the bird. On most birds the differences—especially the barring on the underparts and the overall paleness of northerns—are obvious. The cautions apply because every year there are a few shrikes found in winter that drive bird watchers to distraction, especially in the areas just south of the Canadian border. A bird with barely visible barring could be a young loggerhead that is late getting rid of the last remnants of juvenal plumage. Or it could be a northern with reduced barring and all the brown tones gone. When you see one of these birds, you have to look at all the possible characters, including the mask, the rump, and the overall color. But in the end, really confusing birds are rare, and if you take your time and put all the field marks together, you will have the name of your shrike.

PLAIN-WINGED VIREOS

Red-eyed, warbling, and Philadelphia vireos

ALL WINTER LONG, BIRD WATCHERS ANTICIPATE THE arrival of spring migrant landbirds. By late April, the first of the much-anticipated Neotropical migrants have appeared across much of North America, and by May they have set up territories continent-wide. Along with the influx of colorful warblers and tanagers comes a smaller contingent of less colorful flycatchers and vireos. Most members of these latter groups have confusingly similar hues of gray, green, olive, and white. Flycatcher identification stymies everyone, even the experts, but vireo identification doesn't have to confuse anyone at all. To sort the vireos into easily identifiable groups, immediately point your binoculars at the wings. Of the fifteen species of vireos in North America, ten have two (or one, in Bell's vireo) bold whitish wing bars, and five species lack wing bars entirely.

VIREOS WITHOUT WING BARS

Two of the plain-winged vireos, the yellow-green vireo and black-whiskered vireo, are infrequently encountered because they have incredibly limited ranges in the southern United States. The yellow-green vireo is an accidental spring and summer visitor to southern Texas (less than

Philadelphia vireo
adult

warbling vireo
adult

red-eyed vireo
adult

one record per year), New Mexico, and Arizona (very few records), and a casual fall migrant to California (several each fall). Encountering this denizen of Mexico and tropical America in the United States is a matter of luck and requires an intimate familiarity with the similar plumages of the red-eyed vireo. It will not be treated here, nor will the black-whiskered vireo. Although this species does breed commonly in the coastal mangroves in the southern half of Florida, and has strayed to Texas (about ten times), as well as a few times each to Louisiana, Alabama, Mississippi, Georgia, South Carolina, North Carolina, and Virginia (once), it is unlikely to be encountered more than a mile from the immediate coast. It can be eliminated because of geographical probability and is best identified by a single, well-known field mark, its black whisker.

The other three species, red-eyed, warbling, and Philadelphia vireos, are fairly similar and can be confusing even for experienced birders. If we can learn which field marks are the important ones and which ones to ignore, then the identification difficulties will be surmountable.

HOW DO WE KNOW IT'S A VIREO?

Vireos are superficially similar to North American wood warblers. Both frequent the mid- to upper levels of trees; both feed on insects gleaned from the surfaces of leaves, twigs, and branches; and both migrate at similar times of year and appear in similar habitats, sometimes in mixed flocks. Vireos typically move much more slowly than warblers, and they methodically search twigs for insects. They tend not to flick their wings or tails, as many warblers do. No species of vireo will make an aerial flycatching sally to chase down a winged bug, but many warblers will.

One species of warbler in particular, the Tennessee, is notorious for causing confusion with the similarly patterned Philadelphia vireo. (Orange-crowned warblers can also be superficially similar to Tennessees, but differ from vireos in the same basic ways as Tennessees do.) Concentrate first on bill shape. All vireos have fairly thick bills that taper slightly throughout their length, curving near the tip to a blunt point with a slight hook that may recall a shrike in a close view. Notice the blunt tip, however, and you will fully understand the bill shape difference. Vireo bills more closely resemble tanager bills, whereas warbler bills tend to be narrow and pointed like those of kinglets. Note finally that the Tennessee warbler (but not the orange-crowned) has white undertail coverts. The undertail coverts of Philadelphia vireo are always yellowish.

LOCATION, LOCATION, LOCATION

The secret that many experts use for bird identification is knowing the details of distribution and abundance inside out. If a midsized vireolike bird were to fly across the road while I was driving through a forest in Maryland in July, I wouldn't hesitate to call it a red-eyed vireo. This isn't because I noted the eye color, but because I know that Philadelphia vireos never occur there in July, that warbling vireos are scarce and breed locally only along rivers and not in the deep woods, and that red-eyed vireos are one of the most common breeding birds in the forests of Maryland. I wouldn't dare try the same trick in September, when all three species are migrating through my area. Knowing the birds' distribution and abundance throughout the year is invaluable and gives you a starting point for any identification.

The red-eyed vireo nests commonly in almost any deciduous woodland east of the Mississippi River. West of the Mississippi, it occurs sparingly throughout the Great Plains to eastern Colorado and across the northern tier states west to Washington and Oregon. In Canada, it breeds across most of the country below the timberline, but is less common in the West than in the East. Migrants may occur anywhere in the United States or Canada, but stay mostly east of the Rocky Mountains except for the occasional vagrant.

The warbling vireo is almost as widespread. It breeds from the Northeast across the entire Midwest, all of southern Canada, the western United States, and the West Coast. It is absent as a breeder only from the Southeast (Carolinas, Georgia, Florida, Alabama), Texas, and higher montane areas. It is found along rivers (exclusively in the East, preferentially in the West), where it breeds in the tall trees along riverbanks. As a migrant, it may occur almost anywhere except the Southeast, where it remains extremely rare.

The Philadelphia vireo has the most restricted range of the three. It breeds in deciduous woods only across southern Canada from Nova Scotia west to Saskatchewan and very sparingly in the extreme northern tier of the United States, including Minnesota, New York, and Maine. As a migrant, it passes mostly through the center of the country, in a band that stretches from Texas to the Appalachians. East of the Appalachians it is rare in spring, uncommon in fall. It is an extremely rare vagrant to the West Coast.

Spring migration of all species begins in early April (in Texas and Florida) and continues as late as the first week of June, with the peaks across much of North America occurring in mid-May. Fall migration starts in mid-August, but peaks strongly in September, with stragglers occurring through mid-October in some areas. All three vireos are unknown in winter in the United States (actually, they are only almost unknown — California has successfully wintered nearly every landbird including these three vireos). The brief habitat notes given above cease to be of much use in migration, when any species may occur in any wooded habitat from coastal scrub to pine forest.

EYE COLOR AND SIZE

The red-eyed vireo is an aptly named bird. In a close view, you should have no trouble noticing that its iris is a fairly bright brick red with a contrasting black pupil. The other two species of vireos have dark brown eyes that often appear black.

However, in fall (July to November) you must take care, because immature red-eyed vireos have dull red or red-brown eyes. You should still be able to detect the dark pupil contrasting with the rest of the eye, and you may note a reddish tone that will tip you off. Unless you get a good close view, however, eye color can be difficult, especially on young birds. It can be a diagnostic field mark but is usually supporting evidence for other easier-to-see characters. The red-eyed vireo is somewhat larger than warbling or Philadelphia vireos, and it has a proportionately thicker and longer bill. Red-eyed vireos always appear to be very elongated, whereas warbling and Philadelphia (which are nearly identical in size and shape) are more compact.

YELLOW BELLIES

The Philadelphia vireo is usually quite yellowish below, and red-eyed vireos are typically whitish below. As you might guess, though, it is not that simple. In fall plumage, adults and immatures of both red-eyed and warbling vireos have strong yellowish washes below. Philadelphias tend to have bright lemon yellow underparts, from the throat to the undertail coverts, with the strongest concentration on the central chest. Both of the other species have the strongest yellow concentration on the flanks, belly, and undertail coverts. Warbling and red-eyed vireos always have whitish on the throat and especially the central breast. Some warbling vireos can be as bright as (or brighter than) Philadelphia vireos, but the concentration of color always differs.

HEAD PATTERN

This is the single most important area to focus on for any vireo, or perhaps for any landbird at all. A good look at head pattern identifies any of the three species. The red-eyed vireo is distinctive, with a brownish olive face and nape, whitish throat, prominent dark eye line (the line through the eye), pale supercilium (the line over the eye), and dark lateral crown stripes (the stripes along the side of the head, above the supercilium) setting off a gray crown. The result is a head that appears to have at least two stripes running along it and a crown that contrasts markedly with the rest of the face.

The Philadelphia vireo is the most similar, as it, too, has a gray crown, pale supercilium, and dark eye line. Note, however, that it does not have any dark lateral crown stripes separating the pale supercilium from the grayish crown, as does the red-eyed vireo. The crown does not appear as sharply contrasting as on red-eyed vireos and looks slightly grayer or slightly darker than the rest of the face. Concentrate on the lores (the area between the eye and the bill), and you will note that the Philadelphia's dark eye line extends straight through the eye to meet the base of the bill. This is an important distinguishing characteristic from warbling vireos, which always have pale lores.

Philadelphia vireo   warbling vireo   red-eyed vireo

The face pattern of the warbling vireo is very indistinct. It has a faint hint of a pale supercilium, which contrasts very slightly with a darker eye line and darker crown, but the departure is never more than pale gray contrasting with medium gray. This gives the warbling vireo a very blank-faced look, with its dark eye standing totally isolated in the middle of a pale gray face. To sum up: warbling vireos have no dark facial stripes, Philadelphia vireos have one (through the eye), and red-eyed vireos have two (through the eye and along the edge of the crown).

BACK COLOR

The warbling vireo usually appears entirely pale gray, perhaps with very faint olive tones, and the red-eyed vireo is a very distinctly olive or dull green-backed bird in all plumages. The back color alone serves to instantly distinguish warbling from red-eyed vireos. The Philadelphia vireo is a bit trickier, because its back tends toward olive green, falling somewhere between the red-eyed and warbling vireos. Note also that the back color extends up to the nape and onto the face of the Philadelphia vireo, just in case your view is in profile and not back-on.

STOP LOOKING AND LISTEN

As any experienced birder will tell you, birding in the woods, especially in spring and summer, involves much more listening than looking. Is your mystery vireo making any sound? If it is singing, the warbling versus Philadelphia question should be easy to solve. If it is only giving call notes (not singing the full song), the identification may be a bit more elusive. Vireos have several common noises that they make. For the red-eyed vireo, the common call is a single note, a catlike *mew* that descends in pitch. This call is usually given when the bird is somewhat agitated, often in response to pishing or in flock interaction of some sort. It is given commonly in fall. Unfortunately, both the warbling and Philadelphia have similar calls that they give under similar circumstances. A less common call, given under more extreme circumstances (such as the mobbing of an owl), is a several-note descending chatter *che-che-che-chew-chew*. Warbling and Philadelphia vireos have similar notes, and the call notes are not useful for separating them.

The songs, however, are useful for separating the warbling vireo from the others. Warbling vireos have a galloping song that runs along up and down the scale for at least a couple seconds. The song is repeated at short intervals but always gallops in a similar fashion, with individuals notes blending and blurring into one another. It is one of the most common couch potato birdsongs — TV and movie producers dub it into commercials, sitcoms, and movies practically any time one of the characters is standing outside.

Red-eyed and Philadelphia vireos have songs that are nearly identical to one another, but quite different from the warbling vireo. Both give short two- or three-note phrases repeatedly, with very slight variations in each phrase. To some birders the up-and-down phrasing sung by these two vireos sounds like the birds are asking a question and then answering it, over and over again. No phrase lasts more than a fraction of a second, and they are repeated with pauses of little more than a second between them. Even expert birders have great difficulty telling the songs of Philadelphia and red-eyed vireos apart. The Philadelphia's tends to be a little higher pitched, has slightly clearer notes, and its phrases are delivered somewhat more slowly. Separate these two species with caution, but note that the distinctive song of the warbling vireo should eliminate any confusion with the other two species, if you are lucky enough to find a singing bird.

IN SUM

Learn which species breeds in your area and be sure to try to note every field mark when you encounter one in the field in summer. Focus on the head pattern, color of the chest and flanks, color of the back, color of the eyes, and habits (to separate vireos from warblers). After having studied these breeding-season birds carefully, you should find the plain-winged migrant vireos much easier to recognize. Focus first on the head pattern (two, one, or zero dark stripes). Double-check the lores: are they dark (Philadelphia, red-eyed) or pale (warbling)? Then check the breast: is it yellow centrally (Philadelphia) or only along the flanks (warbling, red-eyed)? Is the eye red? Does the back have strong olive or green tones, or is it more gray? As with everything in birding, practice and careful study will yield rewards. ➤

"SPECTACULAR" VIREOS

Bespectacled vireos that are almost spectacularly subtle

THE WORDS "SPECTACULAR" AND "VIREO" OCCUR IN THE same sentence infrequently. Something like, "The vireos, as a group, are spectacular in their drabness," is the rule-proving exception.

I'd like to counter such dismissive appraisals — I maintain that the vireo family includes a fair number of strikingly handsome birds, especially as one heads south into Latin America. Even the middle- and long-distance migrant vireos that breed in the United States or Canada (or both) include some pretty spiffy species.

The best example has to be the simply stunning black-capped vireo — if you manage ever to see one. The cards, unfortunately, are stacked against you: the species is rare, localized, and a quintessential skulker. It's more than worth the trip to the Edwards Plateau of central Texas, where the black-capped is making its last stand, to see this gem. If you do make the pilgrimage, identifying the black-capped will not be a problem, because the male's glossy black hood, extensive white spectacles, wine red eye, and dark green and white body leave little room for doubt. Although less colorful, females are distinctive enough to be immediately recognizable, and we will not treat the species further here.

BESPECTACLED BIRDS

Setting aside that obvious standout, I'd nominate the yellow-throated, white-eyed, and all three "solitary" vireos (plumbeous, Cassin's, and blue-headed) as birds that distinguish themselves through their crisp, attractive markings and coloration. All have prominent wing bars and well-

plumbeous vireo
adult

Cassin's vireo
adult

blue-headed
vireo
adult

white-eyed
vireo
adult

white-eyed
vireo
immature

yellow-throated
vireo
adult

defined "spectacles." (The latter feature is my real reason for referring to them as spectacular.) "Bespectacled vireos" would better please the language mavens, but I'd rather think of them as spectacular.

There are a couple of other species that almost made the cut for our spectacular group, but fell a bit short in either the spectacle or wing bar department: the Bell's, gray, and Hutton's vireos. Though all are interesting birds in their own right, they don't quite fit in with our five. In fact, when you first encounter one of these less well marked species, it can be surprisingly difficult to be sure you are actually looking at a vireo and not at a warbler, flycatcher, or something else.

In birding parlance, spectacles are formed by the combination of an eye-ring and a supraloral line that contrast with the rest of the face. They are often white or yellow on drab olive or gray backgrounds. Vireos seem especially prone to showing this pattern, although there are certainly many other birds, such as the Nashville warbler and the solitary sandpiper.

A supraloral line (or simply "supraloral") is a technical-sounding term for the narrow band of feathers that runs over the top of the lores, which are the small brushy feathers that stretch from the eye to the base of the bill. The supraloral is also the forward part of the eyebrow, or supercilium.

Two of our five vireo species, the white-eyed and the yellow-throated, have yellow spectacles; the spectacles of all three solitary types are white. We might be tempted to split our subjects into yellow- and white-spectacled groups, but a little more research shows that the yellow-spectacled yellow-throated vireo actually has many characters in common with the white-spectacled solitaries. The white-eyed is clearly the odd bird out.

WHITE-EYED VIREO

Consider habitat. You'll observe any number of flying pigs before you see a "solitary" or yellow-throated vireo in a waist-high bramble patch, whereas the same tangle might conceal white-eyed vireos behind every third bush. As for your lifetime count of white-eyeds seen foraging high in the forest canopy (the more typical habit of the yellow-throated and the solitary group), it'll probably range from zero to none.

So the white-eyed vireo stands out from the crowd by virtue of its predilection for low, brushy areas rather than forests. It also has the most distinctive song of the group, which you may have seen transliterated as

QUICK bring the beer CHECK. Though this is a highly memorable rendering, nonsense syllables along the lines of *CHICK chuh bree-ear bree-ear CHICK* or *CHICK-uh bree-ear CHICK* even more closely approximate the phrasing and cadence of a classic white-eyed vireo song. Note that variants such as *CHICK shpwee-CHICK* are common, and in some areas — south Texas springs to mind — they are the norm.

Also be aware that the beginning and ending *CHICK* notes that make the white-eyed song so distinctive may occasionally be omitted, especially the last one. Still, the song's explosive, querulous quality gives away the identity of the singer.

There's only one other point about identifying white-eyed vireos: don't expect them always to have white eyes, especially in summer and fall. Like quite a few other species, young birds have different-colored irises than adults. So if you see a bird that in all respects resembles a white-eyed vireo except that it has amber eyes, you are most likely looking at a bird in its first year, especially if the calendar is somewhere past June first.

YELLOW-THROATED VIREO

The yellow-throated vireo, with its amber eyes and yellow spectacles, could momentarily be mistaken for a first-year white-eyed, but remember habitat — the yellow-throated vireo is a forest canopy bird, often found in fairly tall forest near streams. And although white-eyed vireos may be quite yellow on the flanks, their throat and breast are always silvery white, and they show a grayish hind neck. One might say that a white-eyed vireo looks complicated, with odd bits of color here and there. The yellow-throated vireo has a much more unified look. It appears as if someone took a gray above–white below bird and dunked it headfirst into yellow paint. The wings, belly, and lower back remain gray above and white below, while the head, throat, breast, and upper back are coated richly with pigment. The name "yellow-throated" is actually not quite up to the task of representing this handsome bird's look. "Yellow-shirted vireo" might be more accurate.

Vocally, the yellow-throated vireo follows the classic pattern of its family — short, multisyllabic phrases repeated ad infinitum. But while the red-eyed, Philadelphia, and blue-headed vireos all have a sweet quality to their songs, the yellow-throated has a distinctly burry tone. Tanagers are often said to sing like robins with sore throats, and there's a similar difference between the yellow-throated and many other vireos. Plus, I don't think I've ever heard a yellow-throated sing more than three phrases before it gave one that sounded very much like *Three-EIGHT*, a nice handle by which to remember the species.

A number of vireos, including the yellow-throated, are known to sing from the nest. Think about that for a second — singing from the nest. You would think this behavior would be heavily selected against because it would surely lead to nests being discovered and robbed. The fact of its continued existence argues otherwise, though, and it's kind of fun to imagine these birds, supremely confident in their camouflage, perched atop their precious eggs and singing away with aplomb. Certainly neighboring orioles and tanagers, who wouldn't be caught dead doing something so risky, would be scandalized.

> *It's important with groups like the vireos to not lose the forest for the trees.*

THE SOLITARY VIREOS

Finally, let's turn to the three-for-one split that seems to have confused a lot of us: the solitary vireos. The easiest way to summarize this one is to do it by range: the blue-headed vireo breeds in northeastern woodlands, reaching westward through the boreal forest of the prairie provinces to Alberta and south in the Appalachians to the Carolinas. Cassin's vireo summers on the Pacific coast, and plumbeous vireo occupies the southern Rockies and Great Basin in between.

Of course, when migration starts, things get more interesting, and birders are still working out the details of these three species' winter ranges and the routes by which they reach them. But how do we separate them when range may not be foolproof?

We'll begin with the plumbeous, which is least like the other two. It is basically a gray and white bird with the classic "solitary" markings of bright white spectacles and wing bars. Other than an occasional tinge of yellow on the flanks, which shows especially in late summer and early fall,

> *You'll observe any number of flying pigs before you see a "solitary" or yellow-throated vireo peer out at you from a waist-high bramble patch.*

this species is immaculately two-toned, elegant in platinum and porcelain.

The Cassin's and the blue-headed present us with a thornier problem, and there are individual birds that even the experts leave unidentified. Most of the time, though, the blue-headed looks quite colorful, with a rich gray crown, face, and neck set off from bright white underparts, and finished with a green-gray back and yellow-green flanks. Just don't expect it to have a blue head.

Cassin's vireos are like toned-down blue-headeds. They have less contrast overall, especially between the face and throat, which blend into each other more than they do on age- and sex-equivalent blue-headeds, at least most of the time. Remember that range is going to identify the vast majority of these forms you will encounter in the field.

Voice is a bit less helpful here. Plumbeous has a burry voice, recalling yellow-throated's but drier. Blue-headeds have a sweet song quite like red-eyeds, but higher and slower. The Cassin's is, you guessed it, intermediate between those of the plumbeous and the blue-headed, like a plumbeous but incorporating sweeter notes and phrases.

It's important with groups like the vireos to not lose the forest for the trees. Most of the time identification will be fairly straightforward, with the expected forms showing up in the usual places. The trick is not to take the regulars for granted, but to observe them as long and as carefully as they allow, learning all you can about them before you go out and try to find a Cassin's vireo on Cape Cod or a blue-headed in Oregon — or otherwise making a spectacle of yourself. ➤

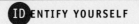
CORVIDS

Crows and ravens:

LET THEM TROUBLE YOU NEVERMORE.

IDENTIFYING RAVENS AND CROWS CAN BE THE WORK OF a second or it can be maddeningly difficult. It all depends on where you are. For all five of the regular species — common raven, Chihuahuan raven, American crow, fish crow, and northwestern crow — the first and most important field mark is the range map in your field guide. In most parts of North America, knowing the range of your bird will at least reduce the problem to telling the difference between a raven and a crow, which is challenging but possible. In ranges where crows and ravens overlap, the problem quickly becomes more difficult.

THE BASIC CHALLENGES

Identifying crows and ravens breaks down into three challenges. The first is telling a raven from a crow and may be fairly easy to moderately hard depending on the circumstances.

The second challenge is telling the crows apart. There are two problems here. The first is telling the difference between fish and American crows, which is often hard and usually requires hearing the bird. The second problem is telling American and northwestern crows apart, which can be done only by range and habitat, and even then there are uncertainties.

The third challenge is between common and Chihuahuan ravens, which is dauntingly difficult unless you go by range and habitat.

fish crows often
perch on wires

northwestern crow
crows grouping on Pacific
Northwest beaches are likely
to be northwesterns

fish crow

American crow

**Chihuahuan
raven**
southwestern desert
only; neck feathers
show white bases
when ruffled

common raven

If you can master the first challenge, telling ravens from crows, range will settle the issue except in a few areas.

RANGE

The American crow is one of the most abundant and widespread bird species in North America. It breeds from the tree line of northern Canada south through most of the United States and is absent only from western Texas, the lowlands of the Southwest, and some of the higher elevations in the Sierra Nevada. It winters from southern Canada south throughout its range. American crows are surprisingly quiet and shy during the breeding season. In winter, however, they gather in large roosts that sometimes include more than 100,000 birds. Anyone who has been to a crow roost, or has the misfortune to live near one, knows that in winter they are anything but quiet or shy.

Fish crows are nearly resident in the Southeast, occurring from southern New England through the Gulf states to extreme eastern Texas, and generally only a few hundred miles inland. Like American crows, they are fairly quiet and timid during the breeding season, and they gather in moderately large roosts in winter.

Northwestern crows are confined to a narrow section of the Northwest coast from extreme northern Washington north to south coastal Alaska. In winter they are slightly less likely to congregate except at feeding sites.

Common ravens are nearly as widespread as American crows. They are resident from the northern limits of North America south through the western United States into Mexico. In the East they are found south to the United States–Canada border and in the highlands of the Appalachian Mountains.

Chihuahuan ravens are birds of the desert Southwest, resident from southeastern Arizona through southern and eastern New Mexico and western and southern Texas. A few breed north in the Great Plains to southeastern Colorado and southwestern Nebraska. In winter they are more likely to be found in large flocks than common ravens are.

CROWS VERSUS RAVENS

In most areas, once you have decided whether you are looking at a raven or a crow, you have identified the big black bird you saw. The exceptions, as we shall see later, are in the Southeast, parts of the desert Southwest, and along the Pacific Northwest coast. If you are in most of the Great Plains and the north-central United States, you don't even have to worry about what it is you're seeing. Any large black bird in those areas is almost certainly an American crow. In much of the rest of the continent you still need to make the decision. The field marks you should use depend on whether the bird is flying or sitting.

In flight, a raven looks like a large black hawk. The wings are broad and rounded at the tips, and the flight is very hawklike. Ravens often soar when they are up high, a behavior that is rare in crows. The two best field marks on flying birds are the tail and the way the bird flaps its wings. The tail of ravens is moderately to obviously wedge-shaped, as the central portion is longer than the sides. The tail of flying crows is basically squared off at the end and at best shows only a faint hint of a wedge shape. When seen from below, the difference is usually obvious. On birds in the distance, seen at an angle, and flying away from you, the shape of the tail is harder to determine, and other characters have to be added to the mix.

The best of the secondary characters is flight style. Crows fly with a distinct rowing motion, constantly and steadily flapping; they seem to move themselves through the air as if they were propelled by oars rather than wings. Ravens flap more slowly on average and intersperse soaring and gliding. Their flapping is very like that of a red-tailed hawk, and distant ravens are more likely to be mistaken for a hawk than for a crow at first glance.

The differences in the tail and the flight style may seem subtle at first, but almost everyone lives where there are crows. If you spend some time watching them you will find that the rowing flight quickly becomes distinctive. When you finally see a raven, it will probably stand out on flight style alone.

Sitting birds can be trickier, although there are some useful field marks. One problem is that in many areas it is uncommon to get a close look at a sitting raven; another is that the field marks are mostly relative rather than absolute and often require experience to be truly useful.

To start with, ravens are bigger than crows, usually noticeably so — common ravens are on average about 50 percent bigger than American crows. The difference is most useful when you have both birds in view at once and can compare them, but with experience, size is usually a good indicator on even single birds.

American crow
fast, rowing wing-
beats, short tail

common raven
often soars like a
hawk, wedge-
shaped tail

Two other field marks can be used on sitting birds. Crows are sleek birds and ravens are shaggy birds, especially on the throat and upper breast. The shaggy throat feathers of ravens are easy to see in most instances and, except under very windy conditions, are never shown by crows. Ravens sometimes show some shagginess on the crown as well, with feathers sticking up, a character not shown by crows.

Bill size can also be useful, although it is slightly harder to use. Ravens have noticeably thicker bills than crows, and usually the feathering on top of the bill is thicker and more visible. Although the raven's overall bill length is not short, its thickness and the size of the bird often leave the impression of a slightly shorter, stockier bill than the crow's.

A single sitting bird at a distance away can be hard to identify. Ravens can look sleek, and in windy conditions crows can look disheveled. When that happens, the best thing to do is wait for the bird to fly, which is usually within a minute or two. This allows you to watch the tail and the flight style to confirm your initial guess.

The bird may also call during takeoff and, despite the fact that both crows and ravens have fairly wide vocabularies, call will usually settle the question quickly. Outside of the breeding season, the most frequent vocalizations of each are easy to distinguish. Crows give a loud, nearly clear *caw* note, often in a series, and it can hardly be confused with any other bird. Ravens typically give a hoarse, guttural, slightly lengthy call variously transcribed as *kraaak*, *croak*, and *gronk*. No matter how it is written, what matters is the deep, hoarse quality of the note.

All of the above characters apply to all ravens and crows. Chihuahuan ravens are very slightly smaller and smaller-billed than common ravens, although the differences are not enough to separate them. The differences still serve to separate Chihuahuan ravens from American crows in the very small area where both might occur.

TELLING THE CROWS APART
NORTHWESTERN VERSUS AMERICAN CROW

Telling one crow from another is only a problem in the Southeast and along the Pacific Northwest coast. Everywhere else they are American crows.

The problem of northwestern and American crows is the easy one — easy because it can't be done. There are no known reliable characters for telling the northwestern from the American crow. Not plumage, not behavior, and not voice. In fact, many ornithologists consider the northwestern crow to be merely a poorly defined subspecies of American crow.

If you want to add the northwestern crow to your life list, you have one option. Go to where they occur, like the coast of southern British Columbia. Go to the beach. Find a crow, or preferably a small group of crows, feeding on marine organisms along the beach. Put northwestern crow on your list.

Once you move 500 yards inland, however, you can no longer be certain, although most of the birds you see may be northwesterns. Observers who have spent years in the region say they cannot tell them apart. Some say they are slightly more social than American crows, some say slightly less. Some claim the voice is, on average, slightly higher-pitched, while others say it is slightly lower. The bills of northwestern crows do average slightly thinner, but there is overlap and it is not a diagnostic mark. In fact, there is overlap in every character. It would seem that American crows in the area are very rare right along the coast, although they have been reported there in the nonbreeding season.

All this may sound a little silly, and maybe it is. But the best bird watchers in North America have thrown themselves at this problem for more than fifty years, and it refuses to yield.

FISH VERSUS AMERICAN CROW

In the Southeast there are two crows, and they provide one of the most challenging field problems we have. Although there are average differ-

ences in some characters and behaviors, absolute identification almost always depends on hearing the bird — and hearing the right call.

The diagnostic call of the fish crow is a double-noted, distinctly nasal *aaah-aaah*. It is important that the call is nasal, and that you hear both notes, because young American crows can give a fairly nasal call — but even when it is given in a series, the call is not double-noted. The second note of the fish crow's call is slightly lower than the first, which is another tip-off.

The nasal quality of fish crow calls can be a strong indicator of species no matter what the vocalization, but except in the case of the double-noted call, it should not be considered diagnostic unless you have a lot of experience with both species. In some situations, the calls of American crows may be higher-pitched than normal, which makes them sound slightly nasal.

There are some structural and behavioral clues to watch for as well. Fish crows are slightly smaller than American crows, although there is overlap. They also have, on average, slightly thinner bills and shorter legs. The differences are not large, and even the most experienced bird watchers will admit that they are, at best, making an educated guess when identifying a single silent crow.

One behavioral character that may help is this: if you are in the Southeast and see a crow sitting on a telephone wire, it is most likely a fish crow. American crows are not as likely to perch on wires, although some certainly do. Still, if you need to be absolutely sure, stop for a while, and hope the bird calls.

Some bird watchers believe that the slightly quicker, stiffer wingbeats, the very slightly more pointed wings, and the smaller head can be clues on flying fish crows. The differences are real, but they are small and subject to many variables. Some of the best observers in the country use them, and they get it right as much as two-thirds of the time. For the rest of us, those small differences are fun to watch for and use to make guesses, but they do not identify birds.

It helps that the two species tend to segregate themselves in the non-breeding season. Single flocks are frequently composed of just one species. Mixing most frequently occurs at feeding concentration spots such as landfills and sewage lagoons, places that allow you to compare the two.

TELLING THE RAVENS APART

Fortunately there is only a very small area where Chihuahuan and common ravens might be found together. This is fortunate because they are nearly as hard to tell apart as American crow and northwestern crow. In virtually every character there is overlap, and the only absolutely diagnostic plumage or structural field mark is only rarely seen, no matter how close you get to the birds. Chihuahuan ravens have white bases to the neck feathers; common ravens have dirty gray bases. The difference is diagnostic if you can see it, but the bases to the neck feathers show in only high winds or when the bird is preening.

Range and habitat are good field marks, though they aren't diagnostic. Chihuahuan ravens are birds of open grasslands and scrub desert lowlands. In the area where they overlap with common ravens, the commons are almost always birds of higher elevations and more wooded habitats. Chihuahuan ravens are also thought to be more social than common ravens, especially in the winter, and if you are in the desert areas of the Southwest and come upon a decent-sized flock of ravens, the odds are extremely high that they are Chihuahuans.

No other character even approaches being diagnostic, although, on average, there are some slight physical differences. Chihuahuan ravens are a little sleeker than common ravens. The bill is smaller and the wings are shorter. The tail is slightly shorter and slightly less wedge-shaped. The calls average higher and less hoarse. All these differences are only averages, however, and they are all slight. In combination they might provide the basis for a good guess, at least after you have considerable experience with both birds. Single ravens in the tiny range of overlap must usually be logged as unidentified raven species.

If you have gotten this far, the parts you remember are probably the parts saying you can't tell this species from that. But it's not that bad. In most of North America, the only challenge is deciding if it is a crow or a raven. Except in the case of fish and American crows, in which voice is diagnostic, there is little geographic overlap between the impossible pairs. There is no reason not to confidently identify almost every large black bird you see, as long as you start with the basic field mark — the range map. ➘

BASICS OF SWALLOW ID

Just getting a good look can be a challenge.

SWALLOWS ARE TOUGH. ONLY TWO GROUPS OF BIRD watchers fail to understand how challenging swallow identification can be: those who have ignored them, and those who have mastered all the subtleties and can recognize any swallow at any distance. The first group is large, the second quite small. Most of us are somewhere in the middle. We recognize swallows when they cooperate, at least most of the time, and have trouble with them more often than we'd like.

At first glance it would not seem that swallows are one of the tougher identification challenges. There are not a lot of them to worry about. Including the purple martin, there are only seven in most parts of the continent, which is not a very big number compared with the flycatchers or warblers. Why do swallows challenge so many of us when we see so many of them?

One reason is that we see most of them as migrants, zipping past overhead, and if we get any look at all it is often brief. To the inexpert eye, all flying swallows look distressingly similar. Even when we come across a feeding flock out over a marsh, pond, or field, we are distracted by how fast they are, how quickly they change direction, and how hard it is to see the field marks. Just tracking a flying swallow takes most of our concentration. Trying to find a field mark at the same time can seem impossible.

Take heart. It is not that hard to get a handle on swallow identification. It just takes patience and acceptance of the fact that some birds will get

SWALLOWS

away. If you take your time, you will find that more and more of the birds seem easier to identify. Or at least your guesses will get better.

The main problem is that swallows are so common we try to master the identification of all of them at the same time. This can lead to field mark overload. North American swallows break naturally into three easy groups. The first is tree and violet-green. The second is barn, cliff, and cave. The third is northern rough-winged, bank, and purple martin.

There really is not much overlap in identification between groups once you learn the field marks that separate them. For example, barn, cliff, and cave swallows have orange or red on the throat and the cliff–cave duo has pale rumps. Rough-winged and bank swallows are brown above and have some brown below. Martins are big and dark (but all-brown juvenile martins and some brownish young females can be confused with the dark bank and rough-winged swallows and with European starling). Tree and violet-green are the only North American swallows that are entirely white below (with a small exception I will get to later). Get the group, and you have reduced the problem to manageable proportions.

A few final tips for swallow watchers. One or two swallows zipping over the middle of a field will be hard to see well. A better bet is to find them where they congregate in large numbers, at their nest sites, feeding areas, and migration gathering spots. Find a barn with several barn swallow nests, an active purple martin colony, a culvert or bridge with cliff or cave swallow nests, or a sandy bank with rough-winged or bank swallow nests. Ponds, lakes, and rivers with their abundant insect populations can attract dozens of foraging swallows. In late summer many swallows gather in huge mixed-species roosting flocks prior to the start of migration.

These natural collections of swallows offer an excellent opportunity to study these birds in a variety of poses, both in flight and at rest. You'll also be able to tune in to their chattering calls, often your first clue to a swooping swallow's presence. ⼇

GREEN SWALLOWS

Tree and violet-green swallows

EASIER AND HARDER THAN THEY LOOK

THE TREE SWALLOW IS ONE OF THE MOST ABUNDANT and widespread birds in North America, and no matter where you are you will see them, sometimes in immense numbers. Also, tree swallows are the earliest spring and latest fall migrant in the family and the only swallow that regularly winters in eastern North America. In the eastern half of the continent they are also the only swallow that commonly uses nest boxes, providing most of us with the chance to spend time studying them during the breeding season. In the West violet-green swallows — the main identification challenge — also use nest boxes.

RANGE AND HABITAT

Tree swallows breed from the tree line in northern Canada south to at least the central United States and almost to the U.S.–Mexico border in the West and to the northern edge of the Gulf Coast states in the East. They can be seen anywhere as migrants, and they winter in the Southwest and the Southeast. Migrant flocks, especially in fall, can number in the tens of thousands and sometimes in the millions. Like all swallows they feed primarily on flying insects, although they will take berries in winter and when the weather is bad.

Violet-green swallows breed from northern Alaska south into Mexico and east to the edge of the Great Plains. They are typically a higher-elevation bird than the tree swallow in the breeding season, but that is more true in the southern part of their range. They are, however, resident along the coast of southern California and can be found there year-round. Despite subtle differences in timing and habitat, any time you see a swallow in the West that is pure white underneath you have to consider both tree and violet-green swallows. Violet-greens are not as abundant as tree swallows, but they are common in many areas. They tend to migrate in small groups and even singly, and although a huge flock may contain violet-greens it is unlikely to be all violet-greens. They have also been found in many parts of the Great Plains as migrants and should be looked for there in spring and fall. In recent years, with observers scouring the immense flocks of migrant tree swallows in the East, a few violet-greens have shown up, and they are undoubtedly more frequent than the few reports would indicate. Close scrutiny of eastern tree swallow flocks in the fall might produce more records, but when you are faced with hundreds of thousands of birds it is easy to take a pass on the problem.

THE GENERIC TREE/VIOLET-GREEN SWALLOW

Both are dark above with dark rumps and only slightly forked tails, eliminating barn, cave, and cliff swallows. Both are entirely white below except for young birds in the fall. Any bird that is all-white below cannot be a rough-winged or a bank. Martins are big and dark. In the breeding season, if the birds are using a nest box (usually a bluebird box), you are looking at a tree or a violet-green swallow. Note that martins use boxes of a sort, but martins nest colonially so it's rare to have a single pair of martins or a single martin house. Tree and violet-green swallows will try to use a martin house for nesting on occasion. They shy away from those that have martins, however, and they don't tolerate close neighbors, so if there are a lot of birds at the house they are almost certainly martins, starlings, or house sparrows.

TELLING TREE FROM VIOLET-GREEN

Both species are blue-green to brown above and white below, but the field marks that separate them can be surprisingly easy to see with practice. Start with sitting birds and when you have a good picture in your head, try

violet-green swallow
adult male

violet-green swallow
adult female

violet-green swallow
juvenile

tree swallow
adult male

tree swallow
adult female

tree swallow
juvenile

rough-winged swallow
adult

bank swallow
adult

seeing the same field marks on flying birds. It is simpler than it looks.

The key field marks for separating tree and violet-green swallows are the face and the sides of the rump. The face works on both flying and sitting birds except juveniles. The rump is hard to see on sitting birds but easy on flying birds and works in all plumages.

Adult violet-green swallows have a mostly white face. They have a dark cap and nape but the face is white and it stands out in almost every condition. The face of tree swallows is dark, and the cap extends down past the eye so that only the throat and chin are white. The difference sounds subtle, but it can really jump out at you in the field.

Young violet-greens have dark faces and are much more similar to young tree swallows. The simple rule here is that if the bird has a white face it is an adult violet-green swallow. If it has a dark face, and is greenish or blue-green above or entirely white below, it is a tree swallow.

On flying birds the sides of the rump are the key. On violet-green swallows in all plumages the white of the underside of the bird comes up over the sides of the rump, sometimes appearing to almost meet in the middle of the rump. That means that from the side or from above you can see the white feathers curving up onto the edge of the rump, and if you do, it is a violet-green. If no white shows, it is not. If no white shows and the back is greenish or bluish, the bird is a tree swallow. If no white shows and the bird is brown above, you still have to eliminate rough-winged and bank swallows, which I will get to in a minute.

YOUNG BIRDS

The bigger problem involves young birds in the fall that are sitting. Young violet-green swallows, and a few drab females in the spring, have dusky faces, making them very similar to tree swallows. There is a difference and it can be seen if you get a good look, which is often possible with sitting birds. The dusky on these birds actually extends farther down the face than does the dark on the face of the tree swallow, and it tends to blend into the lower face and throat with no clear line of demarcation between the dark and the pale. On tree swallows the line between the dark on the face and the white on the throat is sharp and clear and tends to be higher up on the face, just below the eye.

There are other, more subtle differences that have been proposed as field marks for separating tree and violet-green swallows, but they are tricky at best and confounding and overlapping at worst. More important, if you can see them you have certainly gotten a good enough look to identify the bird using the face and the rump. The two that bear further study are size and the color of the upperparts on adults.

The tree is our largest swallow except for the purple martin and, although it is only a half-inch larger than violet-green on average, the birds are less than 6 inches long, and the difference can be evident on birds sitting together. Except in direct comparison I find size of little use, though. There is also a subtle difference in the back color of adults. Tree swallows in the spring tend to be glossy and have a distinctly blue tinge to the upperparts. Violet-greens are a flatter, less glossy color and are typically greener, without the blue tinge. The quality of the light and the circumstances of the observation can make the difference impossible to see much of the time, however, and you should use these characters with caution if at all. Besides, if you get a good enough look to be absolutely certain of the color, you have already seen enough of the face and rump to know which it is.

OTHER SWALLOWS

Young tree and young violet-green swallows are brown above and can be mistaken for rough-winged or bank swallows, especially in the fall when young trees and violet-greens have a dull wash of brownish gray on the chest. This is the only plumage in which they are not all white below.

Compare the Face

violet-green swallow
adult male

tree swallow
adult male

tree swallow
juvenile

CHECK THE RUMP AND THROAT

Young violet-greens are easier to separate from banks and rough-wingeds because of the white on the sides of the rump. Sitting birds are not hard either, if you keep the face pattern in mind. The same characters that help separate young violet-greens from young trees will help eliminate bank and rough-winged swallows. Rough-wingeds are the only brown swallow with a brownish throat and upper chest. All the rest have white throats. Young banks have a brown band across the breast, similar to the brown wash across the breast of some young violet-greens, but the band is sharply defined and darker than the wash on the breast of violet-greens. In addition, bank swallows have a sharp line between the dark of the face and the white of the throat, unlike the blended look of violet-greens.

Tree and violet-green are the only North American swallows that are entirely white below.

Young tree swallows also have a brownish band on the chest. They have a white throat, however, which eliminates the rough-winged swallow. The bigger problem is bank swallows, which have a brown band on the chest and a face pattern very similar to young tree swallows. The key is the breast-band. It is dark and sharply defined in bank swallows, and if you are looking at a sitting bird you will see that it has a sharp tongue of brown that goes an inch or so down the chest. The breasts of young tree swallows have a brownish wash that is not sharply defined and has no tongue of color going down onto the breast.

The difference is not as subtle as it sounds and on most sitting birds you can see it easily. Flying birds are much tougher. Sometimes, if you are close enough, you can see the difference in the darkness and sharpness of the band, but some flying birds just have to be allowed to go on their way unnamed. Trust me, they don't care. They know which they are.

With considerable practice it is possible to make a reasonable identification of the birds on the basis of size alone. Banks are our smallest swallows, almost a full inch smaller than tree swallows. My own experience is that size is much more useful when both birds are present, but practice can make it an almost reliable field mark under most conditions.

VOICE

Many experienced (very experienced) bird watchers regularly identify all the swallows by voice. It is absolutely possible to learn to do so, but it takes determination, effort, and time spent with a good tape of bird calls.

First, every call made by every swallow can, and has been, described as "twittering." It is not hard to learn the generic swallow call. The trick is dividing them once you realize it is a swallow. Because written descriptions of calls are often more confusing than helpful, especially when the call is twittering, if you want to learn the vocalizations you need to get a tape and then take what you have learned into the field and practice, practice, practice.

The song of the tree swallow is typically three longish descending notes that end in twittering. The key is the three notes, the descending quality, and the pattern of having a twittering at the end. In flight and when agitated they also have sharp, thin notes or a repeated clear series that is almost a whistled note. It is the longer series that you need to focus on first.

The song of violet-green swallows is typically a two-noted *chee-chee*, often followed by a series of shorter, sharper notes. Other calls, mostly given in flight, are very similar to those given by tree swallows, although to some ears they are sharper and more abrupt. Unless you have a very good ear or a lot of practice, most vocalizations are not especially helpful in separating the two. They are worth learning mostly because they will, in time, make it easier to eliminate some of the other swallows.

If you have been passing up swallows, take the time to take a longer look. What seems at first glance to be complicated is not, despite the length of this chapter. Remember, the trick is to get to the right group, which is often easy. Once you do, the number of field marks you have to remember is small. In the case of violet-green and tree swallows you can identify the vast majority of the birds you see by looking at the rump and the face and remembering that more white in either place means violet-green. Once that becomes second nature, and it will before you know it, the subtleties won't seem so subtle or hard to recall. ✖

RUSTY SWALLOWS

Cliff, cave, and barn swallows

CLIFF, CAVE, AND BARN SWALLOWS FALL NATURALLY into a group of their own by virtue of the fact that they build nests from mud, with or without other materials. Formerly all placed in the genus *Hirundo*, they share not only a fondness for mud, but steel bluish backs, and throats and foreheads richly colored with some variety of chestnut-buff. Barn swallows are one of the most cosmopolitan of all bird species, and they shouldn't be too difficult to distinguish. Cliff and cave swallows have recently been separated into their own genus, *Petrochelidon*, and the real field challenge here is distinguishing between them.

BARN SWALLOW

Barn swallow is really in a class of its own, although its throat pattern recalls cliff's and its forehead looks a bit like cave's. The most fundamental field mark is that wonderful swallow tail, which is simply one of the most aesthetically pleasing of all avian characters. Swallow tails would look great on just about any bird, lending an air of grace and sophistication like a good sport coat or the perfect little black dress.

The barn swallow's outer tail feathers are so eye-catching that their equally unique white tail band receives little comment. Maybe "band" is too strong a word — it recalls the thick white terminal band on the tail of the eastern kingbird. The barn swallow is more subtly ornamented, with

cliff
swallow

cave swallow

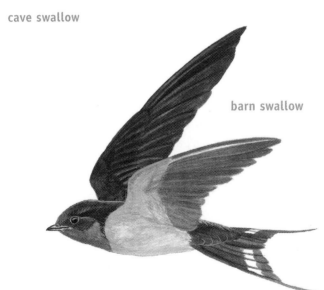

barn swallow

a broken band of small white rectangles a little more than halfway down the tail. The barn swallow's tail pattern is not unlike magnolia warbler's, calling to mind a delicate Chinese fan. The wider the fan (or tail) is spread, the easier it is to see the contrasty pattern.

Individual barn swallows vary quite a bit in appearence. The underparts range from deep buff, even bay, to whitish or pale beige. Juveniles' tails aren't as elongated as adults', though they're still quite long-tailed compared with other swallows; juveniles are also paler overall than adults.

CLIFF AND CAVE SWALLOWS

It's tempting to separate cave and cliff swallows from other common swallows by their pale rump patches, but be careful. Bank swallows' (see page 232) uppertail areas are distinctly lighter than the rest of their upperparts, particularly when seen in bright sunlight.

Assuming that you really do have a cliff or cave swallow in your sights, how do you pin it down to species? One seemingly obvious answer — range — is less reliable here than in many cases. Though cave swallows in the United States are largely restricted to southern and western Texas and southern New Mexico, they appear to be undergoing a massive range expansion. In fact, the species wasn't even known in the United States until 1915. Restricted to nesting in caverns and sink holes during their first half-century of residence north of the border, cave swallows have figured out how to make use of man-made highway culverts — or perhaps our construction techniques and materials have come more into line with their innate preferences. Cave swallows have even been observed commandeering barn swallow nests and putting them to use. In the 1980s, cave swallows of the Antillean race established a small but successful colony in southern Florida. Moreover, cave swallows have shown a real tendency to wander, especially up and down the Atlantic Coast in late fall, and might conceivably turn up virtually anywhere in North America, though it is still a topic of debate where these vagrants originate.

In a sense, cave swallows are following in the footsteps of cliff swallows. Cliff swallows were historically birds of western canyons and cliff faces, but spread into the East, probably because the clearing of wilderness areas and the construction of barns and bridges provided them with suitable foraging grounds and nesting sites. Cliff swallow populations are believed to have increased steadily, at least until house sparrows became widespread and began competing with them for nests. In any event, the race is on, and it will be interesting to see how the relative distribution and numbers of our three "mud" swallows shifts in the twenty-first century.

BY THE THROAT

Back to telling cave and cliff swallows apart. The single most useful mark is the throat. Cliff swallow has a well-defined dark chestnut bib with a black border along its lower edge that contrasts strongly with the pale beige chest and underparts. Most cliff swallows also have a surprisingly visible white forehead that helps distinguish them from the darker-browed cave swallow. (I say most cliff swallows, as some Mexican forms have dark chestnut foreheads; they still give a different overall impression than cave swallows do.) As well as darker foreheads, cave swallows have throats that are evenly washed with a pale buff that blends relatively gradually into the underparts, rather than sharply contrasting bibs.

The cliff swallow's dark chestnut throat and black cap, combined with its grayish tan collar, make it look like a dark hooded bird; the white forehead doesn't really disrupt this impression. It's an image that may not make much sense initially, but you may find it suddenly pops into sharp relief when you actually see the bird. The head pattern of cave swallow isn't hooded, but capped. The throat, cheeks, and neck are all similar in color and effectively isolate the black coloring around the eyes and nape; cave is a buffy-headed swallow with a dark partial cap.

A few other distinctions are sometimes useful in the field. Cave swallows are smaller than cliff swallows and have darker, more rufous rumps. In general, cliff swallows appear large and buffy-rumped, and caves are smaller and chestnut-rumped.

In summary, the barn swallow is easily differentiated from either cave or cliff by its attenuated, white-paneled tail and longer, more aerodynamic lines. Look at the head patterns of cliff (hooded) and cave (capped) swallows to further distinguish these two look-alikes. You've got the key to identifying the "mud swallows."

Perhaps the greatest identification lesson to be learned from swallows is that it really is possible to identify small songbirds on the wing. There aren't too many swallow species to keep track of, and they can often be studied at some length as they quarter back and forth over a favored field or waterway. ✦

DRAB SWALLOWS

Bank and rough-winged swallows and purple martin

IN LATE SUMMER, BEFORE THE FIRST MIGRANTS HEAD south with the start of fall migration, swallow numbers are at their peak in most parts of North America. Adults are joined by newly fledged young of the year. When a large swarm of swallows is seen swirling over a field, pond, or marsh, or even perched along a wire at this time of year, some confusing identification problems can be encountered.

Among the least-colorful (and perhaps least-appreciated) of our swallows are the bank and rough-winged swallows. Telling these birds apart in late summer is complicated by the addition of young tree swallows, which are brown on the back and lack the metallic blue-green of their adult plumage. Taken together, this trio of brownish-backed swallows can be both difficult and easy to tell apart. Add in our other dull-colored swallows and the larger juvenile purple martin, and you've got a set of confusing similar birds we might call the "drab swallows." Looking only at their backs as they zip past below you may leave you guessing. Get a good look at their breasts, however, and the identification becomes much easier.

ROUGH-WINGED SWALLOW

Rough-winged swallows are the easiest to identify, and in many parts of the continent they are more commonly encountered than the other two. They are the only brown swallows with a brownish throat and upper chest. Rough-winged swallows are the same size as tree swallows but slightly larger than bank swallows. From above, the rough-winged's back appears uniformly medium brown, and its throat and upper breast appears to be washed with a dull gray-brown. There is no sharp contrast between the dark head and the lighter throat. Instead, "roughies" appear to have an even gradation from dark to light. Both bank swallows and young tree swallows show a definite contrast from dark head to light throat.

Compare an adult rough-winged with a juvenile and you'll notice that the youngsters have a cinnamon tinge to the breast and back feathers and light cinnamon wing bars. This can be a good field mark to look for when scanning through a fall flock of perched "brown" swallows. These wing bars fade when the rough-winged molts into adult plumage.

BANK SWALLOW

Bank swallows are our smallest swallow species. Although they appear quite similar to rough-winged swallows, when the two are seen side by side, the bank is noticeably smaller. From above, the bank and rough-winged are nearly identical, though in perfect light you might notice that the bank swallow's tail and wings appear to be a darker brown than its head and back (the rough-winged is uniformly brown in these areas). Young bank swallows can be singled out from adults by their contrasting buffy rump — a field mark than can be seen in flight.

On its underside, the bank swallow always shows a well-defined breast-band across the white throat and belly. On flying birds, this dark band is the field mark most bird watchers use to tell banks and rough-wingeds apart. Some banks also show a spike of dark brown that points from the breast-band down onto the white belly.

If you cannot see the white belly, look at the side of the bird's head. If you see sharp contrast, dark above and white below, you're looking at either a bank swallow or a young tree swallow (see below). Rough-winged swallows do not show a clear contrast between the head and the throat when viewed from the side.

JUVENILE TREE SWALLOW

Young tree swallows are plain gray-brown above and show a gray (not dark brown) breast-band. This band is heavier on the sides than in the middle of the breast; in the middle of the breast, it often appears indistinct. Bigger than a bank swallow and whiter underneath than a rough-winged, young tree swallows have a sharply contrasting dark head and white throat similar to banks'. One glimpse of this white throat, and you can eliminate rough-winged swallow from consideration. In flight, tree swallows are broader-winged than either bank or rough-winged. (The wing shape of the flying tree swallow almost approaches the triangular shape of the starling's wings.)

In the West, there is the possibility of confusion with juvenile violet-green swallows, which also have brown backs and a dull brownish wash on the breast. At any time of year except fall, young violet-green swallows are all-white below. The other obvious field mark differentiating the young violet-green swallow from these other brown swallows is the amount of white on the face (violet-greens have a lot of white on the face) and on the rump — the violet-green is the only one that shows a white rump.

JUVENILE PURPLE MARTIN

Juvenile purple martins also show the dirty-chested, brown-washed look of the rough-winged swallow, but they usually have steel blue feathers scattered through the upperparts. A young martin is nearly twice the size of a rough-winged swallow, something that should become clear as you watch the martin flying or perched among other swallows. Martins have wide, triangular wings, and they soar more and flap less in flight than other swallows do.

The European starling can also be confused with a young purple martin, because of its triangular-winged silhouette. If you give them a good long look, though, you'll see that the starlings' more labored "buzz-bomb" flight sets them apart. Though they glide for short distances, starlings lack the graceful circling, soaring, and diving flight of martins and other swallows. The starling's tail is square-tipped (not notched like the martin's) and its bill is long and pointed (not tiny and dark like the martin's).

SWALLOW VOICES

Swallows are, as often as not, dark shapes whizzing over against a bright sky. Luckily, they are quite vocal birds, talking back and forth as they fly. I almost always hear them before I see them. This is especially true for the rough-winged swallow, which seems to sing its low, hoarse, buzzy *trip*

rough-winged
swallow
adult

bank
swallow
adult

tree swallow
juvenile

rough-
winged
swallow
juvenile, showing
bright rusty
wing bars

purple
martin
juvenile female
(not to scale)

trip trip trip song everywhere it goes. The bank swallow's call is less rolling and drier, but it also tends to give a series of low, scratchy calls as it flies. In contrast, the tree swallow's silvery, liquid twitter sounds to me like someone jingling paper clips in a glass tumbler. It is the signal song of spring on the hay meadows. Purple martins announce themselves with a deep, unique, chortling *chwerp chworp* call, changing pitch with each note.

A FINAL WORD

Swallows can also be identified by other factors, including voice, nest-site preference, and range, but plumage is often the best clue. Though the differences can be subtle, a good look at a mystery bird's underside plumage will reveal enough evidence for you to make a very solid guess at its identity. ✹

CHICKADEES

Black-capped or Carolina?
It's a chickadee mystery!

SEPARATING BLACK-CAPPED AND CAROLINA CHICKADEES in the field may be one of the most difficult and underappreciated problems bird watchers face. To understand why they are a problem, you need to know something about where each species occurs, what happens where they both occur, and what happens in invasion years.

Black-capped and Carolina chickadees are fairly closely related, which should be clear to anyone who looks at the pictures in the field guide. It is not so obvious that they are not each other's closest relatives. The latest evidence shows that black-cappeds are more closely related to mountain chickadees than they are to Carolinas, despite the fact that telling black-capped from mountain is not usually difficult.

Black-cappeds are the more northern species and Carolinas are southern. In all but a very few years, the only identification problem exists where the range of the two species overlap — a line running roughly through central New Jersey, southern Pennsylvania, and central Ohio, Indiana, and Illinois, and south in the Appalachian Mountains. Finding the precise area of overlap requires checking local sources, such as a state breeding bird atlas or regional bird lists and books.

The good news is that if you live north of the range of Carolina chickadees, every bird you see is a black-capped. There is virtually no evidence that Carolinas ever wander north, although I am not sure how you would tell for certain if one did. South of the range of black-capped, all the birds

Carolina chickadee
note clean-cut bib edge, gray wing coverts

black-capped chickadee
note ragged bib edge, whitish wing coverts

Carolina chickadee
whitish wing stripe is limited to tertials

black-capped chickadee
whitish wing stripe includes tertial edges and secondary coverts, in a hockey-stick shape

are Carolinas. Black-cappeds do move south in some years, at least a few hundred miles into the range of Carolinas. According to data from banders and other sources, it appears that these movements have happened once, and only once, per decade in this century. Otherwise there is no discernible pattern, and the movements do not seem related to the movements of other northern birds. Black-cappeds do what black-cappeds do.

The problem of chickadee identification can be divided into two sections: the range of overlap and invasion years. As you will see, they are very different problems, indeed.

Banding returns show that in invasion years, the black-cappeds that move into the range of Carolinas do not come from areas close to the overlap zone. They come from the Far North, and that makes it considerably easier. Black-capped chickadees from north of the Canada border are much larger than black-cappeds from farther south, so the other differences between the two species become more obvious. In the region where the two meet during the breeding season, they are most alike in size, plumage, and vocalizations. The reasons are too complicated to go into here. Just be glad that the invaders travel a long way.

Over the past 100 years, a number of characters have been used to separate the black-cappeds and Carolinas. Many of these clues have made it into field guides, and others have become locally established. Many of them are helpful, but only two clues are completely reliable, and one requires a bird in the hand. If you investigate the problem, you will eventually come across the following field marks. Remember, though, these field marks apply only in an invasion year. Why they cannot be used in the range of contact will be explained later.

SIZE

Black-cappeds are bigger than Carolinas. When birds from the North invade, the difference can sometimes be striking; black-cappeds often appear closer in size to a titmouse than a chickadee. The sizes of both species are somewhat variable, however, and for many birds it is not a useful character. In the hand, banders can almost always tell which is which by calculating the ratio between the length of the wing and the length of the tail. (The black-capped has a proportionally longer tail.) Forget trying this in the field.

BREAST

On average, and the word "average" is crucial here, the border between the black bib and the pale gray chest is more ragged on black-cappeds than on Carolinas. On freshly plumaged black-cappeds (and birds in the fall and early winter are in fresh plumage) the black feathers of the bib intrude into the gray chest in an irregular pattern. The border between the bib and the breast is almost always a neat straight line on Carolinas. This is not always an easy character to assess, and it should be used with caution.

FACE

It has been suggested that the size and brightness of the white face patch may be useful in separating the two. Although there may be a small difference in some birds, the amount of overlap is so great that this character is essentially useless. Once you have already identified a bird you can check to see if there appears to be a difference, but chances are you will come to no real conclusion. In fact, the size of the face patch may vary even between individual black-cappeds.

BEHAVIOR

It has been suggested that black-capped chickadees tend to feed closer to the ground than Carolinas. Some observers claim that if a flock of chickadees is responding to pishing, the black-capped will come in low while the Carolinas come in high. Could be. I have seen that happen, but I have also seen black-cappeds up high and Carolinas down low.

SONG

The song of the black-capped is typically described as a two-noted whistle, *fee-bee*, and the song of Carolina as a four-noted whistle, *fee-bee fee-bay*. On the breeding grounds those descriptions hold true most of the time, but they don't typically sing in winter. Both species have variable songs. Some Carolinas sing two-note songs. Some black-cappeds sing four-note songs. Some of both sing three-note songs. To make matters worse, they imitate each other. Hearing a typical black-capped two-note song coming from a flock of Carolinas should make you look more closely at the singer, but do not be a bit surprised if it turns out to be a Carolina.

So much for the characters that don't work, or work only part of the time. Now for the ones that do, more or less.

WHITE IN THE WINGS

In fresh plumage, sitting Carolinas and black-cappeds both have fresh pale feather edges on some of the wing feathers. (We will only be discussing sitting birds. Trying to separate the two in flight is insane.) The result of these pale edges is the appearance of a strong white line running down the wing from the shoulder almost to the rump (see the illustration on page 238). Some field guides have suggested that black-cappeds have this white line and Carolinas do not. As a matter of fact, they both do, and it can be as bright on a Carolina as on a black-capped.

On black-cappeds, the edges to the greater coverts are broad and very white. The result is a miniature hockey stick of white coming up the wing and jutting downward across the shoulder.

The real difference between the two birds shows in the greater coverts, which are the feathers that show on the shoulder of the folded wing. On black-cappeds, the edges of the greater coverts are broad and very white. As you can see in the illustration, these edges look a bit like a miniature hockey stick. The white line on the back that comes up to the shoulder is the handle, and the white on the shoulder, which curves slightly downward, is the blade of the stick. On fresh birds, before the edges wear, this pattern is usually quite striking. If you see it, you are almost certainly looking at a black-capped. On fresh Carolinas, the greater covert edges are often gray rather than white. They are not as broad, they do not contrast as sharply with the edge of the wing, and they are usually a little darker than the white stripe on the back.

CALL

The basic chickadee call, *dee-dee-dee*, is different from the song, in part because it is less a product of learning and imitation. Both Carolinas and black-cappeds regularly give the *dee-dee-dee* call, and the number of notes can vary from one or two to a dozen, depending on the bird and the circumstance. In Carolinas, the *dee-dee-dee* call is usually rapid and somewhat high-pitched. In black-cappeds it is noticeably slower and hoarser, and the difference between the two is easy to recognize with practice. Often, the first hint you get of a black-capped in a flock of Carolinas is hearing a slow, hoarse *dee-dee-dee* call obviously different from the other calls emanating from the flock. The one caution is that when birds are agitated, as they are when mobbing an owl or responding to pishing, the calls of both species tend to speed up and sound slightly higher-pitched. However, the difference should still be obvious in almost all cases.

Both species have a variety of other calls, including gargles and contact notes, but there is, as yet, no evidence that any of them can be used in the field to separate the two.

A word about numbers. In invasion years, black-cappeds move into the northern range of Carolina chickadees. It is not unusual to find black-cappeds in groups, almost always with Carolinas, and the Carolinas will outnumber the black-cappeds at least two to one. If you find one definite black-capped in the flock, you can be fairly certain there are others.

Now for the bad news: you cannot identify the chickadees in the range of overlap. If local research establishes that you are within twenty-five miles of the point where the two species come into contact, it is impossible to put an exact name on the birds you are seeing. Many, and perhaps most, of the birds in that zone are the result of hybridization.

Despite the fact that scientists have established that Carolina and black-capped chickadees are separate species, they do hybridize where they come into contact. It was generally thought that the hybridization involved only a few birds and was confined to a very, very, narrow band of the overlap area. The recent evidence indicates that the zone of hybridization is at least fifty miles wide. In that zone, most of the birds show genetic evidence of belonging to both species. It is a bird-watching mess. Even when a bird looks like a Carolina, sounds like a Carolina, and is twenty

miles south of where black-cappeds occur, it usually has a few black-capped genes in it — and the same is true in reverse.

Audio playback studies have only complicated the problem. A researcher in Virginia went to the contact zone and played the song of a Carolina chickadee. A bird flew in and responded lustily with a typical Carolina song. The researcher changed the tape and played the song of a black-capped chickadee. The bird immediately switched to a typical black-capped song! And it happened over and over. Measurements and other characters don't help, either. In fact, only genetic testing provides any evidence of hybrid birds' parentage, and most of the birds tested in the overlap area show that at least somewhere in the past, the two species mingled genetically. Genetic testing is not a useful field technique for most of us.

Even when a bird looks like a Carolina, sounds like a Carolina, and is 20 miles south of where black-cappeds occur, it usually has a few black-capped genes in it.

So if you are in the range of overlap, and a bird looks and sounds like a typical Carolina, what should you call it? There is no good answer. In many areas where the two species overlap, local bird watchers call all birds on one side of the line Carolinas, and all the birds on the other side of the line black-cappeds. They go with the "if it looks and sounds like one I am going to call it one" technique. Who cares if the bird's grandfather and grandmother dallied a bit?

This technique is fine as long as you recognize that you will be wrong some of the time, and that much of the time you may be dealing with hybrids. And sometimes, you just need to write some birds off. During ten years of breeding bird atlas work, much of it in areas where these two species of chickadee come into contact, I ran across birds I simply could not name. First they would look like a black-capped. Then they would

Invasion-Year Cautions

Black-cappeds invade about once a decade. The evidence comes from banders, mostly those working in their backyards. Banders are required to use measurements to separate the two species, so we can be fairly confident that they get most of the identifications right. There are always a few birds that resist classification, but there are enough banders to allow us to plot the invasions with confidence. We have learned a couple of crucial facts from these efforts.

1. Black-cappeds invade about once a decade; they do not occur south of their normal range every year. After an invasion year, when observers have gotten used to looking at black-cappeds, there are always reports in the next one or two years. In some areas, black-cappeds are reported every year. There is no evidence from the banding that these reports are accurate. Except in invasion years, banders capture no black-cappeds south of the range, a direct contradiction of the reports from people in the field. I know there are more watchers than banders, but until banders catch a few birds, I am skeptical of these "mini-invasions," especially because I was once a major contributor to those reports. Back in the days when I was first learning to tell the two species apart, I was considerably more confident than I should have been, and following invasion years I always "found" a few black-cappeds. I was wrong.

2. Black-capped invasions penetrate only a couple of hundred miles, at most, into the range of Carolinas. Banding results show the movement to be from the Northeast, with the birds moving southwest, through the mountains and the Piedmont. Even in years of large movements, it is rare to get black-cappeds along the coast or on the coastal plain south of the normal range.

3. In the years when black-cappeds move south, they start arriving in the range of Carolinas in late October and stay until the end of March.

look like a Carolina. Then the mate would show up and look like neither one, or a blend of both. I learned that there are some birds I simply cannot put a name on.

The more we learn about the two species, the more complicated the issues becomes and the more fascinating. There is a massive body of literature about Carolinas and black-cappeds, and it grows constantly. Those of you who become intrigued should find a good ornithological library and settle in for some pleasant, contradictory reading. For everyone else, take heart. Once you learn where and when to look, and learn the field marks that separate the two, you can put a name on most of the chickadees you see. Just be willing to occasionally throw up your hands and admit it when you can't tell if your bird is one species or the other. Apparently the chickadees have the same problem sometimes. *

SMALL WRENS

The tiny, brown, overlooked field problem

WRENS AND KINGLETS

THE MOST OVERLOOKED FIELD IDENTIFICATION CHALLENGE in North America may well be the LBWs, or little brown wrens. While experts are struggling with the subtle distinctions between gulls and shorebirds and *Empidonax* flycatchers, many bird watchers find themselves struggling to answer a simpler question: was that a house wren or a winter wren?

A look at the field guide range maps gives us a clue as to why so little has been written about the problem. Except along the West Coast, there is very little overlap between the two in the breeding season, and house wrens largely leave North America in the fall. In winter they are generally confined to the southern edge of the United States, but it is at that season that they overlap with winter wrens there. In addition, house wrens are found in small numbers north almost to the Canada border, usually on Christmas Bird Counts.

There is some overlap during migration, when either species can be seen almost anywhere, but winter wrens tend to show up late in most areas, after house wrens have left. Still, the combination of a few early winter wrens and a few lingering house wrens creates an opportunity for a bird watcher in almost any part of the continent to struggle with this identification at some point. A small wren can confuse us but a good look and a little attention to a few key field marks can make naming wrens almost as easy as naming male ducks.

THE SIMILARITIES

House and winter wrens have a lot in common. They are small, mostly brown, and have longish thin bills and stubby tails. They are quick and active and tend to stay low and hang out in brushy piles and thickets, especially in winter. They are both curious and will usually respond to *pishing* or squeaking, at least to take several quick peeks at the observer, if nothing more.

The physical similarities, and the tendency to provide a brief view and then dart back into cover, are what make the identification a challenge.

THE BASIC FIELD MARKS

Field guides tend to emphasize the size difference between house and winter wrens, but most observers find size a difficult field mark at best. For one thing, it is extremely rare to have an opportunity to directly compare the two birds in the field. House wrens are usually almost an inch longer than winter wrens, but unless you have a well-developed sense of the size of both, that isn't much help. At best, use the impression of size as an indicator. If it looks big, it may well be a house wren. If it looks small, it is probably a winter wren. But the first impression is only a starting point: be careful not to ignore the more useful characters.

TALE OF THE TAILS

Tail length is a good field mark, although it is also somewhat subjective. Both have relatively short tails. However, a short tail alone is not a field mark. The key is that the winter wren appears to have almost no tail at all, but merely the stub of one. The tail often looks like it has been bobbed or hasn't grown out yet. The tail of a house wren is short, but it still looks like a tail. The tail of a winter wren looks like an afterthought.

These diminutive dynamos would be much easier to identify if only they'd sit still long enough.

winter wren

house wren

It is not only the length of the tail that can be helpful, but what the bird does with it. House wrens may hold their tails up, down, or in-between, but if you watch the bird for a few seconds, it will almost always move a bit, and the tail rarely stays cocked up for long. The tail of the winter wren, in comparison, is almost always cocked straight up, a tiny flag held in an uncomfortable position (although it obviously isn't to the wren). The cocked-up, stubby tail is one of the best characters for winter wrens and can push your confidence level up to nearly 100 percent.

If you aren't completely satisfied with the tail as a field mark and want to run your confidence level up the final few notches, turn to plumage.

PLUMAGE

Yes, both birds are generally brown, but there are differences that with a little practice can become fairly obvious.

One of the best, quick-look field marks is overall color. All browns are not equal. Winter wrens are darker than house wrens. The color of the upperparts is typically a little darker brown than that of house wrens; the underparts are also darker and more uniform. The result is that in the field, a winter wren often appears as an almost uniformly dark brown bird. House wrens, in comparison, are paler overall, especially on the underparts, and they virtually always show a contrasting pale throat and upper breast. They are also a little grayer on the back, especially in the West. The differences may sound small when described, but they don't seem small when you are looking at the bird. When you have carefully studied a few house wrens and winter wrens through binoculars, you will begin to realize they don't look very much alike at all.

The most obvious plumage difference is the barring on the flanks. Because both house and winter wrens are often observed below eye level in the nonbreeding season, it sometimes takes a little effort to see the flanks, but when you do the difference between the two is useful.

Both birds have barred flanks, but on the winter wren the barring shows more contrast, almost black and white and striking. The barring on the flanks of the house wren is much more subdued, a brown on buffy that lacks the contrast of the winter wren's. The distinctiveness of the dis-similarity depends a lot on the observer's point of view and the light, so use a little caution. If the barring contrasts strongly, your bird is almost certainly a winter wren. If there appears to be no barring at all, and you have had a good look, it is most likely a house wren. In the case of anything in between, check out the other field marks before putting a name on the bird.

OTHER SUBTLE CLUES

Other, more subtle, characters can help and are worth looking for, at least for the fun of learning the differences. (If all this field stuff weren't fun we wouldn't be doing it, would we?)

The head patterns are sometimes helpful, especially since often the best view we get is head-on, as it peers at us from the thick part of a bush or from under a downed log. The house wren has a faint buffy eye line, which is easy to overlook on most birds. Unless you check carefully, many house wrens give the impression of having no eye line at all. The generally plain head and face contrast with the pale throat and (sometimes) cheeks, but even on the most contrasty birds, the overall impression is of plainness about the head.

Winter wrens tend to have an even, more uniform head color — brown everywhere. The face is usually the same color as the throat and the top of the head is darker, but overall, it looks like a medium- to dark-headed bird. The key is that many winter wrens show an obvious pale eye line that is almost white in the eastern part of the continent and buffier in the West. A word of caution: as discussed earlier, house wrens can show a faint buffy eye line, and the eye line on winter wrens is not always striking. Overall head color, especially the contrast between throat and face, is very helpful, but the distinction in the winter wren's eye line should be used judiciously.

SONGS

Song quickly distinguishes the two, of course, but song is not much use in winter on most birds. Wrens can be a little different from other birds, though. Both species occasionally sing even in December, at least on warm days. It isn't common by any stretch, but it does happen. If you are lucky enough, your bird will feel exuberant and break into song, but I don't sit around too long waiting for it to happen.

Almost every bird watcher in North America knows the song of the house wren — a bubbling, whistling jumble of notes that can be heard in many backyards in summer. The song of the winter wren is far less familiar to most of us because it nests in the North or in higher mountain woodlands. It's not much of a backyard bird unless you happen to have a great big brush pile there in winter. The winter wren's song is not like the song of the house wren. It is a series of relatively high-pitched trills, melodious and pleasing, with a slight change in pitch between trills. In the breeding season, the winter wren's song is notable because it seems to last forever, although in reality it is usually only a few seconds long — that's a long time compared to the songs of most birds, though. In winter, if the bird happens to sing, the song is often truncated, so length is a less useful indicator. For most observers, the song of the house wren is familiar and immediately recognizable, even when it comes at the wrong time of year. The song of winter wren, for most of us, is greeted with a puzzled "What was that?"

Wren in Doubt...

There are regional distinctions in both wrens that can complicate the identification problem somewhat. Fortunately, they are geographically restricted; we aren't going to delve into all the subtleties here, but stick with the short version.

1. **WINTER WRENS** in Alaska's Aleutian Islands (where there are no house wrens) are as big as any house wren in the continental U.S.

2. **SOME HOUSE WRENS** in the desert Southwest have distinctly brown throats, and were once considered a separate species: the brown-throated wren. They can be devilishly difficult to separate from other house wrens, but the characters that separate house and winter wrens still work. The brown-throated variant looks like a house wren without a contrasting throat.

Neither the Aleutian winter wren, nor the southwestern brown-throated house wren are serious problems for 99.9 percent of North American bird watchers, but it's good to know they're there, just in case.

Call notes are more useful than song during all but the summer months. The call of the winter wren is a distinctive double-noted *chimp-chimp*. (Imagine the call of the song sparrow, but doubled.) The notes are quick and loud, and once you learn them you will find a lot more winter wrens. They call throughout the winter, and most birders hear a lot more of them than they see. The call notes of house wrens are varied but are much buzzier. The commonest call is a single note that is more or less untranscribable. It sounds most like *bschzze*rt, but every person describes it a little differently. The key is the short, strong, buzzy quality, somewhat similar to the notes of common yellowthroats, and marsh and sedge wrens. They are very different from the call notes of winter wrens. If you see and hear the bird, the identification should be easy.

Both birds may give a chattering series of notes when scolding, which they sometimes do in response to pishing. The chattering of a winter wren tends to be dry and quick, and the chattering of a house wren more varied and buzzy. The observer should focus on the quality of the sound, not the pattern or the number of notes.

HABITAT

Habitat is not much of a help, but it can be useful in some cases. In winter, winter wrens can often be found along streams, rivers, and swamps where there is standing water. They especially like areas with downed trees that they can hide under and explore, and they can be found hopping around rocks on wooded hillsides.

House wrens in winter favor brush piles and thickets, often in drier areas — but winter wrens can be found in the same habitats. The difference is that on average, winter wrens tend to prefer slightly wetter places than house wrens. The habitat difference holds up well, but it is not diagnostic.

It's easier than you think to tell a winter wren from the look-alike house wren.

Although most of the differences discussed here may seem somewhat subjective (size, tail length, contrast), the amount of overlap in most of the characters is not great. I have yet to see a bird anywhere in North America that showed such sufficiently confusing field marks that I couldn't tell what it was. An individual winter wren might show a slightly more contrasting throat or an individual house wren a more striking eye line, but overall they still look like what they are. Look at the whole bird, and any confusion should disappear — just about the time the bird ducks back under a log. ❦

KINGLETS

Kinglet identification takes patience and practice.

THE SECRET TO IDENTIFYING KINGLETS IS PATIENCE. Our first glimpse of a kinglet is often brief and unsatisfactory. We spot a small greenish bird high in a tree and can see only the underside, or we see one pop out of low, thick brush and just as quickly disappear behind a leaf. Being bird watchers, we do the natural thing and try to put a name on the bird. Even if our quick peek has persuaded us to eliminate similar groups such as warblers and vireos, we are often left wondering which kinglet it was.

If we can resist the urge to name every bird the instant we see it, the problem will usually resolve itself fairly quickly. If the bird is a kinglet, it will be in constant motion, and our second or third look will allow us to see the field marks we need to confirm the identification.

Golden-crowned and ruby-crowned kinglets are among our most widely distributed species, and, depending on the season, it is possible to see either species almost anywhere on the continent.

RANGE

Golden-crowned kinglets breed from the boreal forests of central Canada and southern Alaska south through the mountain ranges in the West to the Mexico border, and in the East, through the Appalachians to Tennessee. They winter throughout the continental United States north to the Canadian maritimes in the East and to Alaska in the West. As migrants, they can show up anywhere and are somewhat irruptive. In some years, they move far south in large numbers. In other years they are much scarcer.

Ruby-crowned kinglets breed from the tree line south to the United States–Canada border except in the West, where they breed in the mountains almost to the Mexican border. Their winter range is more restricted than that of the golden-crowned, primarily in the southern third of the United States — except in the West, where they can be found north along the coast to southeastern Alaska, and in the intermountain region north to extreme southern Canada. They, too, can show up anywhere in migration.

Both kinglets are late and early migrants, arriving in the fall after the main passage of warblers and heading north again in front of the waves of migrants coming out of the tropics. A few birds linger late or arrive early, though, and you cannot eliminate warblers and vireos from contention solely on the timing of the migration.

THE GENERIC KINGLET

Kinglets are tiny, active, gray-green birds with short tails and plump bodies, which make them look like little round balls of energy. Both species have tiny, thin, pointed bills. Their size, rounded appearance, small bills, and constant motion are the characters that draw our attention at first glance and are usually enough to let us know that we are looking at a kinglet.

ELIMINATING THE LOOK-ALIKES

The first step in kinglet identification is to make certain we are not looking at one of the plainer warblers or vireos. Most can be eliminated quickly by size, shape, and behavior. No warbler or vireo is as short-tailed and dumpy-looking as a kinglet, and no warbler or vireo is as constantly on the move. Only two warblers, Tennessee and orange-crowned, are similar enough to cause confusion, but even they can be eliminated if you get more than a two-second look.

Warblers seem small, but compared with kinglets they are huge, lumbering creatures. Size here is just as distinctive as shape. Most warblers, including Tennessee and orange-crowned, are long-tailed compared to kinglets, and they have longer, heavier bills. The result is a bird that looks

golden-crowned kinglet
adult male

ruby-crowned kinglet
adult male with crest raised

ruby-crowned kinglet
adult male

orange-crowned warbler
adult

Hutton's vireo
adult

sort of slender and elongated. Spend a few minutes watching one of each, and the differences will be striking.

Both kinglets have two white wing bars, a plumage feature neither the orange-crowned nor Tennessee warbler shows. The orange-crowned can sometimes have a single faint wing bar, but basically it is a featureless bird. The reason observers sometimes confuse orange-crowned warblers with one of the kinglets is the warbler's orange crown. It is true that the warbler has an orange patch on the top of its head, but the patch is usually hidden, and many bird watchers go years without seeing it. Tennessee warblers can also show a single faint wing bar, but share no other plumage character with kinglets. Also, they always have a white or yellow line above the eye, which stands out on an otherwise unmarked head.

No warbler or vireo is as short-tailed and dumpy-looking as a kinglet, and no warbler or vireo is as constantly on the move.

Some of the plainer vireos might be confused with kinglets, at least for a second or two, but once again, shape and behavior are key. Vireos, like warblers, are large compared to kinglets, and they have even thicker, heavier bills than warblers. They also tend to be slow and deliberate, almost lethargic movers, unlike kinglets.

There is one vireo that can cause more than a momentary problem. Hutton's vireo is found along the West Coast and in southwestern mountains and is very similar in plumage to the ruby-crowned kinglet. It is smallish (for a vireo), gray-green, and has two white wing bars. The confusion arises because birders see the similarity in plumage and ignore the shape differences. If you do not have a lot of experience with the two in the field and want to confirm your identification, look at the wing, focusing on the wing bars.

The lower wing bar, which is large and quite clear, is white on both birds. Behind the wing bar on the ruby-crowned kinglet is a solid black patch of feathers, which contrasts sharply with the wing bar. Hutton's vireo lacks this black patch; the area behind the wing bar is a plain, non-contrasting greenish yellow.

You can also check the face pattern. Both have plainish heads with bold white eye-rings, but Hutton's vireo also has pale lores (the area between the eye and the bill), which the ruby-crowned kinglet lacks. The differences might seem hard to see, but both Hutton's vireo and ruby-crowned kinglet are easy to get close to, and their patterns are surprisingly easy to see in the field. The combination of characters discussed here makes all but poorly seen birds reasonably simple to identify.

SEPARATING THE KINGLETS

Telling a ruby-crowned kinglet from a golden-crowned is a snap if you get a good look at the head. Golden-crowneds have strikingly patterned heads that are very different from the plain heads of ruby-crowneds. Golden-crowneds have a thin black line through the eye, a bold white line above the eye, and a bold patch of yellow outlined in black on top of the head. Males sport an orange central patch, and the females' crowns are all-yellow. As noted, ruby-crowneds are plain gray-green on the head, and the bold white eye-ring is the only character that stands out; it tends to make ruby-crowneds look a little bug-eyed. Male ruby-crowned kinglets get their name from the red patch on the crown, but as in the case of the orange-crowned warbler, it is hidden most of the time and the bird erects its "ruby" crest only when it is agitated. Spotting the ruby on the crown of a ruby-crowned is rare.

If you can see the head, the identification should be easy, but because kinglets are so often up high in trees, it is not always possible to see the head pattern right away. They look just like little balls of feathers flitting through the upper branches. When you see a kinglet up high, especially if it is in an evergreen, the odds are that it is a golden-crowned. This is one of several behavioral differences that can steer you in the right direction, even before the field marks become obvious.

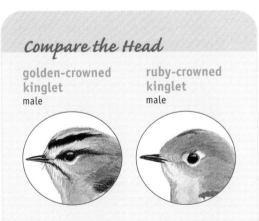

Compare the Head

golden-crowned kinglet
male

ruby-crowned kinglet
male

HABITAT IS A CLUE

In migration and winter, golden-crowned kinglets are birds of the evergreens — especially pine trees and other conifers. They are particularly fond of spruces where they are available. If the bird is flitting around the top of pine trees, and especially if it is hanging upside down from pine cones, it is almost certainly a golden-crowned. Although ruby-crowneds are sometimes found foraging in a pine tree, they do not hang upside down.

If, however, your kinglet is staying low, darting in and out of thickets or foraging on the outer branches of small deciduous trees, it is almost surely a ruby-crowned. Habitat preference is just that — a preference, not a law — but the distinction holds true most of the time and provides clues you should not ignore.

IS IT WITH FRIENDS?

Another useful clue is the number of kinglets there are. In migration and winter, golden-crowneds tend to be a social species, traveling in flocks of a half-dozen to twenty or so birds. If one kinglet in the top of the tree turns into half a dozen, the odds have gone way up that you are looking at golden-crowneds. On rare occasions you can find a ruby-crowned foraging with a flock of golden-crowneds, so it always pays to check as many of the birds as you can. Ruby-crowneds are far more solitary in migration and winter. They are frequently found in flocks of other birds, especially chickadees and late-migrating warblers, but it is rare to encounter a flock of ruby-crowneds. Even when there are several birds in the same area, they don't seem to flock together.

LISTEN CAREFULLY

The most useful field mark after the head is the voice. Maybe it is related to their constant motion and high energy, but kinglets are noisy creatures even in migration and winter, when they are one of the most persistently vocal birds. The good news is that the kinglets do not sound anything alike. Many bird watchers find small flocks of golden-crowned kinglets because they hear them first, which is not a surprise considering the birds' small size and their fondness for the upper branches.

Golden-crowneds are constant talkers, but they are not loud, and if you are not paying attention, you might miss them. The common call is a very high, thin *seet* note, usually given in threes: *see-see-see*. To the ear of most bird watchers, the call is very like that of brown creeper, but creepers rarely call in winter and even more rarely from the tops of pines. A flock of foraging golden-crowneds is distinctive because the soft *seet* notes seem to be constant, dripping down from the trees like mist.

The most useful field mark after the head is the voice.

Ruby-crowned kinglets are not quite as persistently vocal as golden-crowneds in migration and winter. They do call regularly, however, especially when they are agitated, such as when they are responding to pishing. The call is a dry *chit*, often doubled as *chit-chit*. When the bird gets agitated, it often runs a long series of *chit* notes together in a sort of machine gun staccato. For so small a bird, the call is surprisingly loud, and once learned it is distinctive and easy to recognize in the field.

Ruby-crowneds are among the most curious and responsive birds. It is usually easy to draw them close with a little pishing or squeaking, and that is when they are easiest to identify. They come to within a few feet of you, calling almost constantly, and when they call they rapidly flick their wings — another character that eliminates look-alikes such as warblers and vireos.

With a little practice, kinglets are easy, as long as you remember that patience is the key, and fight the urge to put a name on the bird until you get a good look at it. ✒

BLUEBIRDS

North America's three beloved blue thrushes

WITH ALL DEFERENCE TO PURPLE MARTIN FANCIERS, hawk watchers, and the people who feed geese at the local park, no birds in North America are as loved as bluebirds. The obvious reason is that they are among the most visually striking birds (at least the males are), carrying a richness of blue that freezes the observer even after the 100th or 1,000th time they've seen one. There are other reasons, too. Bluebirds evoke a sense of our rural past, of summer fields and farms and open spaces, and a sense of nostalgia for a place and time many of us have experienced only in cultural memory. Even beyond that, we have a special connection with bluebirds. When eastern bluebird numbers fell we rushed to help, erecting boxes for them and then creating trails dedicated to their preservation, all of which amounted to one of the grandest efforts to save a species in all human history, and we did it all as volunteers and amateurs. That it has worked so wonderfully well has strengthened the bond we feel with these birds. Even people who don't know anything about birds know about bluebirds.

One of the reasons people don't think much about bluebird identification is range. Eastern and western bluebirds barely overlap — only in winter in western Texas and year-round in extreme southern Arizona. The amount of overlap is a little greater in winter in the southern Great Plains, when both species may wander a bit, but in general you can figure out which one you are looking at by knowing where you are.

Mountain and western bluebirds do overlap throughout much of the West. In summer, mountain bluebirds tend to live up to their name, favoring higher elevations, whereas western bluebirds are typically lowland birds. There are a few areas where the two are found in proximity, but elevation is a key field mark. In winter, however, mountain bluebirds move into the lowlands, and then it is not unusual to find them together.

Eastern and mountain bluebirds overlap to a greater extent. They both breed in southern Manitoba and Saskatchewan, where they have been recorded using the same bluebird trail. In winter, mountain bluebirds move into southern Arizona, where they encounter both eastern and western bluebirds. In addition, mountain bluebirds are highly migratory and have been recorded throughout the East in winter, although occurrences are rare. There may be more of these wanderers than we think because females are probably overlooked.

Among the three species the only potential confusion exists between eastern and western bluebirds. Male mountain bluebirds are so striking, and so unlike the other two, that it is almost impossible to confuse them. They are an overall blue unmatched by any other bird in North America, and recognition is nearly instantaneous.

Male eastern and western bluebirds are not hard to tell apart, assuming you get a decent look. Both are deep blue on the head and upperparts, with rusty chests and pale bellies and vents. On eastern bluebirds, the rust goes all the way to the chin, whereas on westerns the chin and throat are the same dark blue as the back. In addition, the belly and vent of eastern bluebirds is white; the same area on westerns is darker and grayish.

The southeastern Arizona race of eastern bluebird has a pattern identical to that of eastern birds, but the blue is paler and there is often some rusty streaking on the cheek. The underparts are a paler rust also, but the color extends onto the chin as it does in eastern birds, readily separating them from male western bluebirds.

It is the females that pose a greater possibility for confusion — again the most similar birds are easterns and westerns. There are clear differences that separate them, but it takes a close look, and any bird only casu-

western
bluebird
male

western
bluebird
female

eastern
bluebird
male

eastern
bluebird
female

mountain
bluebird
male

mountain
bluebird
female

ally and quickly observed may be misidentified. Part of the problem is that watchers tend to focus on the males and give the females short shrift, which is more true for bluebirds than for many species.

Both female eastern and western bluebirds are duller versions of the males. Female easterns are grayish blue on the head, nape, and back, with slightly brighter blue, contrasting wings. The underparts are patterned like the male, but the rusty color is noticeably paler.

Female westerns are also patterned like males, but duller. The blue upperparts are washed with gray-brown, as is the throat. The wings contrast less with the upperparts than they do on eastern females, but the difference can be hard to quantify unless the birds are seen in good light. The most striking difference between eastern and western females is the gray-brown throat of westerns. Westerns also have dark grayish flanks that contrast with the paler vent. The vent of female easterns is also pale and contrasts with the flanks, but the flank color is pale rust rather than gray. Some female mountain bluebirds (and even some males) can show a surprising amount of buffy or rufous coloring on the breast and throat, similar to western bluebirds. Even with these plumage aberrations, mountain bluebirds still appear slimmer overall with a slender, all-black bill.

It is the females that pose the possibility of confusion. Part of the problem is that watchers tend to focus on the males and give the females short shrift.

Gray female mountain bluebirds differ from both female eastern and western bluebirds by having no rust on the underparts. They are extensively gray below, although the vent is paler. Above, they are a paler grayish blue with paler blue wings than either of the other two species. In most field situations, female mountain bluebirds look almost uniformly colored, with virtually no contrast anywhere, although the throat is usually paler than the rest of the underparts.

There are two minor structural differences that help separate all mountain bluebirds from easterns and westerns. Mountain bluebirds have the longest wingspan of our three bluebirds and are slightly longer-bodied, too. This gives them a tall-and-slender appearance. These differences are not great, but with experience they become surprisingly obvious to many observers.

As you would expect with birds so closely related, habits, songs, and behavior are not especially helpful in separating the three. The differences between the species are small, and there is enough overlap in any single character to make reliance on such factors unwise. Calls, however, can be a help. The calls of western and mountain bluebirds are very similar, and even with practice it is difficult for most observers to tell them apart. Both most commonly give a mellow *tew* note, and while to some ears the call of the mountain bluebird is slightly less mellow and a little weaker, it takes a very practiced ear to make a good guess at which species is calling. The call of eastern bluebirds is a two-noted *chur-lee*, the general quality of which is the same as the calls of the other two, but the two notes make it distinctive. Even so, call alone is not enough to identify an out-of-range bird. At best it should be treated as an "I'd better look at this more closely" field mark.

Now you are ready to slap a name tag on any bluebird that graces a fencepost or telephone line in front of you. When you are through being transfixed by the elegance of the males, however, pay some attention to the females. They are elegant in their own way, and you may find that you have been overlooking the unexpected. 🖋

BROWN THRUSHES

Earth-toned singers of ethereal songs

SEPARATING THE BROWN THRUSHES FROM ONE ANOTHER is not as difficult as many other bird identification challenges. It lacks the seasonal changes in plumage of the confusing fall warblers (pages 292, 296, and 302). Nor does it have the sex-and-size confusion of "It could be a big female sharpie, or a small male Cooper's" (page 88). And it certainly comes nowhere close to long-billed versus short-billed dowitcher. Yet the presence of an unfamiliar brown thrush can produce an unsettling wave of anxiety as we struggle to remember the important field marks of these gifted singers. It's a lack of practice, due to the fact that most of us have only one or two of them with us for the breeding season, that keeps us unfamiliar with the identities of the brown thrushes. The rest of our experience comes from seeing them in migration or perhaps on their breeding range in the high mountains and in the forests of the Far North.

There are five brown, spotted thrushes on the accompanying illustration, but there are six such thrush species in North America. We need to set aside one species the identification and field marks of which are still being worked out: the Bicknell's thrush. The Bicknell's was officially made a separate species only in 1995, though speculation as to

Swainson's
thrush
adult

hermit
thrush
adult

gray-
cheeked
thrush
adult

veery
adult

wood
thrush
adult

how closely related Bicknell's is to the visually similar gray-cheeked thrush had been going on since the 1880s. Field guides published since the "birthday" of the Bicknell's thrush in 1995 use phrases like "averages shorter wings" and "tends to have more yellow on the lower mandible." At the moment the only way to identify a Bicknell's thrush in North America with any certainty is to go to its limited breeding range — mountaintop forests in New England and easternmost Canada — during the breeding season and look for a gray-cheeked thrush look-alike.

The brown spotted thrushes are notable as world-class singers. Their flutelike songs are produced by a complex system of syringeal muscles that are able to create multiple notes simultaneously. These rich vocalizations, which have inspired naturalists and poets for centuries, have evolved to be heard in the thick vegetation of the woodland habitats where these thrushes breed.

Some thrush songs, such as the *ee-oo-layyy* of the wood thrush or the downward spiraling melody of the veery, are familiar and fairly easily identifiable. But many of our thrush encounters happen during migration when these songsters do not normally sing. We then must rely on our eyes to help us identify the brown thrushes.

There are three visual clues to remember about thrush identification: back color, breast spots, and eye-rings. These field marks are not always easy to see, because the thrushes' preferred habitat is deep woodland, where light can be limited even on a bright, sunny day. Add to this that the thrushes are fairly shy birds and are also swift fliers, offering just a quick glimpse as they slip across an opening in the woods or move from one thicket to the next.

BACK COLOR

Our five thrushes can be most simply divided into two groups: those with rusty backs (wood thrush, veery, and some hermit thrushes in the East) and those with drab, olive-gray backs (Swainson's and gray-cheeked thrush). When you see a mystery thrush, the first question to ask yourself is: what color is the bird's back? If your bird has an obviously rusty back, your choices are narrowed to wood thrush and veery. Let's begin with these two birds.

WOOD THRUSH

The wood thrush, the largest of the five species, has the boldest markings of all. A bright rusty back from head to tail is set off by a white breast with large black spots from throat to belly. Wood thrushes nest all across the eastern half of the United States, and their range includes just a bit of southeastern Canada. True to their name, wood thrushes are birds of older deciduous woods and can be found nesting in suburban parks and backyards with large trees. Among these five thrush species, the wood thrush stands out for its snow-white breast spangled with round black spots and its bright white eye-ring. Wood thrushes stand or perch in an upright posture. In fact, with this posture and the bold markings, the wood thrush might, at a glance, be mistaken for a short-tailed brown thrasher.

VEERY

The veery shares the wood thrush's rusty back but little else. Its breast is lightly spotted with warm brown; it has the faintest and most indistinct spots of all the brown thrushes. The veery has almost no eye-ring at all; it has a plain face. Whereas the wood thrush is a bird of bold markings and contrasting colors, the veery is colored by a muted wash of reddish brown, gray, and dull white. The veery's back is evenly rusty from head to tail. Veeries can be seen across the eastern two-thirds of North America in migration. Their breeding range is more northerly than the wood thrush's, covering the southern third of Canada, the northern tier of the United States, and all of New England. Farther south, veeries breed at higher elevations in the Appalachians and Rocky Mountains.

Back to your mystery bird. Let's say it gave you no impression of a rusty back. What now?

HERMIT THRUSH

One of our remaining candidates — the hermit thrush — has a grayish back and a rusty-brown tail; it is the only brown thrush with this color difference. The hermit thrush is an interesting anomaly among the five thrushes in a variety of ways. Hermit thrushes have a huge breeding range that comprises most of Canada, all of New England and the high-elevation East, and nearly all of the wooded, mountainous West. The hermit is also the only spotted thrush likely to be seen in the United States in winter. Its rufous tail is notable not only for its color, but for the bird's habit of flicking it upward and slowly lowering it back down.

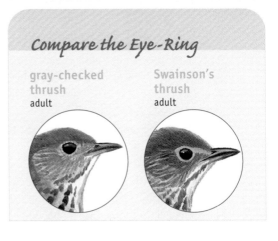

Compare the Eye-Ring

gray-checked thrush
adult

Swainson's thrush
adult

The hermit thrush is generally considered more vocal than other thrushes, and more curious. In fall and winter, the hermit thrush can be located by its soft *chup* note. Hermits will often respond to pishing by scolding and coming in for a closer look. Close up, you can see the hermit thrush's noticeable and complete eye-ring. On its upper breast, the hermit thrush has dark spots that fade out toward the belly; they are about halfway between those of a veery and wood thrush in intensity. There is quite a bit of regional variation in the coloration of hermit thrushes; western birds are more grayish on the back and eastern birds are more brownish. The best clues for the hermit thrush are a rusty tail contrasting with a brownish olive back and a complete buffy-white eye-ring. See it flick that rusty tail upward and you've clinched your hermit thrush ID.

A bird that is not rusty on the back or tail, but looks grayish overall, leaves you with two possibilities: gray-cheeked thrush and Swainson's thrush. Let's stick to the eye-ring as a field mark for a moment. We humans instinctively look to the eyes of each other and our fellow creatures for signs of life, emotion, and communication. It's no different with the mystery thrushes. If you can remember this handy field identification tip, you'll be the Lord of the Eye-Rings.

SWAINSON'S THRUSH

The Swainson's thrush was formerly known as the olive-backed thrush. Olive is a good way to describe the Swainson's back color, but the gray-cheeked thrush's back color is very similar, so this is not a very helpful field mark. The key to telling these two *Catharus* thrushes apart is the always-present buff-colored eye-ring and spectacles on the Swainson's — a field mark utterly absent in the gray-cheeked thrush.

Swainson's thrushes come in two typical color forms, a russet-backed form found along the Pacific coast (which is vaguely similar to a veery), and an olive-backed form found throughout the rest of the species' range. Both forms and all ages of Swainson's thrush always show the eye-ring and spectacles.

The breeding range of the Swainson's thrush is quite similar to that of the hermit thrush. But the Swainson's is perhaps most commonly seen by bird watchers during migration in late spring and early fall, when they are en route from or to their wintering grounds in Mexico or South America. During migration, Swainson's thrushes give a distinctive frog-like flight call that some birders liken to a spring peeper's *hweep!*

Back to that mystery thrush for the last time. If you've seen the bird well enough to note that its back and tail are olive-colored, and it does not have an obvious eye-ring or spectacles, you've narrowed the field to our one remaining thrush species.

GRAY-CHEEKED THRUSH

Would that it were simply a matter of saying, "If it has gray cheeks, it's a gray-cheeked thrush!" Alas, that doesn't really work. The cheeks are hard to get a good look at on a bird skulking in deep cover, and several of these thrushes could be described as having gray cheeks. It becomes a process of elimination. Other than a heavily spotted upper breast, the gray-cheeked thrush lacks distinctive field marks. It has no bright rust on the back or tail, no eye-ring, no noticeable facial markings, no habit of flicking its tail. The spotting on the upper breast is more concentrated than that of the veery, hermit, or Swainson's thrush, but it is nowhere near as striking as the wood thrush's bold spotting.

When you have a plain-faced, olive-gray bird with some upper breast spots, gray-cheeked is your thrush. You may notice that it's smaller and more delicate than other thrushes as well. The wood thrush is a giant by comparison.

Gray-cheeked thrushes breed exclusively in the Far North; Alaska is the only state in the United States that can claim them as breeders. Because their breeding range comprises the upper reaches of Canada and Alaska, and their winter range is in South America, most field encounters with gray-cheeked thrushes occur during migration. Gray-cheeked thrushes migrate in spring and fall across the eastern half of North America.

THE RUSH OF THRUSHES

The pleasure of seeing and identifying North America's brown, spotted thrushes is almost as wonderful as hearing their ethereal songs. The steps outlined here for thrush identification are only suggestions, tools that might come in handy in the field. There will undoubtedly be mystery thrushes that get away from you unidentified, but it's the mystery that makes watching birds so much fun. ➴

WAXWINGS

The brown wanderers: cedar versus Bohemian

MOST BIRDERS HAVE LITTLE DIFFICULTY RECOGNIZING a waxwing. They are well represented on postcards, nature calendars, and Christmas cards, where their habit of feeding on holly berries is perfect for the season.

Waxwings are sleek and attractive birds, with showy cardinal-like crests, small black masks, dark throats, and bright yellow tail tips. They are extremely gregarious, almost always occurring in small flocks and sometimes banding together by the hundreds. When one of these large flocks descends upon a fruiting crabapple, holly, or hackberry, the birds can provide hours of entertainment as they strip the tree of its fruit. The lisping, high-pitched calls of waxwings are unique and easy to recognize.

Across much of the country, waxwing identification is not an issue. The Bohemian waxwing is a bird of northern climes; the cedar waxwing may be found throughout the United States, most of Canada, and well into Mexico and Central America. Bohemians breed exclusively in northern Canada and Alaska and winter throughout the Rocky Mountain states in the West at least as far south as northern New Mexico and northern Arizona. Across the Great Plains, Bohemians regularly stray south to northern Colorado and Nebraska, but in the East they can be expected no farther south than Maine, New Hampshire, Vermont, western Massachusetts, and upstate New York. It is a rare bird that appears as far south as Pennsylvania or Long Island, and it is strictly accidental farther south than that.

Birders in the Southeast, Texas, southern Arizona, and southern California can call every waxwing they see a cedar and be right 100 percent of the time.

cedar waxwing
adult

Bohemian waxwing
adult

> *They look essentially the same year-round, whether male or female, adult or immature, fresh or worn.*

Both species of waxwings, like finches and certain owls and hawks, are irruptive, showing a large variation in their numbers in any given area from year to year. You may have hundreds of waxwings in your yard one winter and not see a single one for three years thereafter. Don't be alarmed: this is the nature of waxwings — they wander widely in search of suitable food sources and are very responsive to changes in local food availability.

So how do we go about identifying a waxwing when we see it? Both species are similar in overall pattern and color, and it requires a good look to confirm the relatively obscure field marks. Fortunately, waxwings have only one plumage. They look essentially the same year-round, whether male or female, adult or immature, fresh or worn. This should come as a refreshing change to anyone who has been struggling with warblers, shorebirds, hawks, terns, or (worst of all) gulls. Once waxwing identification is learned, it can be applied any time or place without exception.

Well, almost without exception. For a brief period in midsummer (July–August) freshly hatched waxwings hold their juvenal plumage. These birds look somewhat like adults but are broadly streaked below and mostly lack the dark mask and throat shown by adults. Even identifying these birds as waxwings may be difficult, so concentrate on the crest and yellow tail tip. (No other bird in North America has a yellow tail tip.) Once you realize it is a waxwing, you can probably guess its species based simply on breeding range. If you are in an area where either species is possible, focus on the size, color, and undertail covert characteristics discussed here. These field marks are shared by juveniles as well as adults.

Waxwing identification uses several specific field marks, each of which requires a different point of view.

UNDERTAIL COVERTS

The undertail coverts are the feathers that grow right below the base of the tail. This is the group of feathers that covers the bird's vent. (This area is also known as the crissum; hence the crissal thrasher, which has distinctively bright chestnut undertail coverts.) The undertail coverts of waxwings, which can frequently be seen as they feed on berries overhead, are definitive field marks. The Bohemian waxwing has rich chestnut undertail coverts, and those of cedar waxwings are whitish or yellowish.

WING PATTERN

Waxwings are named for the distinctive colorful waxy tips on the secondary feathers of their wings. On both species these tips are red, and if you ever get a chance to examine a waxwing in the hand, you'll find these tips to have a very interesting consistency, almost like drops of red lacquer.

When the undertail coverts cannot be seen, examining the wing pattern is the best approach. The cedar waxwing has reddish waxy tips on the secondary feathers, so that the rear part of the folded wing is tipped with red. The wings of Bohemian waxwings are much more colorful. They, too, have red tips on the secondaries, but they also have prominent patches of yellow and white elsewhere on the wing. On the Bohemian, the tips of the primaries (the long feathers that form the wingtips that are visible at rest) are marked with brilliant yellow, like the tail tip. Whether or not you fully understand where the yellow patch in the wing is, it is safe to say that if it is there, your bird is a Bohemian waxwing. On the cedar, the wingtips are dullish black and much less showy.

Bohemian waxwings also have two brilliant white patches in the wing. One occurs at the tips of the primary coverts and appears as a white wing patch or "pocket handkerchief." A second showy patch of white occurs just above the waxy red tips on the secondary feathers.

One note of caution is that the cedar waxwing can sometimes show an edge of white along the inner edge of the tertial feathers of the wing. This can be mistaken for the white in the wing of a Bohemian waxwing by unwary observers, but by noting the placement of the white, and by making sure to watch for the yellow in the wing as well, confusion can easily be avoided.

SIZE

The Bohemian waxwing is a significantly larger bird than the cedar waxwing, and while experienced birders may notice this size difference on lone birds, the rest of us will see it only in direct comparison. Fortunately, it is not unusual to find mixed flocks of waxwings where both species occur. (Sometimes they mix with other fruit eaters as well, such as robins and starlings.) When seen side by side with the cedar, the larger size of the Bohemian waxwing is obvious to anyone. The Bohemian about matches European starlings in size; the cedar waxwing is more the size of a bluebird.

OVERALL COLOR

Overall color of the waxwing in question is another useful characteristic, but one that is best used when the observer is experienced with one or the other species. In general, the cedar waxwing is brown with a yellow belly, and the Bohemian is largely gray. More specifically, cedar waxwings have a rich brown head, nape, and breast and a back that is slightly duller. The wings are darker brown and mixed with gray tones; the belly is usually pale yellow below the chest. Bohemian waxwings have a similar brown color to the head, but that color contrasts with an entirely gray body. The breast, belly, back, and wings are all medium gray and lack the contrasting yellow belly or darker wings shown by cedars. If you know the cedar waxwing well, the ghostly gray of the Bohemian waxwing will be immediately obvious even in a distant view.

CALL

For observers who get a special thrill out of birding by ear, these two waxwing species can be separated by call. Both give high-pitched, whispery calls that are not always easy to hear and will probably be inaudible to some people. In the Bohemian, though, those calls are lower, longer, and buzzier in quality than in the cedars. To those familiar with one species, the different quality of the other will be obvious.

THROAT

One final characteristic is of little use in the field, but is worth noting to fully appreciate the differences between these two species. The chin patch on Bohemian waxwings is sharp and well defined, whereas on cedar waxwings it bleeds smoothly into the chest at its lower margin.

DON'T BE FOOLED

Many birders are occasionally tempted to assume that any bird not showing the expected field marks must be a different species. Most of us have made this mistake. Imagine you are watching a flock of cedar waxwings in your yard and enjoying their antics as they pillage the berries from a small holly next door. You are especially enjoying the yellow tail tips that the birds alternately fan and fold as they feed, when suddenly you notice that one bird has an orange tail tip. You are surprised and confused, but you check again. Yes, that tail tip is definitely orange, and all the other ones are yellow. You must have a different species of waxwing here. Checking your book, you note that the Bohemian is the only other possible waxwing. Excited, you call your fellow birders.

Both cedar and Bohemian waxwings can occasionally have orange or even reddish tail tips.

Both cedar and Bohemian waxwings can occasionally have orange or even reddish tail tips. It is not a mark shown by different species, ages, or sexes of birds. In waxwings, production of the yellow color in the tail tip is highly dependent on diet, and studies have shown that the waxwings with diets that influence the production of pigments occasionally have off-color tail tips. It is not particularly uncommon or unusual and can often be seen in a small percentage of the birds in any large group of waxwings.

BE SURE

Overall, waxwing identification is not particularly difficult; it simply requires focusing on the proper field marks. The chestnut undertail coverts and yellow wing stripe of the Bohemian, when seen, are 100 percent diagnostic, and other characteristics, such as size, color, and call, can be useful points for confirmation. However, it is important to be certain. Across most of the United States, the Bohemian is a red-letter bird, and reports would surely be mentioned on the rare bird alert and might draw a crowd of birders. You should make certain that you have checked all the field marks before claiming to have seen a Bohemian waxwing, but, when you are certain, you can take great joy in the discovery of this unusual nomad from the boreal forests.

BASICS OF WARBLER ID

Identifying warblers from head to tail

FOR THE VAST MAJORITY OF BIRD WATCHERS, SPRING means warblers. Or perhaps it is the other way around: warblers mean spring! It doesn't really matter which comes first, because the two are inextricably linked in the minds of watchers from Boston to Santa Barbara, from Pt. Pelee to the upper Texas coast. No matter when spring comes to your part of the world, warblers will be coming with it.

Spring warbler watching means calling up information that has been stored, unused in the memory banks, for nearly a year. This chapter is designed as an exercise to stretch and warm up the mental muscles in preparation for the coming waves. When you have the right mind-set, you will be amazed by how quickly you start to remember.

One reason spring warbler watching appeals to so many people is that the birds are so striking. Most of them are easy to identify — although not always easy to see! There is little chance of confusion when you see a male, hooded warbler, an American redstart, a red-faced warbler, or a black-throated gray. Open up any field guide and the picture jumps off the page.

Females are often as easy; in many cases they are simply slightly duller versions of the males. A bird watcher who sees a spring warbler and draws a blank usually does so because he or she has not seen the bird before, or because so many birds have been seen in such a short period of time that he or she is suffering from memory lock. After all, more than fifty war-

WARBLERS

blers regularly occur in North America in the spring, and in some parts of the country it is possible to see more than twenty species on a good day. Spring warblers can sometimes be almost too much of a good thing.

For those anticipating their first spring with warblers, or who have not been able to spend as much time with these birds as they would like, we are going to start with some basic warbler watching and identification tips that should make it easier to put a name on any bird.

BASIC WARBLER WATCHING — A CHECKLIST

First, decide if what you are looking at is a warbler. This is not hard most of the time. The only real area of confusion involves the vireos, which tend to be plain greenish birds. In general, vireos are less colorful, slower-moving, and have thicker bills than warblers. When you do find a bird that you don't recognize immediately, work your way quickly through a mental checklist. Do this before you look at the book! The bird may fly away before you get another look, but the book will always be there.

Start your checklist with an overall impression of color and pattern. Many warblers are so striking that you may be tempted to stop there. Don't! An all-yellow bird can be any of a half-dozen warblers, and if all you note is its color, you will end up frustrated. Once you have the general color and pattern, start on the specifics.

START AT THE HEAD AND WORK BACK. Check the head and face pattern for cap, eye lines, and color. Face pattern is often critical in identifying similar species.

> CHECK FOR WING BARS. Warblers break down into two broad groups, those with wing bars and those without. Noting whether the bird has wing bars will cut in half the number of birds under consideration.
>
> CHECK THE UNDERPARTS. Are there streaks or a breast-band? If the bird has yellow below, does it go all the way to the tail, or is it just on the chest? If you can see the back, check for streaks or other patterns. It is difficult to see the backs of warblers because they spend so much time near the treetops. Fortunately, the back pattern is rarely a key character.
>
> CHECK THE TAIL. Many bird watchers forget to check the tails of warblers. Some warbler species can be easily recognized by their bright yellow or white tail spots. A few species flash white outer tail feath-

ers. The palm warbler wags its tail as it forages, often on the ground.
CHECK THE UNDERTAIL COVERTS, which are the feathers that cover
the underside of the tail; usually, they extend about halfway out the
length of the tail. Checking undertail coverts may seem a bit over-
technical to many people, but it is often a snap because a lot of warblers are seen only from below.

It takes only a few seconds to run through this checklist, and it can be
the difference between identifying a bird and letting it get away. After
using it a couple of times, it becomes second nature, and you can identify
nearly every warbler you see.

Many people find it helpful to use a reference species, one bird with
which they are familiar, as a starting point when they see a new warbler.
Then they can say, "Well, it looks like a ___, but it has more yellow below."

A reference bird can be a valuable tool. It can be any species you
already know well. One good choice might be yellow-rumped warbler.
Yellow-rumped has the advantage of being widespread and fairly common, and in many parts of the continent it can be seen in winter as well
as in fall and spring. In addition, yellow-rumpeds are very responsive to
pishing, so it is easy to get great looks at them.

The yellow-rumped warbler comes in two flavors. In the East, these
birds are the "myrtle" yellow-rumped warblers of the older field guides.
In the West, they are "Audubon's" yellow-rumped warblers. At present,
they are considered one species, but the names "myrtle" and "Audubon's"
are still useful because it is possible to tell the two forms apart visually.

USING THE BREEDING-PLUMAGED MALE "myrtle" yellow-rumped warbler as our reference bird, let's run down the checklist. The exercise will be
almost the same for Audubon's warbler, and the differences will be noted.

GENERAL APPEARANCE:
Dark above; dark and light
below. Maybe a little larger than
a typical warbler.
HEAD: Mostly dark, blacker below the eye, a thin
white line above the eye. Bright white throat.
(Audubon's is similar but the face is plainer, with
just a broken white eye-ring, and the throat is
bright yellow.)

UPPERPARTS: Dark blue-gray. Two broad white wing bars.

UNDERPARTS: Mostly white but with a band of heavy streaks across the breast and down the sides. Looks like an inverted U. Bright patch of yellow on the sides of the breast.

TAIL: Bright yellow rump. Underside of the tail has two big white spots.

After this simple little run-through, which takes only a few seconds, you are going to open the field guide and settle almost immediately on yellow-rumped warbler. If you had stopped at dark above, mostly pale below, with wing bars, you would have had to choose from half a dozen birds.

If the bird happened to be a female, you would have gone through the same process. Many of the field marks would have been the same. Consider the myrtle yellow-rumped warbler in relation to the Audubon's yellow-rumped warbler. Although many of their field marks are similar, Audubon's has a yellow throat and large, square, white wing patches formed by fringes on its secondary coverts.

Now consider both these birds in relation to the magnolia warbler. All three have blue-and-black heads and yellow rumps. The most obvious differences in the magnolia are the extensive yellow on the underparts and the bold black "necklace" streaks. In any plumage, the magnolia's bold white tail panels, which make its tail appear to be divided in half, are easy to see and are diagnostic. Without the checklist, you could spend quite a while staring at your field guide trying to put a name on your dark-headed yellow-rumped mystery bird and still end up with nothing but a "warbler sp." note in your field log. It takes the whole package to identify the bird. ❧

CONFUSING SPRING WARBLERS

Separating the look-alikes is not that hard.

FEW GROUPS OF BIRDS HAVE LURED MORE PEOPLE INTO becoming bird watchers than the North American warblers. In springtime these birds are at their finest — with their bright, flashy breeding plumage and stunningly beautiful songs. Imagine how wonderful they would be if they would just sit still and let us admire them! Instead, they are often so active that it's hard to get a good look at them, or they are so skulky and secretive that trying to find them tries our patience.

Every birder has heard about confusing fall warblers (see pages 292, 296, and 302). Although many spring warblers are fairly easy to identify, some are not. In this chapter we'll give you a brief roadmap for sorting out these confusing spring warblers.

MAGNOLIA AND YELLOW-RUMPED "MYRTLE" WARBLERS

If you study the pictures in a field guide, you will see that magnolia and "myrtle" yellow-rumped warblers are not hard to separate. When all you have is a quick look at a bird high in the trees, however, magnolias and "myrtles" can cause confusion. Both have yellow rumps (isn't it amazing how many warblers we first see flying away from us?), white eye lines, white wing bars on dark wings, and dark face patches. It is not easy to identify one of these birds if you can't see, or don't remember, the right field marks.

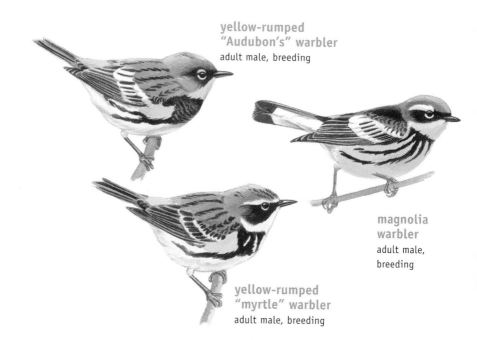

yellow-rumped
"Audubon's" warbler
adult male, breeding

magnolia
warbler
adult male,
breeding

yellow-rumped
"myrtle" warbler
adult male, breeding

The most basic difference between the two is that magnolias are solid yellow below with strong black streaks on the chest and belly. Yellow-rumpeds are basically white below, with just a little yellow at the sides of the breast. They normally have solid black patches on the breast and a thin black line across the breast. The pattern of black on the underparts forms a distinctive, inverted U shape.

Both magnolias and yellow-rumped warblers sing weak-sounding songs. The Maggie's song is a variation on *weeta, weeeta, weeta, teo*. The yellow-rumped's song is a weak, segmented series of trilling notes, that sounds like the jingling of a small silver bell: *tsing, tsing, tsing, tsing*. Yellow-rumps also give a *tschup* call note that is distinctive.

TENNESSEE AND ORANGE-CROWNED WARBLERS

Tennessee and orange-crowned warblers pose one of the toughest spring identification problems, although the challenge doesn't come up as often as many observers might wish. That is because Tennessee warblers are acci-

Philadelphia vireo
adult

Tennessee warbler
adult male

red-eyed vireo
adult

ruby-crowned kinglet
male

orange-crowned warbler
adult male, breeding

dental in the West, where orange-crowneds are numerous. On the other hand, orange-crowneds are scarce in the East, although they do occur.

These two warblers are so plain that it can sometimes be difficult to distinguish them from vireos or kinglets. Both Philadelphia and red-eyed vireos have heavier, more strongly hooked bills than any warbler (except the yellow-breasted chat). Although the Philadelphia vireo is similar in size and coloration to a Tennessee warbler, it has a yellowish, not white, breast; and overall, it shows less contrast between its olive back and yellowish underparts than the Tennessee. Red-eyed vireos have clean white underparts but sport much heavier bills than Tennessees do; they are also bigger and have stronger dark lines above and below the eye line.

Ruby-crowned kinglets can also be confused with orange-crowned warbler. Note the kinglet's minute, fine bill, prominent white eye-ring, and bold wing bars in contrast to the orange-crowned's overall olive-drab coloration. The kinglet's habit of hovering under branch tips as it gleans quickly sets it apart from most warblers.

Both the Tennessee and the orange-crowned are plain warblers without wing bars. In general, the spring Tennessee has the more contrasty features, with distinctly greenish upperparts and white underparts; sometimes there is a faint tinge of yellow at the sides of the breast. Orange-crowneds are duller both above and below; most show dull yellow or buff on the underparts, making them closer in color to the back. In addition, the Tennessee has a brighter, more noticeable white eye line than the orange-crowned. Even the plainest orange-crowneds should show some indistinct, blurry streaking on the breast, although it is not always easy to see. Both species have a dark line through the eye, but the orange-crowned has a yellowish eye-ring as well, which is lacking on the Tennessee. If you can see the undertail coverts, they solve the problem. The undertail coverts of the Tennessee are white. On orange-crowneds, they are yellow. It is easier to see the area on a Tennessee because the bird is often found high in the trees. Orange-crowneds skulk more, staying lower, although they do occasionally forage above eye level.

One more note on plumage: don't be confused by the orange-crowned's name. It's a rare and lucky occasion when you get to see the orange crown on a breeding-plumaged male. (You're more likely to see the red belly on a red-bellied woodpecker!)

These two warblers not only look alike, but they have fairly similar songs. The Tennessee's song is the more complicated, and much louder, song. It starts out with a series of spaced single notes and gradually increases in volume and tempo until it ends with a loud smacking trill: *seebit seebit seebit twit twit twit twack, twack, twack, twack!* Two bird watchers I know argue over whether the Tennessee's song is "cloyingly sweet" or "annoyingly percussive." I think it's both! The orange-crowned's high-pitched song is a long staccato trill that is more mechanical and less musical than the Tennessee's. It often drops slightly in pitch, most noticeably on the last two or three notes.

BLACK-AND-WHITE VERSUS BLACKPOLL

Our next two birds are black and white warblers, although only one of them is a black-and-white warbler. The similarity between the latter and the blackpoll warbler causes many watchers to stop and sort through the memory banks trying to recall the field marks.

The most obvious difference between the two is that the black-and-white warbler has a black-and-white-striped head and the blackpoll has a

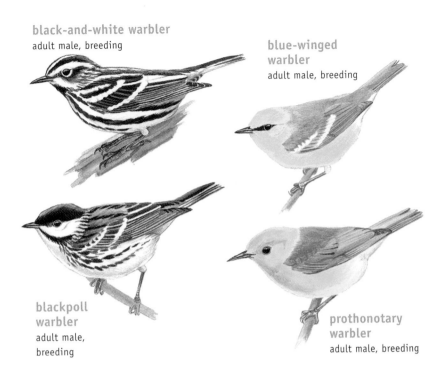

black-and-white warbler
adult male, breeding

blue-winged warbler
adult male, breeding

blackpoll warbler
adult male, breeding

prothonotary warbler
adult male, breeding

solid black cap. There is a mnemonic device many bird watchers use to remember the difference. The name "black-and-white" has hyphens, which are the same as streaks. Blackpoll has a dark "poll," or head (think of the poll tax, which is a sort of head count).

Black-and-white warblers have black and white stripes on the back and underparts; blackpolls do not. Both species have dark wings with white wing bars. The male black-and-white warbler has a black throat; the blackpoll has black streaks on the sides of the throat.

When you do not see the bird in question well, behavior can be a good clue. Black-and-white warblers are creepers, working steadily along tree branches and trunks. Only rarely do you see them foraging out on the smallest limbs or picking insects from leaves and buds. They tend to forage closer to the ground (and to the observer) than blackpolls do. Blackpolls are more typical warblers in this regard, foraging in the tops of trees and on smaller branches, even darting out to catch insects on occasion. Blackpoll warblers are often hidden in the leaves at the very tops of the tallest trees, making it hard to get a glimpse of them. They are slower than many other warblers, but they are not creepers.

Voice can also be a clue. When blackpolls come through in the spring, they often seem to be one of the most vocal migrants, and they typically arrive later than the other warblers. In many areas, they are the last warblers to be found passing through in spring. Black-and-whites are generally earlier migrants and are already on territory in many areas by the time blackpolls arrive. The songs of these birds are superficially similar because both are very high and thin, consisting of short wheezy notes. The song of the black-and-white is a series of paired notes, *wee-see wee-see wee-see* — as many as a dozen pairs at a time — that sounds rather like a squeaky wheel. Blackpoll songs are even higher and thinner, consisting of single short, hurried notes in a series, *seet, seet, SEET, SEET, SEET, seet, seet,* sometimes speeding up or gaining volume in the middle of the song and losing steam at the end.

BLUE-WINGED AND PROTHONOTARY WARBLERS

You would not think, looking at the pictures in a field guide, that blue-winged and prothonotary warblers would be an identification problem, but birds seen through binoculars are not always as distinctive as the pictures in the book. Both of these birds are yellow below and olive above, with extensive yellow on the face. No matter which sex you are looking at, two characters — on the wings and head — should quickly solve the problem, if you remember to look for them. Blue-winged warblers have two white wing bars. The wings of prothonotary warblers are plain. Blue-winged warblers have a strong black line from the bill through the eye, which contrasts strongly with the face. The head of the prothonotary warbler is plain and mostly yellow.

Habitat and song can also be good clues to separate these species. Prothonotaries prefer swampy woodlands with large old trees; they use old woodpecker holes and other tree cavities for nesting. The prothonotary's loud, ringing song, *sweet, sweet, sweet, sweet, sweet* is an excellent clue to this bright golden yellow bird's presence. Blue-winged warblers are commonly found in old fields that are slowly reverting to woodland, with lots of brush and saplings. They are often encountered along woodland edges where they use a lofty, exposed perched to sing their typical *beee-buzzzz* song. Later in the season, blue-wingeds may switch to an alternate song, an insectlike *chicker-cherwee!*

northern
waterthrush
adult

ovenbird
adult

Louisiana
waterthrush
adult

THE WATERTHRUSHES AND OVENBIRD

Because of their names, and because waterthrushes and ovenbirds are brown skulking birds that live close to the ground, many bird watchers forget that they are warblers. When they see one of these three species, confused birders may spend time wandering through their field guide's sparrow plates until the memory banks catch up. All three birds are dull brown above and white below, with fairly heavy streaks on the breast. (Worm-eating and Swainson's, the other two plain brownish warblers that live close to the ground, do not have any streaks on the chest.)

Separating ovenbird from the two waterthrushes is the first step. Ovenbirds have an orange crown bordered with black streaks and a bright white eye-ring. Waterthrushes have a plain crown and a white line above the eye. The streaking on the chest of an ovenbird is bolder and heavier than on a waterthrush. Ovenbirds are usually found in dry woods, walking around in the leaves. Waterthrushes are typically found along streams and in bogs and swamps. In migration, though, any warbler can show up anywhere.

They are often so active that it's hard to get a good look at them, or . . .

Separating the waterthrushes is a bit more challenging. Louisiana and northern waterthrushes are very similar and have confused many observers. When you see a waterthrush, the first step is to look at the white line above the eye. It is the easiest and most certain way to tell the two species apart. On the Louisiana waterthrush, the line is narrow and slightly duller in front of the eye but gets noticeably wider and more brightly white behind the eye. On a northern waterthrush, the line is narrow all the way back and is usually, but not always, tinged with yellow.

Next, check the underparts. The streaks on the Louisiana's underparts are somewhat disorganized, lighter and more blurred. The streaking on the chest of northerns is heavier, with spots that seem to form long streaks. Most northerns have a yellowish wash on the chest, but some are as white as Louisianas, and many Louisiana waterthrushes have noticeably buffy flanks. Most northerns also have spotting on the throat, and most Louisianas have plain white throats. Many observers rely on the Louisiana's larger bill and bubblegum pink legs to distinguish it from the finer-billed, dark-legged northern. But in the low-light situations in which we often see the waterthrushes, leg color can be difficult to determine.

Both waterthrushes sing loud songs that are a series of musical, slurred whistles. The northern waterthrush's song has three parts: *sweet sweet sweet, sugar sweet, chew chew, chew, chew.* The last part, *chew-chew-chew,* is diagnostic. The Louisiana waterthrush sings a loud, ringing song that begins with several slurred *tee-eet* notes, which seem to swoop in tone. The *tee-eet* notes are followed by a jumble of percussive whistled tones at the end. Both species also give a loud *chink!*, especially when flying along woodland streams.

. . . they are so skulky and secretive that trying to find them tries our patience.

HAVE PATIENCE

The biggest trick to spring warbler watching is patience. When you see a bird you don't recognize, stay with it for a while. Warblers are flitty, and identifying them takes some practice, but their constant movement can also be a boon because it means you get to see all of the bird, not just the underside or the back.

When you think that you have seen everything there is to see on an individual bird, it is time to turn to the field guide. In most cases you will identify the bird fairly quickly. After all, spring warblers are pretty gaudy. But even when a bird seems unmistakable, run through the checklist on page 280. Sometimes an "unmistakable" bird is anything but, and there are few frustrations as keen as seeing a real eye-popper and then discovering, after it has disappeared, that you don't know what species it was. If the occasional mystery bird gets away, don't worry. One of the advantages of spring warbler watching is that there are always more birds to see, and sometimes the pleasure is in the looking, not the identifying. 🐦

CONFUSING FALL WARBLERS

Most don't change plumage in fall. But there are a few...

EVERY YEAR AROUND SEPTEMBER 1, A POTENT VIRUS infects the minds of bird watchers. The virus has become so common, so much a part of bird watching culture, that it has achieved mythical status. It is known as Confusing Fall Warbler Syndrome, or CFWS.

Many bird watchers are infected with CFWS. The primary symptom is a habit of throwing up one's hands in dismay anytime one sees a warbler in fall. CFWS leads one to think that warblers are tough enough in spring, when they are dressed in their breeding finery and singing, and that in the fall, when they are drab, quiet little green and yellow birds, identifying them is hopeless. The good news is that while the symptoms are real, CFWS itself is mostly a myth. Warblers in fall are only marginally more difficult than warblers in spring.

Let's run the numbers. Pick up your favorite field guide and page through it. All told, you come up with about fifty-three warblers, give or take a few vagrants. The only antidote needed for CFWS: forty-three of the fifty-three, or slightly more than 80 percent of warblers, look exactly the same in the fall as they do in the spring! Repeat those numbers to yourself several times. Amazing, isn't it? If you have mastered 80 percent of the spring warblers, you can easily identify 80 percent of the warblers you see in fall.

The prothonotaries, blue-wingeds, black-throated grays, chats, ovenbirds, waterthrushes, and almost three dozen other warblers are no harder to identify in the fall than they are in spring, because they look almost exactly the same in both seasons. Sometimes fall plumages are a little

American
redstart
immature male,
first fall

American
redstart
adult male,
breeding

duller, with slightly muted colors, but the field marks do not change. If you can identify an American redstart in spring, you can identify one in fall.

Even erring on the side of caution, there are no more than ten fall warblers that are sufficiently different to represent a challenge to our field skills and knowledge, and they can be divided into two general categories. The first is the immature/female group. These fall warblers look like faded versions of the adults in breeding plumage, and thus offer fairly obvious visual clues to their identity. The second category contains the bay-breasted/blackpoll/pine and the magnolia/Cape May/yellow-rumped groups. These are the classic confusing fall warblers — the birds that, in their fall plumage, look nothing like the adults do in breeding plumage. These warblers can be further divided into two categories: streaky and unstreaky fall warblers (see pages 296 and 302 for more about these groups).

The immature/female group includes birds like chestnut-sided, black-throated green, Townsend's, and palm warblers. Although fall adults in this category look pretty much the way they do in spring, the youngsters are duller and can be confusing. Because we see the youngsters only in fall — and don't see many of them — it's easy to forget their field marks. Spend a little time in early fall boning up on the field marks, and about half of our ten confusing fall warblers won't be confusing any longer. Each of these birds is distinctive in its own way. The fall immature chestnut-sided, for example, bears a clean grayish breast and bright, lime green upperparts. With its white wing bars and eye-ring, it stands out. Most of the other warblers in this category retain enough of the adult's markings that they are fairly easy to identify: they look like washed-out versions of the adult females. The immature black-throated green might lack the adult's black "beard," but it does have its green upperparts and yellow face. The Townsend's face pattern is consistent in all plumages. Although the immature palm can look quite dull in fall, its yellow undertail coverts and constantly pumping tail betray its identity.

The second category consists of two groups. Fall bay-breasted and blackpoll warblers can look very different than they do in the spring, especially immature birds. The two species look much alike and might also be mistaken for dull pine warblers. The same similarity problems exist for Cape May, magnolia, and yellow-rumped warblers — a trio that requires a little work to sort out. (See Streaky Fall Warblers, on page 296.)

If this sounds intimidating, add it up, and you'll realize we're talking about only five or six species. The Everest that seemed insurmountable turns out to be a fairly small hill.

The notion that identifying fall warblers is harder than learning to speak Chinese is so deeply entrenched that it is treated as fact. How did that happen?

The problem may be over-reliance on field guides. Faced with constraints of format and space, field guides focus on the the birds most likely to cause confusion. Reading the guide, we subconsciously adopt the idea that fall warblers are hard. Specialty guides feed the paranoia. They are wonderful sources of information and are far more complete and detailed than general guides. Unfortunately, many bird watchers look at the sheer size of most specialty guides and automatically conclude that it would be simpler to build a particle accelerator in their backyard than to put a name on a fall warbler. Remember, a specialty guide is not a field guide. The purpose of a field guide is to help you identify birds. The purpose of a specialty guide is to provide information that won't fit into the field guide — but most of the time that information isn't needed to identify a bird in the field.

The trick is to not become overwhelmed by the amount of information out there. Step back and look at the big picture — only ten of fifty warblers actually fall under the "confusing" banner — and you will be cured of Confusing Fall Warbler Syndrome. A little time spent thumbing through the field guide will refresh your memory on the few birds that are truly challenging. Then you will be ready to tackle warblers in fall with the same enthusiasm you greet them with in spring. ✒

STREAKY FALL WARBLERS

Immature females in drab disguise

WATCHING WARBLERS IN SPRING IS PURE FUN. THE occasional identification challenge might intrude, but they are easily solved, and we're free to appreciate the birds in all their gaudy glory. With few exceptions (such as the black-throated blue warbler), female warblers are strikingly similar to males; even those females with radically different coloration (American redstart, for example) give more than enough pattern clues to betray their identity.

Watching warblers in fall is another game entirely. Like all games, it's fun, and it shouldn't cause consternation even if it is a bit more challenging. In fall, we're often dealing with immatures wearing their fresh juvenal plumage. (They don't molt into breeding plumage until after their migration south. Breeding plumage comes in in late winter, usually before they make the flight back north to us.) Fall plumage is dull and cryptic, and that's where the fun begins. In this chapter, we'll discuss a few hints that should make you look forward to your next "baypoll" warbler (a made-up term used to describe the hard-to-discern blackpoll and bay-breasted warblers in nonbreeding plumage). The species we'll focus on are the streaky fall immatures of magnolia, prairie, pine, Cape May, bay-breasted, and blackpoll warblers. Each of them is dusky greenish above, with varying amounts of yellowish below, and all show some streaking on back, breast, or both. We'll proceed from easiest to not-so-easy, dispelling clouds of qualm all the way.

Streaky fall warblers: immature females

magnolia warbler

pine warbler

Cape May warbler

blackpoll warbler

bay-breasted warbler

prairie warbler

STREAKY, WITH OBVIOUS CLUES

It's always nice when a species displays a feature that amounts to an identification clincher, one that is dependable in every plumage. Magnolia warblers always carry a lot of yellow from bill to belly, which contrasts nicely with their white undertail coverts. Though the immature "Maggie" may show none of the thick black streaking on the flanks that adults do, the bright white panel in the middle of its tail will clinch the identification. The white undertail coverts add to the impression that the bird's white tail has been dipped in ink. Another generous hint is the magnolia's bright yellow rump patch. Get that square white panel bisecting the tail, add a yellow rump, and you've clinched the magnolia's identification.

Another yellow-bellied species with a lot of white showing in the tail is the prairie warbler. Immature female prairies in fall show dull yellowish wing bars, bright yellow underparts with dark streaking, and white outer tail feathers. The best mark to look for is on its face, where the prairie has a yellow crescent beneath the eye. It has the most heavily patterned face among this group of confusing warblers. Round-headed and active, the prairie wins my vote for cutest face of all the the warblers. Behavioral clues are important here as well, because the prairie's tail almost never stops pumping. You'll see it low in old field vegetation, showing juncolike flashes of white when it flits from shrub to shrub.

STREAKY, WITH LESS OBVIOUS CLUES

The Cape May warbler, highly variable in fall plumage, is less generous with its identification hints, but a careful observer can collect several. Though the type specimen was collected in Cape May, New Jersey, the Cape May warbler doesn't breed there, any more than the palm warbler breeds in palms. But its Latin name, *Dendroica tigrina*, makes perfect sense, even in fall. The "little tiger" carries its stripes, which go from throat to vent, year-round. Immature female Cape Mays may not have any yellow at all and may have only a hint of the breast streaks. The cheek patch, brilliant cinnamon on the adult male, may be dullest olive, only barely outlined, and there's usually a pale yellowish patch running up behind the cheek. Also look for a glimmer of olive-yellow on the rump, an echo of the male's bright yellow backside. But fall immature Cape Mays are always well streaked below.

Cape Mays are dumpy, short-tailed warblers. They may fool you momentarily, hover–gleaning like kinglets at the tips of branches — small, light warblers can do acrobatic things like that. (You won't find the large pine, blackpoll, or bay-breasted warblers doing much hover–gleaning.) Cape Mays have a long, slightly decurved bill, which they use to glean fruit and probe flowers for nectar. Check for yellow-ish patches on the hindneck and rump and tigerish streaking on the lower flanks. If you've got all three, you probably have a Cape May warbler.

> *Fall warblers flock together, and flash and flit tail spots and panels continuously, signaling their flockmates to follow.*

FLASHES AND FLITS

When fall warblers flock together, they flash and flit tail spots and panels continuously, signaling their flockmates to follow. Most of the confusing fall warblers have white tail spots. The pine's are the largest, making its closed tail appear entirely whitish from below. Rump patches, which are bright yellow on magnolia, myrtle, Audubon's, and most Cape May warblers, are another flocking signal. You'll see much more of this tail action in fall than in spring; this probably has to do with the birds' tendency to stay in flocks as they search for fruiting plants. When the birds are look-ing for insects, as they do in spring, they're seeking a scarce but evenly distributed resource, so flocking won't necessarily help. In fall, birds exploit more fruit, which is an abundant but patchily distributed resource. When one member of a flock finds a fruiting shrub, they can all exploit it together and move on with full crops. So when fall comes, war-blers flit and flash and wag their tails, helping each other hang together.

STREAKY, BUT LEAST OBVIOUS

There are three *Dendroica*s that can be devilish to separate, and the clues are even more subtle than those we've already discussed. They are the pine, bay-breasted, and blackpoll warblers. Perhaps the easiest to eliminate is the pine warbler. While many adult pine warblers have a strong suffusion of yellow on head and breast, a dull immature female pine warbler is drabber than drab, without yellow or warm buff tones anywhere. Let that drabness work for you! Lack of information is information! White wing bars are the only discernible field mark, but they are often ill-defined. Streaks on the side of the breast may be blurred and indistinct. Nothing is sharp and clear on the fall immature pine warbler. Look first for an unstreaked back, as this is the best mark to separate it from the other two species. You may have to look hard, because some immature bay-breasts and blackpolls have back streaking so faint it looks plain. On the breast, look for faint, blurry streaks below and broad white panels, not spots, in the outer tail feathers, that make the closed tail look white from below. While bay-breasted and blackpolls give the impression of having a line through the eye, the pine has more of a spectacled look, with pale lores and a broken eye-ring.

There isn't a nickel's worth of difference between the upperparts of fall immature bay-breasted and blackpoll warblers.

On a holistic level, the pine is a big, heavy, sluggish warbler, and it will probably creep around and let you puzzle over it for as long as you like. Pine warblers work along the larger horizontal limbs of trees, methodically gleaning insects. Here, the bird's name can help. I see the vast majority of my pine warblers in pine trees.

There isn't a nickel's worth of difference between the upperparts of fall immature bay-breasted and blackpoll warblers. Both are olive-green with streaked backs. Seen from below, however, it is often apparent which is which. The best clues are all in the underpart coloration. An adult male bay-breasted still has bright chestnut on its flanks in fall and even the dullest immature is suffused with a warm buff below that gets warmer toward the rear. The undertail coverts are noticeably buffy, not white. The best character of an immature bay-breasted warbler is the clean, even, warm buff tone of its underparts, which is rarely broken by streaks. Here, the bay-breasted's name can help us remember its field marks, even in fall.

The blackpoll warbler, in contrast, shows distinct breaks in coloration from the yellow on its throat and breast to its grayish olive flanks to its white belly and undertail coverts. Its coloring isn't even, and is further broken up by streaks on the sides of the breast. Blackpolls are more likely than bay-breasteds to show a dark line through the eye and a strong, pale yellowish superciliary line. Bay-breasted warblers appear plainer in the face, giving them a sweeter look than blackpolls, which always look a little mean to me.

I usually get laughed at when I mention leg color as a field mark on warblers. Ditto for the color of the soles of their feet. Such tiny birds, moving so quickly . . . how can anyone get a look at their leg color, much less at the soles of their feet? If you're lucky, the yellow legs of fall blackpoll warblers will jump out at you. Some tricky immature blackpolls will show dark legs and yellow feet, and some immatures (such as the one pictured on page 297) may have yellow only on the soles of their feet. If you're looking closely at eye lines and undertail coverts, you might as well have a look at their legs and feet. They can be a clincher in separating blackpoll from bay-breasted warblers. Bay-breasteds, Cape Mays, and most pines have dark to medium-gray legs and feet.

Now that you're feeling more at ease about streaky fall warblers, let me offer a word about variability among these birds. Some that you encounter will be textbook birds showing all the distinctive field marks well. A few individuals may be so oddly or subtly marked that you'll just have to guess at their identities. I am still puzzling over an immature female warbler that could have been a Wilson's or a hooded. A friend saw white in the tail when it flew. I missed it. We're still wondering what it was. And sometimes, when the light's wrong, and you just can't get a good look at the soles of a warbler's feet (!), you have to write "baypoll warbler" in your notebook. But if you keep these tips in mind, there will be fewer every year, and those fall mystery warblers will be the ones that get you out in the morning. 🐦

PLAIN FALL WARBLERS

Drabness is a field mark among these plain janes.

THE PLAIN, UNSTREAKED FALL WARBLERS CAN REALLY give the birder a hard time. Suddenly, there's a yellowish bird in front of you. It's got a shoebutton eye and no discernible field marks. There are no wing bars or white tail spots. Unsure what you're looking at, your mind jumps from genus to genus. There's so little to go on. What fun!

I'd like to try to demystify these plain little birds and encourage you to look at the differences and similarities between them on a genus (not genius!) level. Three of the plain fall warblers pictured here belong to the genus *Vermivora*. They all share certain characteristics: small body size, rather short legs, and sharp, almost needle-tipped bills. They are the Nashville, Tennessee, and orange-crowned warblers. The other three birds discussed here are bulkier than the *Vermivora*s, so it makes sense to discuss them separately.

THIN-BILLED VERMIVORAS

Of the three, the Nashville is probably easiest to identify. No matter what plumage it's in, the Nashville always sports a complete white to whitish eye-ring. Though colors are muted in fall immatures, they closely follow the pattern and hue of adult plumage. The Nashville has a yellow throat, which contrasts nicely with its gray hood. At 4³/₄ inches, the Nashville is a really tiny warbler, and it leaps around actively, occasionally pumping its tail. (The Nashville's tail-pumping lacks the conviction of the palm warbler's or prairie warbler's, however.) The occasional dusky-fronted Nashville is a much smaller, more agile (and more easily seen) bird than the similarly marked Connecticut warbler, with which it might be confused. If it's right out in the open looking back at you (and lacks an overall dark hood) it's probably a Nashville. Connecticuts are notorious skulkers, spending all their time on or near the ground.

The Nashville's cousin, the Tennessee warbler, is just as badly named: neither can be found in Tennessee, except during migration. Tennessees vary a lot in fall; some are almost pure white below, mimicking spring plumage, while immatures like the one pictured on page 304 can be quite yellow below. Even yellowish immatures, though, usually have white undertail coverts, in contrast to the other warblers in this group. The Tennessee warbler always shows a dark line through the eye and a strong pale superciliary line over the eye. The upperparts are a distinctive grass green. The Tennessee's shape is also distinctive — its short tail makes it look a bit top-heavy. Long primary wing feathers and long white undertail coverts, which extend to within ½ inch of the tail tip, accentuate the short-tailed impression. Then there's that needle-sharp *Vermivora* bill. In spring, with their plain greenish upperparts, white underparts, strong white superciliary line, and gray caps (on adult males), Tennessees are most often mistaken for red-eyed vireos — vireos that must have had their bills in a pencil sharpener, at least. You'll often see Tennessees in nice little same-species flocks, which will help you sort out the variations in their plumage. The immature female pictured on page 304 looks least like the spring male — most males are whiter than this.

Common in much of the West, the orange-crowned warbler (our third *Vermivora*) is a rare prize for the warbler watcher east of the Mississippi. Furthermore, they're late migrants, showing up in late September, often after the bulk of the Tennessees have passed through. You'll see them singly, as they don't often travel in flocks with other orange-crowneds. There's nothing very striking about the orange-crowned's plumage; it's blurry and indistinctly marked, with no wing bars. One patch of color does stand out, and that is the bird's yellow undertail coverts. They show stronger color than any other part of the bird. (Compare this to the white undertail coverts of the similar Tennessee.) Shorter wings and a longer tail give orange-crowned a more balanced silhouette than the Tennessee,

Unstreaked fall warblers: immature females

Nashville warbler

Tennessee warbler

orange-crowned warbler

yellow warbler

common yellowthroat

black-throated blue warbler

as well. Blurry streaks mark the breast, and an indistinct dark eye line and pale superciliary line point toward the sharp, thin *Vermivora* bill. Feel free to look for the hidden orangish spot on the crown— it may not be there on fall immatures, but it's a thrill to see it when it appears.

In fall, common yellowthroats often give me pause before I remember to look at the structure of the bird.

BULKY WARBLERS

The next three warblers are larger, bulkier birds: the yellow warbler and the female black-throated blue, genus *Dendroica*, and the common yellowthroat, genus *Geothlypis*. The immature yellow warbler is perhaps the plainest of all the birds discussed here, especially in the face. A black eye stares out of a perfectly plain face, and that's your first hint. Your next hint is the large bill, which is thicker than those of the *Vermivoras*. Perhaps the most distinctive thing about a fall immature yellow warbler is its yellow tail spots, which are unique among warblers. Notice, too, that the yellow suffusion in the tail even carries over into the legs. Some immature yellows can be extremely drab — the one pictured here is a bit yellower than the dullest female. But check for those yellow tail spots when there's nothing else to go on, and they may clinch the identification for you.

A deceptively plain-looking bird, the female black-throated blue warbler has a couple of neat hints to her identity that, once discovered, close the case. Nine out of ten immature females carry the "pocket handkerchief" that distinguishes adult females: a tiny whitish spot at the base of the primary wing feathers, that stands out on the otherwise olive-drab plumage. Look for a small white crescent under the eye, and a nice yellowish superciliary line over the eye. Overall, she's chunky and short-tailed, and her golden-olive underparts are distinctive. This is one of the few warblers in which the female is drastically different from the male in all plumages, and she's all the more fun to find for that fact.

In fall, common yellowthroats often give me pause before I remember to look at the structure of the bird. Yellowthroats have a large range of plumages, from fully masked males to females with eye-rings to brownish immatures. This is one of the brownest of the immature warblers, with a strong wash of brown on the flanks. A nice contrast always exists, though, between the dark cheek and the yellowish throat, and a broken eye-ring gives it an inquisitive look. Drab juvenile yellowthroats can be confused with one or more of the *Oporornis* warblers (Kentucky, Connecticut, mourning, and MacGillivray's warblers) but the shorter, stockier yellowthroat lacks the yellow belly that all these birds show. The long broad tail of the common yellowthroat is often flicked and flirted as the bird clambers through low, dense vegetation. Extremely short, rounded wings with little primary extension give the impression of a tail-heavy bird. The yellowthroat is fairly large, with long strong legs and an athletic, wrenlike manner. It clings to low vertical stems, cocks its head, and makes eye contact as it gives a low, dry *chup!* call. Yellowthroats are not shy; they're curious, and they often respond well to *pishing* and squeaking.

When faced with a dull, unstreaked fall warbler, look at the face pattern — or note the lack thereof. A complete white eye-ring suggests Nashville; superciliary lines narrow it down to Tennesee, female black-throated blue, or orange-crowned. Then check under the tail, for undertail covert color. White points to Tennessee; yellow on an otherwise all-drab bird suggests orange-crowned. Yellow tail spots clinch yellow warbler. A pocket hanky of white on the wing betrays the black-throated blue female. If you're out of field marks, look at the overall structure of the bird, and watch for the tail-heavy, short-winged, leggy build of the confiding common yellowthroat. Congratulations. You've just navigated through the sometimes murky waters of fall warbler watching! 🐦

TANAGERS

Sorting out
THE FOUR TANAGER SPECIES
REGULARLY FOUND NESTING IN NORTH AMERICA

THERE ARE A LOT OF EYE-CATCHING, COLORFUL BIRDS in North America. Warblers, darting bolts of light, make us think of spring; orioles, bold and public, are summer. Tanagers have a special message, too. The sight of one immediately evokes a vision of the tropics, of dense jungles and deep green forests. Perhaps it is the stunning reds, or the deliberate, tropical movements, but no day with a tanager is a bad one.

Over most of North America, tanager identification is straightforward, depending both on range and on the obvious plumage of the males, which is almost unmistakable. It is the females that are most likely to give us pause with their subtle shades of green and yellow.

There are four species of tanagers that regularly breed north of the United States–Mexico border. Three of the four breed in the West, and two of the four breed in the East. Except for vagrants, the identification problems are limited. In the East, the challenge is summer and scarlet tanagers. In the Southwest, the problem is summer and hepatic tanagers. Western tanagers, widespread in the West, cause few identification problems even when they show up at feeders in the East during winter.

Let's start in the East, where the ranges of summer and scarlet tanagers overlap widely, allowing the greatest opportunity for missteps.

Males are easy. In breeding plumage, male scarlet tanagers are a deep, riveting scarlet, with contrasting jet black wings. Nothing else looks like a male scarlet tanager. The male summer tanager is a more subdued, rosy red, but it is still a striking bird. The wings are red, not black. The

TANAGERS AND BUNTINGS

only bird it can be confused with is the northern cardinal, though the confusion should be only momentary because of the cardinal's heavier bill and prominent crest.

Male summer tanagers remain red all year. Male scarlets, which arrive in full plumage in the spring, lose the red in the fall as they head south. This occasionally leads to one of the stranger and more confusing tanager plumages: a bird with a patchy red and green body, with abrupt edges between the two colors. These birds often confuse the inexperienced observer, at least at first, but noting the thick tanager bill and the black wings should quickly right the picture.

These patchy scarlets can also be mistaken for older female summer tanagers, whose yellowish body plumage is sometimes washed with soft red. The female summer tanagers lack the black wings of the scarlet, however, and the red wash blends into the yellow without abrupt edges.

THE FEMALES

Female scarlet and summer tanagers are the real identification problem in the East. Both are plain yellowish or yellow-green or yellow-brown. During the summer, two clues will help you tell which is which: range and the company they keep. Summer tanagers are more southerly in range, and any bird in deep southern pine and pine-oak woodlands is almost certainly a summer. Scarlets are more northerly, favoring hardwood forests. In the middle range it is possible to find either, although habitat preferences usually (but not always) keep them from occurring in the same woods. In migration, either bird might be found almost anywhere, and every spring a few summer tanagers show up far north of where they are expected.

Female scarlet tanagers are olive-yellow, the green tint usually obvious if the bird is seen well. There is also a greenish cast to the browner upperparts, and the wings are dusky, contrasting with the olive body plumage. The yellow under the tail is typically bright and contrasts with the rest of the underparts. Female summer tanagers are similar, but the underparts are a plainer yellow, and the brownish upperparts lack any olive tones. They show little or no contrast between wing and body hue. The differences can be subtle at times.

The bill of the summer tanager is larger than the bill of the scarlet. This character is useful only when the observer has experience with both

summer
tanager
male

hepatic
tanager
male

older
female

summer
tanager
female

hepatic
tanager
female

western
tanager
female

scarlet
tanager
female

winter
male

molting
fall male

western
tanager
male

scarlet
tanager
male

Male tanager heads at a glance

summer tanager   hepatic tanager   western tanager

species or is comparing the two side by side (and wouldn't I love to have that happen someday). Bill color can also be a clue. The bill of the summer tanager is always pale, usually yellowish, while the bill of the scarlet tanager is frequently (but not always) dusky.

IN THE SOUTHWEST

The only other area where tanager identification is a problem is the Southwest, where three species, summer, hepatic, and western, occur. The western tanager is the least likely to be confused with the others and should be recognizable at all seasons. The only significant problem is that the species might be mistaken for an oriole. The heavy tanager bill and the more sluggish, deliberate movements should sort out the confusion fairly quickly.

Male western tanagers are as close to unmistakable as birds get. The bright yellow body, black wings with broad white and yellow wing bars, and the bright red head make this one of the most recognizable birds in the West. Even in the fall, when birds are slipping into winter dress, there is still red around the base of the bill, a dead giveaway.

Even the females are distinctive, although their color is more muted than that of their mates. The underparts are a dull yellow and the upperparts are a darker, grayer color that contrasts with a yellower nape and rump. The wings, though not quite black, are still dark and have two diffuse but obvious whitish wing bars. The wing bars alone eliminate the other tanagers in the region.

scarlet tanager
adult male

scarlet tanager
molting fall male

The real problem in the Southwest is differentiating between hepatic and summer tanagers, which mimic each other in both male and female plumages.

Male hepatic tanagers are bigger and duller than male summers, with a distinct gray wash on the red back and flanks and a contrasting dark, grayish ear patch. The females are more difficult, but the overall differences are the same. The female hepatic is grayer on the back and sides. The ear patch is both grayer and more visible, and it contrasts with the hepatic's brighter, yellowish crown and brighter yellow throat. Female summer tanagers show little or no contrast on the crown, and the throat is barely brighter than the breast. Some female summer tanagers, especially in the Southwest, can have a gray wash on the back, but even these birds lack gray on the underparts and do not have the contrasting crown and darker ear patch. The hepatic tanager's larger, darker bill, with its curved culmen (the ridge on top of the bill), gives it a slightly "meaner" look than the pale-billed summer tanager wears.

Tanager identification is not usually difficult, as long as one sees the bird well. A few scarlet tanagers are found in the West every year, and a few western tanagers are found in the East, but both are reasonably easy to identify. Oddly, it is the summer tanager, the more southern bird, that is most likely to winter at a feeder in most parts of the country (especially females or young males) and they are sometimes found far to the north of their normal range. But wherever you are, no matter what the season, any day with a tanager is a treat.

BUNTINGS

Love those males!
Work on those females!

BUNTINGS ARE AMONG BIRD WATCHERS' FAVORITE BIRDS, in part because the "B" seems to stand for blue, at least for the males. The same observers largely ignore females except in the breeding season, when they are identified by the company they keep or by range. Buntings deserve a closer look, and with a little in-the-field experience, most females and immatures can be identified with confidence. You may discover that your expectations have been limiting the number of birds you see.

BUNTING BREAKDOWN

There are four regularly occurring buntings in North America and a look-alike that occasionally confuses people. The four are indigo bunting, lazuli bunting, varied bunting, and painted bunting. The look-alike is blue grosbeak. A fifth bunting, the blue bunting, is a rare vagrant to extreme south Texas.

Painted buntings are the gaudiest and easiest to identify. They breed in the coastal areas of the Southeast and in the southern Great Plains. They are notable wanderers to the Southwest and the Atlantic Coast, and have been recorded as far north as the Canadian Maritimes. Most out-of-range records are at feeders in fall and winter, but they have shown up during every season.

Varied buntings are confined to the border regions of south Texas and extreme southern Arizona and New Mexico and, except for a few records in California, are not known to wander outside of that range.

Indigo buntings are generally assumed to be birds of the East, and lazuli buntings of the West. That general rule is valid, but indigo and lazuli buntings overlap (and occasionally hybridize) on the Great Plains, and indigos breed in the Southwest, where they overlap with both lazuli and varied buntings.

In addition, indigo buntings are regular vagrants throughout the West, and lazuli buntings are rarer but somewhat regular wanderers to the East. Thus, there is more than enough opportunity to see either in many parts of the continent, especially in migration and winter.

Blue grosbeaks breed across most of the southern two-thirds of the United States.

All these species winter south of the United States border, but all have been found in this country in winter. Painted buntings are regular in Florida in winter, especially at feeders.

THE MALES

The first and simplest challenge is males. They present few serious identification problems. Most field guides cover the differences well, and we can content ourselves with a short summary of the field marks.

Male painted bunting: This one is almost impossible to misidentify. It is so striking and colorful that it evokes images of tropical species. The deep blue head, red body, and greenish back and wings are like no other bird you are likely to run across outside of a zoo. It's an overused term, but male painted buntings are as close to unmistakable as a bird gets.

Male varied bunting: They are almost as distinctive as the painteds, but the contrasts are smaller and you need to get a good look to see the color. Varied has a reddish nape, a blue body and face, and a variably reddish wash on the breast. If you get even a semidecent look, most male varied buntings will be easy to identify.

Male indigo and lazuli bunting: These two are not hard to tell apart, and the most likely source of confusion is not each other, but other bluish birds. Male indigo buntings are deep blue — indigo — all over. The only other remarkably blue birds in North America are the bluebirds and

lazuli
bunting
female

varied
bunting
female

lazuli
bunting
male

indigo
bunting
female

varied
bunting
male

indigo
bunting
male

blue grosbeak
female

painted
bunting
female

painted
bunting
male

blue grosbeak
male

some of the jays. Jays are large, however, and bluebirds are not blue all over except for the mountain bluebird, which is sky blue and larger than the indigo bunting. Male lazuli buntings are easy to separate from the other buntings because they have whitish bellies and bold white wing bars, as well as a wash of rufous across the breast. In fact, they look most like male eastern or western bluebirds, but bluebirds are larger, lack the wing bars, and are usually found in different habitats.

Male blue grosbeak: The outlier in the group is this bird. Males are almost entirely blue, like indigo buntings, but have bold rusty wing bars. Blue grosbeaks are also a bit larger than any of the buntings, and when you have spent time comparing the bills of the buntings and the grosbeak, you will understand how the bird got its name. The bill is strikingly thick, giving the bird a bull-headed look that the buntings do not share.

SONG

Experienced observers regularly separate the buntings by song, but the differences in song between lazuli and indigo buntings are subtle and subject to interpretation. In general, the songs of lazulis are slightly higher-pitched than those of indigos, and tend not to have as many paired phrases. The call notes of the two are nearly indistinguishable. The painted bunting's song is different, full of sweet whistles and warbles, and has been compared to a melodious version of the common yellowthroat's, except that it varies. The song of the varied bunting falls somewhere between the painted and the other two, and varieds often include a hoarse descending *wheer* note. All the differences are small, and identifying most birds entirely on song is an iffy proposition.

ON TO THE DIFFICULT PART

So much for the easy stuff. The females are not nearly so distinctive and cause even experienced observers problems. The trick is to remember a few key field marks, especially the presence or absence of wing bars, the color of the throat, and the presence or absence of diffuse brown streaking on the breast.

With female buntings, the first hurdle is to realize that you are looking

Buntings at a glance

| male
varied bunting | male
lazuli bunting | male
indigo bunting |

at a bunting, and not a sparrow. Especially at feeders, observers tend to overlook female buntings, assuming they are just largish dull sparrows. The generic difference between the female buntings and sparrows is that no sparrows are so plainly brown all over. Sparrows almost never lack some streaking below, or at least some noticeable feature to their plumage. The plainer the bird, the more likely it is you are looking at a female bunting. Finally, the buntings also typically have shorter, more conical bills than sparrows.

FEMALES, YOUNGSTERS, AND WINTER MALES

The rest of the hurdles are a bit more complicated. Females and young birds in the fall are essentially identical and can be treated as a group. First spring males look largely like adult males in the duller, patchy plumage of fall and winter, but they still look like adult males. It is the female and juvenal plumages that cause the most trouble.

START WITH THE EASY ID

Female painted bunting: Once again we start with the easiest of the group, female painted buntings. They cannot be confused with any other bunting and are most likely to be passed off as a warbler. They are yellowish green on the upperparts and greenish yellow on the underparts, reminiscent perhaps of a female tanager or a female Wilson's warbler. Tanagers are quite a bit bigger, however, and warblers are almost always smaller and have thinner bills. There really isn't another bird the color of

**female
varied bunting**

**female
lazuli bunting**

**female
indigo bunting**

a female painted bunting. It's our only all-green bird. Youngsters are the same but somewhat duller, especially underneath.

THE CHALLENGE BEGINS

The real challenge is the female varied, indigo, and lazuli buntings. They are all the same size and generally plain brown all over. It takes a good look and attention to subtlety to separate them with confidence. Even under close observation, some birds, especially female varied buntings, may have to pass unnamed.

Female varied bunting: This one is the plainest of the three. It is, in fact, a bird without field marks. There are no streaks, no pattern to the head save for the faintest hint of a paler brown eyebrow, and no wing bars. The bird is basic pale brown. Plainness is the key identifier when comparing it with the other female buntings.

Female lazuli bunting: Both lazuli and indigo buntings occur in the range of varied buntings, although lazulis are more common as a rule. Female lazulis are also plain brown birds, but they always show pale wing bars. The wing bars are smaller than and lack the contrast of the male's, but they are always present. The birds usually show a short pale eyebrow, although it is sometimes hard to see. The female lazuli's underparts are also different from varied's. Female lazulis are plain below but have a variable buffy wash on the breast that contrasts with a paler, not-quite-white belly. The combination of wing bars and contrast between the breast and belly separates almost all female lazuli from female varied buntings.

Female indigo bunting: These birds fall somewhere in between the other two. They are plain brown all over, usually slightly darker than either lazuli or varied. They have only the faintest indication of wing bars, which are almost always indistinct; when present, they tend to be buffy and lacking white. Female indigos also show fine brownish streaks on the breast. The streaking is not easy to see unless you get a good look, but it is always there and increases the contrast between the breast and the unstreaked underparts. The pattern of contrast is similar to that on the lazuli but is caused by a difference between a darker breast and a pale brown belly, rather than by a buffy breast and a white belly.

The other key to female indigo buntings is the throat, which is always whitish and contrasts with the breast. The female varied's throat is essentially the same color as the breast, and the throat of female lazulis is grayish, not white, and doesn't contrast strongly with the breast.

Female blue grosbeak: These are grossly similar to the female buntings but note again the large size, the disproportionately large bill, and the strong brown wing bars.

ID KEYS

The key to female buntings lies in the pattern of the underparts and the presence or absence of wing bars. Checking females may lead you to turn up an unexpected bird, however. In the East, some winter females turn out to be lazulis, whereas in the West some females are indigos. In migration, either might turn up anywhere. Most out-of-range birds will be in female plumage, however, a pattern that holds for many other birds.

If all this sounds daunting, don't worry — it is. As with all tough birding problems, the rewards are worth it. These clues should help you on your way. ✒

BASICS OF SPARROW ID

Choose one species you know well and go from there.

FOR THE BEGINNING BIRDER FLIPPING THROUGH A FIELD guide, sparrows seem like an endless parade of terribly similar birds. Other bird groups are much easier to grasp — the large egrets and herons, ducks and geese, even breeding-plumage warblers are a cakewalk compared to sparrows. Many beginners avoid the sparrows much like a sensible person avoids Friday rush-hour traffic or haunted castles during a full moon.

North America's sparrow species' appearance and size are the genesis of the term "LBJ" or "little brown job." Of course not all of our sparrows are either little or brown — but most are both. Some sparrows are distinctive enough at a glance that identification should be no problem. (Think lark sparrow, white-crowned sparrow, eastern and spotted towhees, and Harris's sparrow.) It's when we get into the very similar sparrow species that we find identifications more difficult to pin down. Not only are many sparrows LBJs in the truest sense of the phrase, but they are also skulkers — they hide in the underbrush, pop up for a quick peek, then vanish once more. Not all of them cooperate by visiting our feeding stations or perching in an obvious spot for all the world to see.

The purpose of this introductory chapter is to give you an identification tool to help you master the LBJs and put the correct name on most of the sparrows you encounter in the field. If you've read the first chapters of this book you already know that when you see a strange bird — sparrow or otherwise — you should look at the bird, not at your field guide. The temptation, of course, is to take a quick look at the strange

SPARROWS

bird and immediately open your field guide, looking for a matching image. But this isn't practical. If your unfamiliar bird is a sparrow, and your hands deftly turn to the sparrow section of your favorite field guide, you may find yourself glancing at page after page of subtly different LBJs. Back to the bird . . . it's gone.

song sparrow

Instead, try this comparative device. Choose a sparrow species that you are familiar with — one that is common in your area. Study this species so that you know its key plumage characteristics, its shape, its size, and its habits. For most of us in North America, a good choice is the ubiquitous song sparrow. Song sparrows provide an excellent reference point for the aspiring sparrow expert: they are common and easily seen in a variety of habitats, they have streaky breasts and often a central breast spot, and they have striped heads. They are, in short, like a lot of other sparrows.

In *Watership Down*, the novel by Richard Adams, the rabbits could identify two kinds of birds, Hawks and Not-hawks. This is what you will now do with the streak-breasted sparrows you encounter: label them either song sparrow or Something Else.

This may seem like a small accomplishment. But by asking yourself, "Why isn't that a song sparrow?" your attention will be immediately drawn to the key characteristics that lead to a positive identification. For example, the markings on a Savannah sparrow are quite similar to those on a song sparrow, and both species show a lot of variation. But a quick look at the tail tells birders whether they are seeing the short notched tail of the Savannah sparrow or the long rounded tail of the song sparrow. Again, familiarity with one species makes the differences in a new species more apparent.

Another helpful device is to learn what to look for — what sparrow species other than your comparison species might occur in your area and what characteristics make them unique. Be aware of juvenal plumages, so that immature birds don't take you by surprise. Young birds just out of the nest may not be wearing the distinctive plumage of adult birds, but they are shaped just like the adults.

Spend a bit of time at home going over the sparrows in your field guide. This type of practice can really pay off in the field. Not only will you be more familiar with the field marks of the sparrows you encounter, you'll also be more familiar with where they appear in the field guide. This is important because most field guides are organized taxonomically, meaning that closely related bird species are grouped together. So a bird that looks much like a song sparrow might not be a song sparrow, but rather a close relative.

To find the field marks on your unfamiliar sparrow, start at the top of the bird's head and work downward and back toward the tail. As your eyes pass over the bird, make a mental note of the standout plumage, shape, and behavior characteristics. Are there crown stripes? What color are they? Is there an eye-ring or an eye line? Is there a necklace? Breast streaks or spots or an unstreaked breast? Wing bars? What color is the rump? You get the idea. By the time you've reached the end of the bird, you should have enough clues to reveal the bird's identity.

SPARROW SPOTTING

Pick a nice fall day and scour the sparrows in a weedy field to get more familiar with these confusing little birds. Observe them through your binoculars, but also with the naked eye to get a general idea of their behavior, shape, size, and habitat preference. Many times these general impressions will be your first, best clues to sparrow identification. Make note of these general impressions while you consider the more specific field marks and you'll learn a lot about these sparrows in a hurry.

As you became familiar with more sparrows, you'll acquire more "reference species," those birds that you can identify at a glance. As your number of reference species increases, the other sparrows will become increasingly easy to identify, because you'll have more known species with which to compare them.

When the ubiquitous LBJs appear, don't fret. The comparative approach will increase your chances of identifying sparrows in the field and help you feel comfortable with this challenging group of birds. ➤

SONGLIKE SPARROWS

Medium-sized, heavily streaked sparrows

FOR MANY OF US, THE SONG SPARROW IS THE DE FACTO sparrow; it is one of the most common and widespread birds in North America. Most of us feel confident identifying it, but other similar streaky sparrows can present more of a problem. When we see sparrows that don't quite fit the song sparrow profile, the head scratching commences, quickly gives way to a shrug of the shoulders, and ends with a philosophical, "It's just a funny-looking song sparrow, I guess." And maybe it is — but if it isn't, you just missed a new bird. Getting a handle on the other streaky sparrows just might transform the world of LBJs from a murky mystery to an interesting challenge.

AN OVERVIEW

The song sparrow's range extends from central Mexico north to the Aleutians, east to Newfoundland and south to Florida. It is common throughout the United States and most of Canada, so it is a good reference point from which to get to know the less common, or at least less familiar, sparrows in this motley crew. (See Basics of Sparrow ID, page 319.) The group as it is defined here includes song sparrow and the other two species in the genus *Melospiza*, swamp and Lincoln's sparrow. Savannah sparrow, vesper sparrow, and fox sparrow join the lineup of song sparrow–like sparrows, because they are similar in character, if not in genus.

Almost all the birds in the genus *Ammodramus* (with the exception of the grasshopper sparrow) have streaky breasts as well, but as a group they have different habits and body structure and they are not so widespread as the birds examined here (see page 334). One of the problems we face with our six species is that they really do look alike. The field guides point you in the right direction, but there can be no substitute for actual field experience, so practice on these sparrows whenever you have the opportunity to do so.

SONG SPARROW

The song sparrow is a medium-sized sparrow with a fairly stocky build. Its bill is medium-sized, and the breast and flanks are heavily streaked. Overall color varies regionally, but the same pattern is found throughout its range. The head is basically gray, with brown lateral crown stripes and a brown post-ocular stripe (behind the eye), which contrasts with the gray supercilium (the "eyebrow"). The throat is white and offset by very broad, dark, Fu Manchu–like throat stripes. The back, like the face, has a gray base color. Heavy dark brown or black streaks start at the base of the neck and go down the shoulders and back. The wings and tail are reddish brown.

Like many of these streaky sparrows, the song sparrow has a central breast spot, or "stickpin," in the middle of the breast where its coarse brown streaks converge. Because many other sparrows have this "stickpin" field mark, it's not particularly useful in the field. This bird's dark, contrasting pattern is ideal camouflage for the weedy understory habitat it prefers. Song sparrows are often found feeding on the ground, sometimes with other sparrows, hopping about with their tails held either horizontally or, when agitated, slightly cocked up. When flushed, they fly a bit more clumsily than most other sparrows, and they don't fly far — they typically head for the closest cover, be it a bush, a brush pile, or any other dense habitat.

Your first clue to a song sparrow's presence may be the musical *chimp-chimp* call notes it regularly gives. Song sparrows are hearty, persistent singers, and though their song is highly variable among individual birds, most descriptions of the song note two or three short introductory notes followed by a long trill and several bouncy notes at the end.

song sparrow

fox sparrow

Lincoln's
sparrow

Savannah
sparrow

swamp
sparrow

vesper
sparrow

SWAMP SPARROW

The other *Melospiza* sparrows — swamp and Lincoln's — are closest in shape and size to the song sparrow. Some birders say that the breeding-plumaged swamp sparrow is the most attractive of the three. It is slightly smaller than a song sparrow but can appear a little plumper. With rich chestnut and rufous tones to the crown, wings, and flanks that contrast beautifully with the bird's gray face and breast, it appears dark overall and is quite eye-catching. The swamp sparrow is the least streaky of all of these song sparrow–like sparrows. Its breast pattern varies with age and season, but differs from all the other sparrows in this group. Swamp sparrows have only faint, diffuse streaks on the chest (immatures and winter adults) or appear cleanly gray on the breast (breeding adults). They also show a more dramatic difference between breeding season and winter plumages than our other sparrows do. Swamp sparrows in the nonbreeding season look dingier and buffier as the crown becomes darker and less rufous. At all seasons, swamps show an unstreaked white throat and a clean gray patch on the nape and sides of the neck that lacks obvious streaking. This gray patch, combined with the breast pattern and the chestnut wings, makes the swamp sparrow fairly distinctive. As the name suggests, they prefer marshy, swampy areas or moist meadows. Compared to song sparrows, swamps are a bit shyer and more likely to skulk in thick cover.

The song of the swamp sparrow is a regular, repeated series of buzzy trills that seems to trail off before it ends.

SAVANNAH SPARROW

The Savannah sparrow is probably the most frequently encountered sparrow of these six species after the song sparrow. Superficially, the song and Savannah resemble one another. Both are medium-sized streaky sparrows, but the Savannah sparrow is smaller, with a shorter tail and a smaller bill. Almost all Savannah sparrows have at least some yellow in the lores (the area between the bill and the eyes) and a pale central crown stripe. Many bird watchers look for the yellow lores as confirmation that a mystery sparrow is a Savannah but many fall Savannahs do not have obviously yellow lores. Some Savannahs also show a dark central breast spot, increasing the potential for confusion with song sparrows. The streaking on the Savannah sparrow's breast is extensive and crisp and well-demarcated, neither as coarse as it is on a song sparrow, nor as fine as on the Lincoln's. Below the breast streaks, Savannahs have a white belly.

Savannah sparrows have different habits than the *Melospiza* sparrows, too. While the *Melospizas* prefer weedy areas with dense vegetation and plenty of cover, Savannah sparrows prefer more open expanses (as the name would seem to imply — they're actually named for Savannah, Georgia). They are found in fields, on tundra, and along open roadsides. When flushed, they are strong fliers. In winter and during migration, Savannah sparrows are found in loose flocks, and when they are spooked into flight, they often fly rather long distances before landing again. They also like to run along the ground and, when startled, will sometimes sit up on a shrub or stick before taking off. In this way, they can seem quite confiding.

LINCOLN'S SPARROW

Behaviorally, Lincoln's sparrow is similar to the other two *Melospiza* sparrows. They breed in moist, boggy habitats and enjoy weedy, brushy areas near water. More delicate-looking than song sparrow, Lincoln's has a slightly shorter tail and finer bill. It has a streaky breast like song sparrow, but the streaks on the Lincoln's are noticeably finer than the streaks on the other sparrows. The song sparrow's breast streaks look as though they were drawn on with a crayon, but the Lincoln's sparrow's look like they were made with a freshly sharpened pencil. Furthermore, the breast streaks on a song sparrow show against a pale white background; on a Lincoln's sparrow, they show against a buffy wash that extends across the chest and along the flanks. This buffy chest color also extends up into the Lincoln's cheeks, giving the bird an overall warmish tone. Compare the faces of a song sparrow and a Lincoln's sparrow, and you'll notice three differences on the Lincoln's face: a buffy malar stripe (the "mustache"), a buffy eye-ring, and an obvious gray supercilium. Again, the Lincoln's markings are finer and more delicate.

A mystery sparrow with a buffy eye-ring and a buffy breast finely streaked with black can hardly be anything but a Lincoln's.

VESPER SPARROW

The vesper sparrow is slightly bigger than the average song sparrow. Vesper sparrows have large heads and substantial-looking pale, pinkish bills.

In flight, they show white outer feathers on their longish tails. This juncolike flash of white in the tail is a great field mark for identifying this species after only a brief glimpse or from a distance. The chestnut brown shoulder patches that many field guides show are not always obvious on perched birds.

The vesper's head pattern also holds clues to its identity. All vesper sparrows have a white eye-ring, and although it is not bold, it does contrast clearly with the dark eye and dark cheek. A bold white malar stripe, or mustache, drops down from the vesper's lower mandible and is offset above and below by dark throat stripes. Vesper sparrows lack the boldly patterned forehead and eyebrow of the other song sparrow–like species. They are the palest and most nondescript overall — and that in itself is a good hint. Couple overall paleness with white outer tail feathers, and you can be sure you've found a vesper sparrow.

Habitat and behavior can be useful clues in deciding whether an unidentified sparrow is a vesper or a Savannah. Savannahs are birds of wide-open spaces and short grass fields; vespers prefer old pastures and weedy fencerows near a few scattered trees, which they perch in more readily than other grassland sparrows.

The vesper sparrow's song is long and sweetly musical. It is plaintive and seems to be sung in a minor key. It starts with two low whistles, and the trills that follow rise and fall in tone. The vesper sparrow sounds like a song sparrow that has taken professional voice lessons.

FOX SPARROW

The fox sparrow is the most distinctive sparrow of our bunch. It is the largest sparrow of the six — about a third larger than a song sparrow — with a big head and a thick, conical bill. Fox sparrows prefer moist woodlands and woodland edges in winter and migration, and wet deciduous thickets during the breeding season. Many bird watchers first encounter this bird during the winter, as it scratches towhee-style through the leaf litter or beneath a bird feeder.

There are four distinctive color morphs of fox sparrow (and all kinds of intermediate morphs where populations overlap and interbreed). At some point these morphs — red, sooty, slate-colored, and thick-billed — may be split into separate species.

Eastern or "red" fox sparrows are perhaps the most distinctive and are a rich chestnut overall, with contrasting pale gray in the face and on the back and rump. They are heavily streaked with chestnut on the breast, and their rich coloration and large size make them hard to confuse with anything else. Fox sparrows of the interior West and California (called "slate-colored") are grayer, particularly on the head and back, and the streaking on the breast and flanks is blackish. California birds (sometimes called "thick-billed" fox sparrows) have quite heavy, thick bills and finer breast streaking. The birds of the Pacific Northwest (known as "sooty" fox sparrows) are almost wholly dark gray-brown — uniformly so above, with heavy mottled streaking on the breast and belly. No matter which morph they are, all fox sparrows show a rusty tail.

The fox sparrow's large size and chunky body structure set it apart from all other sparrows. Its low-toned, rich, warbling song is reminiscent of the purple finch's — so reminiscent, in fact, that you might not think you are hearing a sparrow at all.

VARIATIONS WITHIN SPECIES

The song sparrow, fox sparrow, and Savannah sparrow are widespread, their ranges spanning much of the North American continent. As is often the case with such cosmopolitan birds, variation within populations exists. A song sparrow in Atlanta, Georgia, looks very different from one in Portland, Oregon. The various morphs of fox sparrows in particular are receiving a lot of attention these days, as we've learned. At one time, the Savannah sparrow was split into two species, but it is currently considered a single species. Researchers are in the process of determining whether it should again be split, perhaps this time into several species. With each of these birds, matters are quite simple in the East, with just one or a couple of different forms. In the West, the geography fragments populations more, and things get more complex. Several forms of each species may occur across a relatively small geographic area.

There are excellent references about the distinct sparrow populations and their subtle differences, and these subtleties are not as important for our purposes as learning the basic characteristics of each species. Familiarity is your best friend in sparrow identification. If you can come to know one or two species fairly well, when you see something different you'll be better prepared to recognize it. ➤

SPIZELLA SPARROWS

small, slender, and subtle

BUT STILL READILY IDENTIFIABLE

THE SPARROWS IN THE GENUS *SPIZELLA* ARE RATHER conspicuous and attractive, making them good place to start. Six species regularly breed in North America, but they are probably more often encountered during the winter, when we see them among loose multispecies flocks in brushy fields. *Spizella*s like open areas with some bushes and maybe a few scattered trees. Sometimes they forage on the ground for seeds, but many times we don't notice them at all until a group of them explodes out of the brush ahead of us on a dirt road or along a trail. Thin little *chips* accompany all this action, and suddenly we realize that we are the ones being watched.

When startled, these birds fly up to a higher vantage point to survey the scene and see what is causing the ruckus, and that's when we get our first good look at them. *Spizella* sparrows are quite small as sparrows go, delicate and slender, with small rounded heads and fine little conical bills. They are fairly long-tailed for their size and are generally elegant, handsome little birds. The black-chinned sparrow of the arid Southwest is unlikely to be confused with any other species, but the remaining five *Spizella* sparrows — American tree sparrow, field sparrow, chipping sparrow, clay-colored sparrow, and Brewer's sparrow — look rather similar to each other. When they are on territory and singing, as they are during the breeding season, they are quite easy to identify, but during winter and migration, things become more complicated. To simplify matters,

American tree sparrow
adult

Brewer's sparrow
adult, nonbreeding

field sparrow
adult

clay-colored sparrow
adult, breeding

chipping sparrow
adult,
nonbreeding

chipping sparrow
adult, breeding

the *Spizella*s can be broadly separated into two categories: those with reddish brown caps and those that are gray-brown overall.

THE RED-CAPPED SPECIES

American tree sparrow, field sparrow, and chipping sparrow fall into the red-capped category. The American tree sparrow breeds in the Far North and winters throughout most of the northern half of the United States.

The field sparrow is an eastern species and can be found in open brushy areas and second-growth habitats of the eastern and midwestern United States. One of the most widespread birds in North America is the chipping sparrow. It breeds in nearly every state in the United States, and in every province in Canada. Its song — a steady, long, rather dry trill — is a constant sound in spring and summer in many places. When these birds aren't singing, however, it is possible that a birder might mistake a "chippy" for another species. In breeding plumage, a chipping sparrow might be taken for either a field sparrow or an American tree sparrow, but there a number of characters that set each of these birds apart.

BILL COLOR

Close inspection of a breeding chipping sparrow reveals that it has an almost all- black bill. There may be a bit of paler gray visible at the base of the lower mandible, but the bill has a dark, blackish appearance overall. In contrast, the field sparrow has a wholly pink bill. The tree sparrow falls in between chipping and field; its bill is bicolored. The upper mandible is dark, and the lower mandible is mostly a pale horn color. When you have a red-capped *Spizella* and you can get a good look at the bill, there may be little else you need to see to achieve a positive identification, but there are still other differences worth noting.

HEAD AND BREAST PATTERN

To solidify your identification, or if you can't see the bill color and pattern, it is worth trying to assess the pattern (or lack of it) on the head and breast of the bird. Chipping sparrow is evenly pale gray below, but the head pattern is quite contrasting. The red-brown cap has a black border above a broad whitish supercilium. Offsetting the supercilium is a very dark, blackish eye line that runs from the bill through the eye to the rear of the crown. This head pattern is quite different from field or American tree sparrows'.

Field sparrows are plain-faced compared to the other two. Rather than the distinctive rufous, black, and white of the chipping sparrow, the field sparrow's head is a study in muted rust and gray, with a white eye-ring that gives it a blank look. Field sparrows also have a warm-buff wash on the breast and flanks.

Largest of the three, the American tree sparrow's rich rusty cap and rusty eye line jump out at the observer, and a closer look reveals its two-tone bill. Spot the "stickpin" — a dark central spot on its clean grayish breast — and you've nailed the tree sparrow's identification.

THE GRAY-BROWN SPECIES

On their breeding grounds, clay-colored, Brewer's, and chipping (yes, chippies belong to both red-capped and gray-brown groups) sparrows are fairly easily separated by range, habitat, and voice. Off-season, though, they look very similar and may be in mixed flocks with several other species. Here's what to look for in winter.

CHIPPING SPARROWS REVISITED

The fall and winter plumage of chipping sparrows is dramatically different from their breeding plumage. And in this nonbreeding plumage, the chipping sparrow is hard to separate from the clay-colored sparrow. The chippy's reddish cap fades to dull brown streaked with black. The black bill pales to gray-brown. The dark eye line remains strong, however, extending into the lores. Rump color is hard to see but is perhaps the best character for distinguishing chipping sparrows from these other birds in winter. The rump is gray on chipping sparrow at all seasons, but is brown on both Brewer's and clay-colored sparrow.

BREWER'S SPARROW

The Brewer's sparrow is the smallest sparrow in North America, but its relative size is not always obvious. Perhaps the most noticeable thing about a Brewer's sparrow is that there is not much noticeable about it — Brewer's sparrows elevate the term "nondescript" to new heights. This ambiguous appearance, however, is in itself quite a good character and can be a good starting point. Compared to the other gray-brown *Spizella* sparrows, the Brewer's is plain-faced. The crown is pale brown, streaked with darker brown, though this central crown stripe (if visible at all) is only poorly defined. The supercilium is better defined than the crown stripe, and a darker brown eye line offsets it slightly. A good view of a Brewer's sparrow should reveal a white eye-ring. The overall dull appearance, the lack of an obvious central crown stripe, the small bill, the plain face, and the white eye-ring are the strongest characters for distinguishing this species.

CLAY-COLORED SPARROW

There are times when Brewer's and clay-colored sparrows are so close in appearance that they really are indistinguishable. These times are fairly rare, however, and most individuals are easily identified, provided they cooperate. At first glance, the clay-colored sparrow might seem as boring and nondescript as Brewer's, but look more closely and you'll see a pretty well marked bird. With their combination of peachy buff, straw yellow, and darker shades of gray and brown, clay-coloreds are really quite handsome. In nonbreeding plumage, most clay-colored sparrows show a nice warm, peachy buff color on the breast and flanks that contrasts slightly with a whiter belly. The head pattern is complex and contrasting, especially when compared with a Brewer's sparrow. Clay-colored sports a white malar stripe that is offset by dark lateral throat stripes, and there is a distinct dark border to the lower edge of the cheek. Finally, all clay-colored sparrows show a nice patch of clean clay gray on the sides and back of the neck. This gray neck collar combined with the bold supercilium and malar stripe, differentiate the clay-colored sparrow from the other *Spizella* sparrows.

Overall, *Spizella* sparrows are a challenge, especially away from the breeding grounds. It takes an initial investment of time to learn how to look at them in the ways that make identification possible. Focus on the birds' bill and head and breast patterns, and try to learn their call notes. Always try to keep in mind the size of the bird. The differences in size between species may seem subtle at first, but they become more apparent when you have a flock of birds to sort through. More than anything else, patience is required, because it can be hard to obtain good views. Not even the best field birders can identify every bird. The key is to take your time and to take advantage of cooperative members of these *Spizella* species when and where you find them. ➤

AMMODRAMUS SPARROWS

Flat heads, short tails, buzzy songs, hard to find

IF YOU ARE LUCKY ENOUGH TO ENCOUNTER ONE OF THE chunky, flat-headed sparrows of the genus *Ammodramus*, chances are you're in a grassland or grassy saltmarsh habitat. In the United States and Canada we have seven separate *Ammodramus* sparrow species: Baird's sparrow, grasshopper sparrow, Henslow's sparrow, Le Conte's sparrow, saltmarsh sharp-tailed sparrow, Nelson's sharp-tailed sparrow, and seaside sparrow. If you've glanced at the illustrations or photographs of these sparrows in your favorite field guide you might have noticed that they all have very streaky backs, relatively flat heads, and several of them might even be called colorful — for sparrows, that is.

To call these sparrows secretive is an understatement. All seven *Ammodramus* sparrows are elusive skulkers that mostly prefer to remain hidden rather than give a bird watcher a honest-to-goodness look. They thrive in thick grassy cover. They almost never perch in the open, unless they are engaged in territorial or courtship singing. Though they may breed closely together in small pieces of appropriate habitat, they are rarely found in flocks — even in winter — as are many other sparrows. If you flush an *Ammodramus* sparrow from cover, you may get almost no view of it. They tend to pop up and drop back down into thick cover rather than fly a long distance. They may even run on the ground to escape danger rather than flush into the air.

The songs of these sparrows really do not deserve to be called songs. They are described as insectlike, buzzy, hissing, and wheezy—not exactly adjectives used in music. Yet song is an important component of knowing these sparrows better and identifying them. If you do not live within the breeding range of one or more of these sparrows, chances are you may not be able to learn their songs. But if you ever go looking for any of the *Ammodramus* sparrows, or if you encounter them singing during spring migration, you'll find it's handy to have a reference set of birdsong recordings to which you can listen.

SEVEN MINUS THREE

Until recently the Nelson's sharp-tailed sparrow and saltmarsh sharp-tailed sparrow were considered one species—the sharp-tailed sparrow, named for its spiky tail feather tips. Field research and DNA studies revealed two separate species, one strictly found along the Atlantic Coast from Maine to Virginia (saltmarsh sharp-tailed) and one breeding coastally in Maine and northward, and inland on the northern Great Plains (Nelson's sharp-tailed sparrow).

Although all of the *Ammodramus* sparrows are superficially similar in appearance, a few are very similar and a few are not. Three of these birds are found in such specific habitat or within such a limited breeding range that they can be eliminated from full examination in this chapter.

SALTY SPARROWS

The seaside sparrow and saltmarsh sharp-tailed sparrow are birds of coastal saltmarsh habitat. Although it's possible that you might encounter both Nelson's sharp-tailed sparrow and saltmarsh sharp-tailed sparrow in winter, you are more likely to encounter both saltmarsh sharp-tailed sparrow and seaside sparrow.

Seaside sparrow is such a large, dark, large-billed bird and so utterly tied to coastal saltmarshes that you are unlikely to confuse it with anything else when given a good look. Its song and call are sufficiently harsh and loud that its vocalizations have been compared to the song of the red-winged blackbird in tone and pattern.

Saltmarsh sharp-tailed sparrow is similar in appearance to the Nelson's sharp-tailed sparrow. The keys to telling them apart lie in the salt-

grasshopper sparrow

Henslow's sparrow

Le Conte's sparrow

Nelson's sharp-tailed sparrow

marsh's paler breast and larger bill and the Nelson's more brightly colored face. Season, location, and likelihood may be your best guides at separating these two sharp-tailed sparrows.

THE RARELY SEEN BAIRD'S

The Baird's sparrow is perhaps the least visually distinctive of all the *Ammodramus* sparrows and it certainly has the smallest breeding range—a kidney-shaped area of remote dry grassland in the western Dakotas and Montana extending into the southern Great Plains in Canada. Most birders seeking Baird's sparrow must make a special trip to North or South Dakota to find this bird. Because it's so rare, we won't spend more time on it here.

THE REST OF THE AMMOS

The rest of the *Ammodramus* sparrows (grasshopper, Le Conte's, Henslow's, and Nelson's sharp-tailed sparrow) are more widely distributed (at all seasons), more often encountered, and more easily confused by birders in the field.

The one non-*Ammodramus* sparrow you need to bear in mind at all times is the Savannah sparrow (which was once considered an *Ammodramus* sparrow). More than one experienced birder has struggled to discern a pale Savannah sparrow from a Henslow's or grasshopper. Like these two *Ammos*, the Savannah is found in grassland habitat and sings a buzzy, insectlike song (see page 324).

GRASSHOPPER SPARROW

During spring and summer breeding season the grasshopper sparrow lives up to its name by singing its *tik, tik tiksseeeeeeeeeeez* song in tall, dense grasslands and dry grassy fields across much of the United States. Of all the U.S. states, only Utah and Arizona lack breeding grasshopper sparrows. It is this insectlike song that is your best clue to a grasshopper sparrow's presence, but many birders miss this fairly common bird because its song can easily be ignored as insect noise.

As a young birder I was told that the grasshopper sparrow has a flat head and a long bill. To remember this I told myself that the grasshopper sparrow's head had been squeezed (making it flatter) and the bill was forced out longer. It's silly, I know, but I've always remembered it.

GRASSHOPPER VERSUS HENSLOW'S AND OTHERS

The most notable visual clues to a grasshopper sparrow's identity (after the flat head) are the plainish, buffy face, the unstreaked breast, and the finely patterned nape. The plain face of the grasshopper sparrow has a few subtle clues. Among these are a slight white eye-ring, a buffy-orange supraloral spot between the eye and the bill and no malar stripes (both Baird's and Henslow's sparrows have obvious dark stripes on the sides of the throat). Like other sparrows, the grasshopper can show lots of variation among individuals, so relying utterly on just one field mark is a mistake.

Other grassland sparrows show some breast streaks, but the adult grasshopper has an unstreaked, buffy breast. If you see a grassland sparrow that is perched, but not singing, check the breast. If it is plain and pale (and the bird is flat-headed), it's probably a grasshopper sparrow.

The nape of the grasshopper's neck is where the fine streaking is located. Though these streaks are described as every color from pink to rufous, the main point is that they are fine, not coarse, streaks set on a gray background.

HENSLOW'S SPARROW

The Henslow's sparrow is much less common and less widely distributed than the grasshopper sparrow, but the two can be found in similar habitat — fields with tall grasses — across much of the upper Midwest. Henslow's sparrows seem to tolerate slightly brushier habitat than do grasshoppers, and although both species seem to be declining, the Henslow's is declining faster — almost to the point of becoming a localized rarity across its range. Many states have started grassland bird surveys in response to the rapid decline of this and other grassland species.

Your best chance at finding and identifying a Henslow's sparrow is to place yourself in the appropriate habitat and listen for the its very unbirdlike song: *tis-slik!* Often sung from a perch even with, or only slightly above, the tops of the grasses, the song of the Henslow's can easily be dismissed as insect noise by the unwary listener. Once you tune into the Henslow's "song" you'll be alert to the presence of this quite shy and special sparrow.

HENSLOW'S VERSUS GRASSHOPPER

Sharing the flat-headed, heavy-billed look with the grasshopper sparrow, the Henslow's also has a white eye-ring. But the similarities end there. An olive-green wash covers the face, head, and nape of the Henslow's sparrow, giving it a dark-headed appearance. Just below the Henslow's plain white throat, offset by dark throat stripes, is a band of fine dark streaks on a buffy breast. These streaks extend down the bird's flanks on either side of the white belly. The back and wings are a boldly patterned mix of rust and black, with white feather edges.

Overall the Henslow's gives a first impression of being olive-headed and rusty-backed, visual clues that can help clinch an identification on distant, obscured, or briefly seen birds. You may be puzzled by the phrase "briefly seen." A Henslow's sparrow spooked from cover flies for a few seconds low over the grasses in a weak, jerky flight, and drops back out of sight. This may be your only look — was it good enough? Your next option is to wait for the bird to tee-up on a perch for its next bout of "singing."

The Henslow's sparrow breeds in weedy fields of the eastern United States and winters in similar habitats in the Southeast, from South Carolina down to Florida and west as far as eastern Texas. But if you think this sparrow is hard to find in its breeding range, looking for it during winter, when it is not singing, can be a fool's errand. Do your looking when the Henslow's is doing what passes for singing and you may be rewarded.

LE CONTE'S SPARROW

There are two birds in North America associated with the name Le Conte: a thrasher and a sparrow. Both are named for Dr. John Le Conte. I'll bet you did not know this, but the Le Conte's thrasher is named for a different Dr. John Le Conte than the sparrow. Dr. "Thrasher" Le Conte and Dr. "Sparrow" Le Conte were cousins, and, ironically, both men were scientists with only a marginal interest in birds. Most of today's bird watchers know the Le Conte's sparrow as a bird of the northern prairie marshes of Wisconsin, Minnesota, and the Dakotas, and as a prized wintering bird in wet meadows, fields, and marshes of the Southeast.

Even though the Le Conte's sparrow is five inches long — the same length as most of our other *Ammodramus* sparrows — it is usually described as "small." Perhaps this is because the Le Conte's has a comparatively small bill or because it is even more secretive and soft-spoken than its close relatives. One thing many bird watchers agree on: the Le Conte's is one of our most beautiful sparrows.

I first heard the song of the Le Conte's sparrow on a field trip to North Dakota, after years of wondering if I'd ever encounter the bird. The song struck me as reminiscent of the sound an old rotary dial phone makes as you dial the number and the wheel spins back to its original position: *tik tik tssshhhhhhhhhhkttt*. I mentioned this to my birding companions and one of them, too young to have ever used a rotary phone, said, "It sounds to me like it's making copies on a cheap photocopier." Fair enough. The song is fairly high in pitch and soft enough that it's hard to hear on a windy day. Fortunately the Le Conte's also sings at dusk and even at night, after the day's wind has died down. But I warn you, unless you want to donate a quart of blood to the mosquitoes that share this bird's preferred habitat, take insect-repelling precautions.

LE CONTE'S VERSUS GRASSHOPPER

The colorful face of the Le Conte's sparrow is surely its most pleasing visual field mark. A buff-orange face surrounds a gray cheek. The top of the head has a white central crown stripe offset by two wider dark stripes, similar to the crown on a grasshopper sparrow. Note that the grasshopper's face is plain and pale by comparison. Overall the Le Conte's sparrow is a much more colorful bird. Still there are times when I see a fresh-plumaged grasshopper sparrow and my blood pressure starts to rise at the prospect of seeing the much rarer Le Conte's.

Some additional clues to identifying this sparrow include the distinct black streaks on the sides of the breast. The adult grasshopper sparrow lacks these. The equally colorful Nelson's sharp-tailed sparrow is found in similar habitat to the Le Conte's, but the Nelson's has an all-dark crown with a gray (not white) central crown stripe.

We may be confused about which Dr. Le Conte this fine sparrow is named for, but if you bear these field marks in mind, get in the right habitat, and have a bit of luck, you'll know for certain when you encounter Le Conte's sparrow.

NELSON'S SHARP-TAILED SPARROW

"Check the wetlands with blackgrass and listen carefully. That's where the Nelson's are!" And with those words of advice from a North Dakota birder we went on a quest to find what many consider to be North America's most beautiful sparrow, the Nelson's sharp-tailed sparrow. Why is it considered so beautiful? I think it's the blend of color — rich ochre, rufous, gray, white, and black. But the Nelson's elusive nature certainly adds to its cachet among bird watchers.

NELSON'S VERSUS LE CONTE'S

Among the *Ammodramus* sparrows, only the Le Conte's compares in richness of color. The closely related saltmarsh sharp-tailed sparrow is

nearly as striking, but has a whiter chest with heavier streaks compared with the warm-buffy, finely streaked breast of the Nelson's.

Inland-breeding (or interior) Nelson's sharp-tailed sparrows are warm-toned overall with bright ochre-orange faces and breasts. The gray cheek patch and nape stand out against these orange areas. Below the finely streaked buff-orange breast is a white belly. The Nelson's back is similar in color and pattern to the Le Conte's sparrow, except for the Nelson's unstreaked gray nape.

Telling a Nelson's sharp-tailed sparrow from a Le Conte's sparrow requires looking at the crown, nape, and back. The Nelson's has a gray central crown stripe (the Le Conte's central crown stripe is white) on a dark crown, and an unstreaked gray nape (the Le Conte's nape is finely streaked). The interior population of the Nelson's also has two obvious white streaks on its dark brown back. Even the songs of these two sparrows are similar, but the long hiss of the Nelson's lacks the sharp introductory notes. Nelson's song can be transcribed as *plk-shhhhhhhh-tsh* ending on a lower note and sounding like someone softly releasing a bit of steam from a radiator.

NELSON'S SHARP-TAILED VERSUS SALTMARSH SHARP-TAILED

Because ornithologists saw fit to separate the sharp-tailed sparrow into two species (the Nelson's sharp-tailed and the saltmarsh sharp-tailed sparrows) birders can now drive themselves nuts when they encounter a sharp-tailed-type sparrow on marshes along the northernmost Atlantic coast or in winter along the Atlantic coast from Virginia to Florida. Both sharp-tailed species occur in these areas, and telling them apart is a matter of deciding whether the chest is buffy and lightly streaked (Nelson's) or white and heavily streaked (saltmarsh). Field guides point to the Nelson's shorter bill and more clearly defined white belly — field marks which would truly be useful if the birds would cooperate by always perching side-by-side. The northeastern-coastal-nesting Nelson's are much duller overall than the inland-nesting Nelson's — even to the point of being less colorful than the saltmarsh sharp-taileds — which helps separate them from the saltmarsh sharp-taileds, at least during breeding season.

The inland population of Nelson's sharp-tailed sparrow nests in prairie wetlands across much of the Canadian Great Plains, reaching far to the north. The heart of the United States nesting range is in North Dakota, but it also includes parts of South Dakota and northwesternmost Minnesota. In migration the Nelson's can be found along the Central Flyway. Perhaps the most reliable shot at seeing them away from their breeding range is in the coastal marshes and wet fields along the Gulf Coast from Texas to Florida and along the southern Atlantic Coast from Maryland to Florida, where they spend the winter.

We were lucky in our quest, finding two singing male Nelson's in a blackgrass marsh, right where they were supposed to be.

A FINAL NOTE

The *Ammodramus* sparrows are a little like space aliens — hard to find, rarely seen well, and perhaps easily overlooked when they are present. As with other sparrow identification challenges, you'll be ahead of the game if you familiarize yourself with the field marks and song of one of the species in the group — grasshopper sparrow is a good choice. Then, when you find a bird that you don't know, an alarm will go off in the birding lobe of your brain and you'll summon all your powers of observation. Perhaps you'll become so fascinated with the *Ammo*s that you'll make a summer trip to the rare sparrow breeding region of the north-central Great Plains. For several years running I've done an annual visit to central North Dakota and the total-immersion approach to learning these sneaky sparrows is definitely helpful. And yet the birds are so spottily distributed and secretive that it's a new challenge every year to locate them. But that, after all, is what makes bird watching such fun. ✈

CROWNED SPARROWS

Members of the genus Zonotrichia

BIG, BOLD, BEAUTIFUL SPARROWS

THE BRUSHY THICKETS AND WEEDY AREAS OF THE NORTH American continent are home to the *Zonotrichia* sparrows. Sometimes referred to as the "crowned sparrows," these birds are found most often between fall and spring in backyards, brushy fields, parks, and woodland edges. The crowned sparrows have a habit very helpful to bird watchers — they vocalize frequently, and in all seasons. They consistently announce themselves, often while concealed from view, with thin *seet* notes or hard, sharp metallic *chips*, and often with full songs. Leaf litter rustles as they scratch for food. We may not see them right away but a little *pishing* will often pique the birds' curiosity and bring them into view. These are fussy, curious birds and that is part of their charm.

The crowned sparrows are handsome as well. Not content to lurk among the LBJs, they sport attractive head patterns and give bold songs that proudly proclaim their presence. Among this group we have such beauties as Harris's sparrow, golden-crowned sparrow, white-throated sparrow, and white-crowned sparrow. They are not just good-looking, either; they also are large as sparrows go. For the most part, adults of these species are easily distinguished. The difficulty comes when a youngster from within this group is encountered for the first time.

white-crowned
sparrow
first-winter immature

white-crowned
sparrow
breeding adult

white-throated
sparrow
first-winter immature

white-throated
sparrow
breeding adult

golden-crowned
sparrow
first-winter immature

golden-crowned
sparrow
breeding adult

Harris's sparrow
first-winter immature

Harris's
sparrow
breeding adult

Immature golden-crowned sparrows lack their namesake character; immature white-crowned sparrows are anything but. What now? Just another Little Brown Job? We can do better than that.

WHITE-CROWNED SPARROW

The most widespread sparrow in this group is the white-crowned sparrow. It breeds from the Arctic willow thickets of Alaska and Canada south into the Rockies and along the Pacific coast. In winter, it prefers weedy areas and is found throughout most of the United States. White-crowned sparrows prefer more open habitat than the other crowned sparrows do. This habitat preference means that white-crowneds are often quite conspicuous; they can be seen boldly perching on top of a shrub and singing at any time of year.

Their most noticeable field mark is head pattern, which on adults is a series of alternating black and white stripes. The cheeks, sides of the neck, and the upper breast are a pale gray or grayish brown, and the flanks are darker brown. The bill is pale, ranging from pinkish to yellowish. Structurally, the white-crowned sparrow is rather long for a crowned sparrow, and it often looks more slender and long-tailed overall. Immature birds are the cause of the most confusion, but they, too, are distinctive. They have a buffy background color to the head and neck, and they have chocolate brown and buff head stripes, rather than the black and white stripes of the adult.

In any plumage, white-crowned sparrows look clean and neat, especially compared to the uneven color and blurry streaking often seen on white-throated sparrows, which often flock with white-crowneds. White-crowneds stand tall and erect, with their crowns often raised and puffed up. With their regal carriage and well-groomed looks, white-crowned sparrows stand out from others in a mixed sparrow flock.

The song of the white-crowned sparrow is a series of clear whistles, buzzes, and trills; it is not as easily transcribed as some other sparrow songs are. Overall, it has a melancholy, minor tone. One birder I know says the white-crowned song sounds like *I gotta go wee-wee now!* This is certainly memorable, if not quite appropriate for sharing with your fellow birders.

WHITE-THROATED SPARROW

The white-throated sparrow nests in mixed woodlands from central western Canada east through New England and Newfoundland. It is widespread and common in the winter throughout most of the eastern United States and locally common west to southeastern Arizona. A few of them also winter along the Pacific coast. This bird is largely absent from the interior western United States, except during migration. It prefers brushy fields, woodland edges, and hedgerows.

There are three things that most bird watchers remember about the white-throated sparrow: its white throat (often combined with white crown stripes); its yellow lores; and its song, which is usually transcribed as *old Sam Peabody, Peabody, Peabody.* (If you live north of the United States border, the white-throated sparrow sings *oh sweet Canada, Canada, Canada.*)

White-throated sparrows appear plump or squat compared to the other crowned sparrows. Adults have well-defined white throats, and their crown stripes come in two flavors: white and tan. It was originally thought the tan-striped birds were immatures, but research has revealed that they are actually a color variation present in adults of both sexes. Both tan-striped and white-striped adults show a variable yellow lore spot, but this tends to be brighter and more noticeable in the white-striped individuals. All white-throateds have quite a bit of chestnut brown in the wing and a pair of pale wing bars. The species' upper breast is gray, becoming paler toward the belly, and browner and streakier toward the flanks.

All ages and color morphs of white-throated sparrow have two field marks: some white on the throat, and a gun-metal gray bill. Breeding-plumaged and winter adults are similar in appearance, though they are more crisply patterned during the breeding season. First-winter birds are less distinctive; they appear similar to adults in structure, but lack the well-defined white crown stripes (making them similar in appearance to tan-striped adults, but juvenile birds usually appear more streaky on the breast and darker overall than tan-striped adults). First-winter white-throated sparrows always show a white throat, gray bill, and hint of the yellow lores. These marks help to separate them from young white-crowneds and golden-crowneds.

Potential identification confusion can occur when an over-eager birder sees the bright white crown stripes on an adult white-throated sparrow and mistakenly calls it a white-crowned sparrow. When you see bright white crown stripes, check the bird's throat. If the throat is white, you'll know you've got a white-throated sparrow. If the throat is gray, you've got a white-crowned. Bill color is another clue — white-throateds always have a gray bill, while white-crowneds' bills are pinkish or yellow.

GOLDEN-CROWNED SPARROW

The golden-crowned sparrow is a bird of the westernmost portions of North America. This large plain-faced sparrow breeds in willow and alder thickets from central and western Alaska south along the West Coast into northern Washington State. It migrates to spend winter farther south, from southwestern British Columbia to Baja, California, in thickets and weedy areas. Many birders describe the song of the golden-crowned sparrow as *oh dear meee*; the species may sing at any time of year.

Adult golden-crowneds have a lovely mustard yellow spot in the middle of the crown, surrounded by broad black lateral crown stripes. The cheeks and sides of the neck are a clean and even gray; the throat is paler. The bill is bicolored gray with a darker upper mandible. Breeding adults are more crisply marked and brightly colored than winter adults.

First-winter golden-crowneds are nondescript and definitely pose an identification challenge. They do have a hint of yellow on the crown, just above the bill, but it can be hard to see and is nearly absent on some birds. The face is a rather plain gray-brown and is darker above the eye, but it offers little pattern — only a faint dark line behind the eye. This rather nondescript appearance (lacking any obvious field marks) is actually quite a good clue to help distinguish this bird from the others in the group.

HARRIS'S SPARROW

Harris's sparrow is probably the least frequently encountered of these four crowned sparrows. It breeds in the spruce forests of central and northern Canada and winters in weedy fields and woodland edges in the Great Plains. Harris's sparrow is the largest species in this group — in fact it is the largest of all our sparrow species, being a quarter-inch larger than a fox sparrow. Its robust size and wholly pink bill (present on all ages and in all plumages) make this bird stick out from its peers.

Adults exhibit extensive black on the crown, throat, and upper breast, making the bird strikingly distinctive. Breeding adults show a gray ground color on the face that becomes a buffy straw in the winter. First-winter Harris's sparrows share this buffy-brown head color. These young birds lack the extensive black present on the forehead, face, throat, and breast of adults and instead show just a suggestion of the head pattern they will acquire in their first spring. The underparts are white, as they are on all Harris's sparrows, with a bit of dark streaking along the flanks. The combination of the white underparts, the pink bill, and the large size distinguishes Harris's sparrows of any age from all other sparrows.

Like the other members of the crowned sparrow clan, the Harris's sparrow is a very vocal species. The song, which is similar in quality to the white-throated's, is two or three *seeeee* notes on the same pitch. Winter flocks of Harris's sparrows create quite a ruckus with a variety of buzzy call notes and short whistled phrases.

OTHER SIMILARITIES AND DIFFERENCES

All the crowned sparrows share a similar back and wing pattern. The upper back is a combination of black, brown, and tan streaks. The lower back and rump are unstreaked and gray-brown in color. All of the crowned sparrows show twin white wing bars that contrast sharply against the otherwise brown and black wings. The white-crowned, golden-crowned, and white-throated sparrows all sport plain grayish breasts and bellies — only the Harris's sparrow is bright white on the belly.

As adults, most of the birds in this group are easily identified at any season. First-winter birds have less crisp and obvious patterns but are still easily separated by the head pattern, bill color, and the bird's overall size.

We often flush members of the crowned sparrow clan from the ground amid the weeds when they are feeding. Range and the subtle differences in habitat choice can provide an observer with good clues as to which bird they have just seen. It would be a lucky day indeed to encounter all four crowned sparrows in the field, as their normal distribution makes this highly unlikely. Still, when you are combing through a winter flock of crowned sparrows, don't rule out the possibility that an unlikely visitor from far away may be present. Sorting through the rustling grasses, you may be lucky enough to scratch up a real prize. ➳

FEMALE BLACKBIRDS

Underappreciated and

SOMETIMES UNWANTED, BUT NOT UNIDENTIFIABLE

JUST WHAT IS A BLACKBIRD? USING COMMON SENSE here leads you into trouble, not out of it. A simple rule like, "blackbirds are birds that are black," means grouping forms as disparate as grackles, anis, and ravens, a taxonomic travesty differing only in degree from trying to shoehorn ivory gulls, snowy egrets, and trumpeter swans into an order called "whitebirds."

On the other hand, the ornithologist's answer — that New World blackbirds are members of the family Icteridae — seems confusingly inclusive, taking in not only species actually called "blackbird," but also grackles, cowbirds, and the bobolink. And it doesn't stop there — orioles and meadowlarks are also, on a genetic level at least, very much blackbirds. And no one needs to be told how to tell grackles from meadowlarks.

In order to address real-world identification issues, we'll focus on just four female Icterids, only two of which are actually blackish: red-winged, Brewer's, and rusty blackbirds, and common grackle.

As they say on *Sesame Street*, "One of these things is not like the others," and certainly the red-winged blackbird, with its prominent streaking above and below, is the odd bird out. But female red-winged blackbirds are the source of more "mystery bird" questions than almost any other bird. They can be seen and studied almost everywhere in the lower forty-eight, and, during the breeding season at least, in much of Canada. So they give us a good place to start.

Female blackbirds

red-winged
blackbird

rusty blackbird

Brewer's
blackbird

common
grackle

RED-WINGED BLACKBIRD

Heavily streaked and obviously smaller than males, female red-wingeds may seem more akin to sparrows than to blackbirds. Even worse, red-wingeds often occur in single-sex flocks; without the giveaway males around, many novice birders conclude that the females are some sort of large sparrow — but no sparrow in the field guide looks quite right.

If only we all learned to look at bills first. The shape of a bird's bill is in most cases the least mutable and most telling clue to its true identity. If you can mentally erase the distracting patterns of those big "sparrows," you will immediately be struck by their lengthy, spikelike bills. (Not struck physically, I hope, as bills that long and sharp might really hurt.)

Such attention to bill structure would not only solve the mystery of the female red-winged, but also make plain the kinship of all the Icterids. Look at the bill on a Baltimore oriole or either of the meadowlarks, and you'll see that they are all quite similar. Even the shorter, more finchlike bills of cowbirds and bobolink belie their family heritage when examined closely.

So the main identification problem posed by female red-wingeds is realizing that they are, in fact, blackbirds. Once you've got that, it's pretty straightforward — they're heavily streaked below, across their entire underparts. Only the female tricolored blackbird is as uniformly striped across the breast and underparts as the female red-winged. But the tricolored inhabits a fairly narrow band along the Pacific Coast and doesn't seem to wander much. If you do need to convince yourself that you haven't stumbled across a female tricolored, begin by looking at the back. If the back is a cold gray black, you've got a candidate that merits further investigation. If the back feathers are at all edged with rufous or warm brown tones, you're looking at a red-winged.

COMMON GRACKLE

The red-winged blackbird exhibits a high degree of sexual dimorphism, as do many of our blackbirds. The common grackle, however, wears a more unisex look, like the meadowlarks and some orioles.

Compared to male common grackles, the female common grackle's significantly smaller size and less obviously keeled tail might tempt you to conclude that you are looking at a male rusty or Brewer's blackbird.

> *Pay attention to those grackles. Really look at them, instead of mentally sifting them out as chaff.*

But common grackles always have bills that are both longer and heavier than either of those species. The common grackle's tail is also longer, both in absolute length and in proportion to its body size.

Even though they don't pose a particularly difficult identification challenge, common grackles do provide those of us who live where they are common a handy point of reference for identifying more unusual species. If you happen to live in a place where the Brewer's blackbird is abundant and common grackle is rare, then study Brewer's.

There is no better preparation for finding rare birds than having a good working knowledge of common species in your area. So pay attention to those grackles. Really look at them, instead of mentally sifting them out as chaff.

BREWER'S AND RUSTY BLACKBIRDS

Brewer's and rusty blackbirds are an interesting pair. Their physical and behavioral traits coincide and contrast in some surprising ways. Both species look a bit like small grackles, but they are given their own genus, *Euphagus*.

Brewer's, basically a bird of open country in western and central North America, has shown classic blackbird resourcefulness by learning to thrive not only in agricultural settings, but also in urban ones. It's not uncommon to see Brewer's blackbirds foraging in parking lots and along sidewalks, and the species appears to be increasing in population and expanding its range eastward.

The rusty is primarily a bird of wet eastern woodlands in winter. It migrates north and west to breed all the way from Newfoundland to the Bering Sea. Though its relatively unpopulated breeding habitat appears fairly secure, the species has been declining. It has shown little or no tendency to diversify in its foraging habits and sticks to flipping wet leaves in search of aquatic insects.

We generally expect the breeding plumage of adult male birds to be the most distinctive for that species — a kind of flagship if you will — while breeding-plumaged females and nonbreeding individuals of both sexes appear more anonymous and cryptic. Brewer's and rusty blackbirds nearly stand this system on its head. The iridescent males are very similar to each other indeed, but the females are usually quite distinctive. Both sexes are generally easiest to diagnose in winter, not summer. The name of the rusty blackbird reflects this unusual state of affairs. Females, juveniles, and winter males display rich brown tones in varying degrees, whereas the male's breeding plumage lacks them entirely.

Rusty versus Brewer's is also a case in which looking at pictures of the birds in a field guide might lead one to conclude that their identification is tougher than it turns out to be in actual practice. Range, habitat, and behavior provide big clues most of the time. You could oversimplify by saying, "In the open, Brewer's; in the woods, rusty," and most of the time, you'd be right.

I'd recommend letting your eye go where it naturally goes first — to the bird's eye. The iris color can tell you a lot.

But let's ponder a lone bird stripped of contextual clues. What do we do?

EYE THE EYES

Let your eye go where it naturally goes first — to the bird's eye. The iris color can tell you a lot. Typical adult female Brewer's have dark eyes; most rusty blackbirds show bright golden yellow eyes.

How do we avoid mistaking the odd yellow-eyed female Brewer's, or

red-winged
blackbird

rusty blackbird

Brewer's
blackbird

common grackle

what if we are not entirely sure that we are looking at a female in the first place? Remember, rusty scaling anywhere on the body, or an overall warm brown tone to the underparts, tells us we have a rusty blackbird. The most critical place to check for this is on the edges of the inner secondaries, often called the tertials. These three feathers, useful in the identification of many birds, cover the lower back–upper rump area on a perched bird and are often fairly easy to see. While you're looking in that general area, note that adult female rusties have a gray rump that contrasts with their browner backs.

OTHER CLUES

Another character to check is the face pattern. The rusty blackbird generally shows a triangular dark area around the eye, setting off its pale buff superciliary, or eyebrow, and giving it a masked look. The Brewer's has a more diffuse, less contrasty face.

Finally, Brewer's have proportionately longer tails, wings, and legs, and tend to walk fairly upright, giving them a more trim appearance than the more powerful, plump-looking rusty.

When a flock of blackbirds descends on your feeders, treat yourself to the pleasure of looking each bird over carefully. This is how avid birders get those rare vagrants on their life lists and onto the rare bird alerts. Looking at the females in winter blackbird flocks can help you pick out species that you might otherwise overlook, and it can sharpen your identification skills at the same time. ➤

FEMALE ORIOLES

These colorful gals are really worth knowing.

ORIOLES ARE A GROUP OF BIRDS YOU CAN KEEP COMING back to, because they present a variety of identification challenges for birders at every level of experience. The adult males are among the most brilliantly colored birds anywhere and are easily distinguished, though their habit of staying well concealed in the upper branches of trees makes them just a little tricky. The females and younger males, however, are more problematic. Most of them are basically similar in appearance; moreover, individuals vary more than many other songbirds.

North America hosts eight breeding oriole species. The ranges of Altamira and Audubon's orioles spill north across the Mexico border only into southernmost Texas; the spot-breasted oriole, native to southwestern Mexico, has been introduced into southeastern Florida. That leaves us with five relatively wide-ranging species: Baltimore, Bullock's, hooded, orchard, and Scott's.

Orchard and Baltimore orioles range over much of the United States and southern Canada from the Great Plains east to the Atlantic Ocean. The Bullock's replaces Baltimore in the West, Scott's occurs in the southern Rocky Mountain and Great Basin regions, and the hooded is found all along the Mexico border from extreme southern Texas to San Diego, northward along the California coast toward southern Oregon. Even though migration shuffles the deck a good bit, most of us go birding in

Bullock's oriole
adult female

Baltimore oriole
adult female

orchard oriole
adult female

hooded oriole
adult female

orchard oriole
immature male

Scott's oriole
adult female

places where only one or two oriole species are expected, and spotting the others is much less likely.

It's still an excellent idea to familiarize yourself with the whole bunch. You may get lucky and find a wanderer far from its normal haunts, or you may travel and suddenly find yourself with unfamiliar oriole species. In either case, it pays to have put in the time to learn your local species backward and forward — that will give you the context in which to place the unfamiliar birds you encounter.

BALTIMORE AND BULLOCK'S

Baltimore and Bullock's orioles epitomize orioles as North American birders know them. Orange and black, with broad, shortish tails and long straight bills perfect for gleaning nectar and catching insects, they are the reference standard against which the others should be judged.

For a time, they were considered to comprise a rather variable "super species," the blandly named northern oriole. But with taxonomic division rather than consolidation being firmly back in fashion, they have regained their status as separate species. However we view them, the two are broadly similar, and they even hybridize where their ranges overlap in the Great Plains.

FACE IT

Most of the time, though, you'll be able to identify females and young males if you remember that in all ages and both sexes, the Bullock's face tends toward yellow-orange, and the Baltimore's tends toward brown-black. Thus, even the youngest, plainest females have at least an echo of the brilliant orange- or black-faced adult males.

If you've got one of the dull orioles, try to study that face pattern as closely as you can manage. The great majority of Baltimores have the brightest orange-yellow on the throat and breast — the cheeks, crown, and nape are darker and less colorful. Bullock's are generally brightest on the cheeks with a duller crown and nape, suggesting the brightly orange-cheeked adult males.

You might also take a look at the back, where Bullock's tends to be smooth and fairly pale grayish, and where the Baltimore looks darker and faintly streaked with brown.

Also remember that most Bullock's females look pretty similar to each other, whereas female Baltimores will run the gamut from extremely dull and Bullock's-like to very heavily marked with orange and brown-black.

SCOTT'S

Scott's oriole can, in some respects, be thought of as a large yellow Baltimore oriole. It has the longest bill of our five species, and that bill usually looks noticeably decurved. The Scott's oriole's bill is also rather broad at the base and fine at the tip, lending it a moderately hooked aspect. Of course, Scott's oriole's overall yellow-green ground color differentiates it from the two "northern" orioles. Its size and often darkly marked head and back help prevent confusion with the also yellowish green orchard and hooded orioles, which are smaller and plainer.

ORCHARD AND HOODED

What of these two smaller species? In practice, geography will allow you to separate orchard and hooded, but how can you be sure? Both females are fairly plain yellow, have whitish wing bars, and generally look pretty similar.

Notice, though, that almost everything about the orchard oriole is small and compact — it has a short straight bill (at least by oriole standards) and a rather short and straight tail. The hooded oriole is nearly an inch longer overall, its tail more rounded and broader across the tip, and its bill longer and more decurved.

Orchards are also more evenly and brightly colored. Hoodeds tend toward gray rather than green on the back, and the hooded's white wing bars typically contrast less sharply than the orchard's.

VARIED PLUMAGE

An issue that surfaces repeatedly concerning these five species is the variety of plumages that one encounters. With many songbirds, most individuals look basically similar. Not so with orioles. Young orioles, especially females, tend to be more or less similar, as do fully adult males. But there is an incredible middle ground of older females and subadult males that ranges between the two extremes.

The orchard oriole is fairly well known for having a "first summer" or subadult male plumage. Overall yellow-green like their mothers, these birds already sport a black or blackish face and throat like their fathers'. They may even show a few flecks of the bay or chestnut they will wear as adults. Be aware that all five species share this trait, so you'll fairly often see female-plumaged birds showing a few malelike characters.

The best clue to an oriole's true sex is its tail pattern.

FURTHER ANDROGYNY

This seeming androgyny can arise in another interesting way. Many female songbirds that have lived to a ripe old age (meaning three or four years) may exhibit some classically male plumage details. For example, an older female Wilson's warbler may have a fairly extensive black cap, and some female western tangers develop red-tinged faces as they age.

Orioles exhibit this more than most songbirds, and it is not unusual to see females, especially Scott's and Baltimore orioles, that are very nearly as bright and contrastingly colored as adult males. To make things even more confusing, in all five of these oriole species the females do occasionally sing, though their songs tend to be simpler and less insistent than those of males.

The best external clue to an oriole's true sex is its tail pattern. Even very heavily marked, bright female Baltimores or Bullock's usually have plain yellow-orange tails — not the boldly orange-and-black tails of their mates. Orchard and hooded males have solidly black tails, whereas those of the females are plainer and yellowish. Scott's females show a more complex tail pattern than that of orchards and hoodeds, with a darker center and pale tips, but not the eye-grabbing black and yellow of the Scott's males.

IT'S A WHAT?

Finally, as you work with potentially confusing groups of birds like female and immature orioles, it's good to remember that not all our challenges involve fine distinctions between close relatives. I am thinking here of a late April morning not so long ago.

The breeze off the Gulf of Mexico was warm and moist, the rays of the rising sun piercing the cloud banks to the east. I was leading a tour group into one of North America's most sacred birding shrines — Boy Scout Woods, a tiny patch of live oak forest on the Texas coast. The place is world renowned for attracting migrant songbirds in the spring, sometimes in astonishing numbers. Approaching such a place, anticipation is always high: will this morning be the one that people talk about for years to come? The one when there seemed to be two birds for every branch?

Entering the scrub at the periphery of the woods, we began to glimpse a few birds here and there. An indigo bunting popped up in a nearby bush, then vanished. A rose-breasted grosbeak zipped by, but few of us saw it. Here and there, the slight chips of various warblers could be heard, but all stayed frustratingly out of view.

Only when we entered a small clearing did we finally find a bird that we could really see. Small and yellowish, our subject showed two white wing bars and a dark line narrowing behind the eye. "Looks like a female blue-winged warbler," I intoned, and began the process of making sure that all members of the group were seeing it.

Most of them found the bird quickly, but it was clear that my diagnosis was garnering little agreement. Finally someone voiced his misgivings. "That's a blue-winged warbler?" he asked politely, doing his best not to bruise my ego, yet obviously confused.

I glassed the bird again, saying a silent prayer that I hadn't blown it and fervently hoping to see the distaff *Vermivora pinus*. It's never a good feeling to misidentify a bird; it's worse when you're the leader. When it's the first bird of the day, well, that really hurts.

Sure enough, the bird I saw was suddenly all wrong for blue-winged, wrong for a warbler, even. Tail too long, bill not black, wings too dull — it was all horribly wrong.

"Hmmmmm — looks like this is actually a female orchard oriole — sorry about that," I murmured. "They can fool you sometimes."

In the end, we had a good morning, seeing a nice assortment of species. But the bird that really sticks with me, more than a decade later, is that little oriole. It was a most humbling reminder that we often don't really know the birds nearly as well as we think we do. ✴

SMALL RED FINCHES

Separating the redpolls and house, purple, and Cassin's finches.

WINTER IS FINCH SEASON, WHEN THOSE NORTHERN nomads sweep down in raiding parties, show up without warning, stay for an hour or a week, and disappear. They are movers, unpredictable, edgy, always peeking over the horizon.

The very inconsistency of finches is one of their greatest attractions. For most bird watchers, there is a spurt of adrenaline when the feeder is suddenly commandeered by evening grosbeaks or pine siskins, or when crossbills put in their not-quite-believable appearance. Chickadees and juncos and downy woodpeckers carry their own brand of pleasure, a comfort born of knowing they are always there, but it is the unexpected that brings a smile to our faces.

There are one or two exceptions, just as you would expect from the unexpected. House finches are ubiquitous and predictable, showing up regularly at nearly every feeder on the continent. Goldfinches, which have their own society and movements, can almost be counted on to appear at certain seasons.

Perhaps it is because we see them so irregularly that many of the finches make us pause, momentarily stymied. What is that thing? Sure, five years ago there was a flock at the feeder for a week, and an instant submersion into finch identification, but since then, nothing. Memory fades and becomes clouded by information and the passage of time. You know that one of them had wing bars, or streaks, or an eye patch, but which one?

In this chapter we'll examine the visual clues that help identify a group of birds that might be called the small red finches. These are

FINCHES

purple finch
male

house finch
male

purple finch
female

house finch
female

Cassin's finch
male

Cassin's finch
female

common redpoll
male

pine siskin
adult

common redpoll
female

hoary redpoll
male

house finch, purple finch, Cassin's finch, common redpoll, and hoary redpoll. The pine siskin is also included here because it can be confused with the females of some of these species. While these species might not be terribly difficult to tell apart, they may be a bit puzzling.

Finch Identification Guidelines

THERE ARE SEVERAL BROAD GUIDELINES FOR IDENTIFYING WINTER FINCHES.

1. **FINCHES TRAVEL IN PACKS.** Yes, people do get one redpoll or a single grosbeak sometimes, but a gang is the norm. If you have one, start by reassuring yourself that it is a finch and not a sparrow or a towhee. Look at the bill. Sparrows and towhees have big bills, but finch bills are bigger, at least in proportion to their bodies. (Excepting siskins and redpolls, of course.)

2. **FINCHES ARE FREQUENTLY LESS SKITTISH THAN OTHER BIRDS.** Maybe it is because they come from the North, where humans and cats are in short supply, but many people have discovered that you can get closer to finches than to other birds.

3. **FEMALES CAN OFTEN BE IDENTIFIED BY THE COMPANY THEY KEEP, BECAUSE MIXED-SPECIES FLOCKS ARE NOT COMMON.** But keep in mind that too much reliance on this general rule can cause you to overlook the occasional red crossbill in the flock of white-winged crossbills, or the female purple finch suffering the company of house finches.

4. **ALMOST ANYTHING CAN APPEAR ANYWHERE.** Winter finches are not only unpredictable, they are great travelers — at least in the years they travel at all. They can, and do, show up in completely unexpected places.

5. **IT DOESN'T HAVE TO BE AN INVASION YEAR.** Even in bad years, when the finches seem to be staying home, there are always a few that take off to see the sights. Just because no one in 500 miles has a redpoll does not mean you have misidentified the one at your feeder.

There is no easy way to break finches into groups for the purpose of discussing identification. Size doesn't help. Neither does likelihood of occurrence, because of rule number four — anything anywhere. The only solution is to compare those closely related species that are most likely to cause confusion, and throw in an occasional caution about unexpected similarities.

THE CARPODACUS FINCHES

Carpodacus (Car-POD-ih-kus) is the Latin name for the genus that includes house, purple, and Cassin's finches, and many bird watchers use the term to avoid having to mention all three each time.

These three are the ones that cause the most identification problems for bird watchers. Although they're nomadic, they are more common than most of the other finches. All three species can be found at the same feeders in some parts of North America, and they look almost alike.

Two decades ago the house finch wasn't even an issue in most of the East, but these birds have spread like, well, finches, and now they are found almost everywhere in the United States. Originally native to the West, eastern house finches started as a fairly small population. As sometimes happens in a limited gene pool, small variations in plumage can spread quickly. As a result, it was fairly common a decade ago to see house finches in the East with big white patches in the wings, a widespread partial albinism. It has died out to a great extent, but it is still possible to find a house finch with white in the wings, and observers should be on the lookout for those individuals. A similar outbreak of partial albinism has occurred in the Pacific Northwest in recent years, although it does not seem to be as common or widespread.

In most of the country, the simplest way of identifying the less common purple and Cassin's finches is to start with the house finch and look for differences. In the East, the problem is simpler because there are only house and purple finches to worry about. Both males and females are fairly easy to tell apart if you get a decent look.

Male purple finches are wine red, or purple-red, compared to the house finch's fire engine red. Many male house finches are pale red, and those are even easier to recognize. The most distinctive difference is that male house finches are streaked with brown on the sides and belly, and the streaks seem to run right into the red on the breast. Male purple

purple finch male
- raspberry-red head, breast, back, wings, tail
- unstreaked white belly/flanks
- large-headed appearance

house finch male
- red only on head and chest
- white belly/flanks streaked with brown
- brown-streaked wings, back

finches are white on the belly, with broad red blotches coming down onto the flanks. Purple finches are also more red on the head and upper back than house finches, lacking the house finch's distinct red forehead band that contrasts with its darker crown.

FEMALES

Females are more difficult to identify, but are still fairly distinctive. Female house finches are basically plain brown birds. Their underparts are light to medium brown, with blurry brown streaks not much darker than the color of the breast. The head is brown with brown crown streaks; the back is darker brown with blurry brown streaks. The female house finch is a plain brown, streaky bird, more apt to be mistaken for a sparrow, or a female indigo or lazuli bunting, than anything else.

In comparison, female purple finches are contrasty brown and white birds. Their underparts are white with bold, contrasting brown streaks. The head and upperparts are dark brown, with a strong pale eye line and a contrasting pale whisker streak. This head patterning is quite unlike that of any house finch.

In invasion years in the East, purple finches may reach the Deep South in large numbers. For the most part, however, they are considered something of a special bird anywhere south of the northern tier of states. They might join house finches at the feeder sometimes, but the house finch is a very domineering species; if there are a lot of house finches around, the purples rarely stay long.

Along the West Coast, observers usually have the same house versus purple finch problem. The characters are the same, although western female purple finches are somewhat duller and the plumage streaking is a little blurrier, which makes the differences between females of the two species a little less pronounced. Even western purple finches have a stronger face pattern than house finches, however, and in all parts of the range, the purple's strongly notched tail can help separate it from the square-tailed house finch.

In the interior West from the Great Basin through the Rocky Mountains, the problem is usually separating house finch from Cassin's finch, a high-elevation bird that sometimes moves downslope in winter. The differences between house and Cassin's are the same as those between house and purple, especially in females. Cassin's shows a much stronger face pattern than does the house finch, more contrast and bold streaking on the underparts, and a notched tail. The males are even easier to separate, because Cassin's have a deep red cap and are a paler, almost rose-colored red on the breast and face. Some male Cassin's do have brown streaks on the sides, below the red; these are darker, more distinct, and more restricted than those on house finches. All Cassin's finches have distinctly streaked undertail coverts.

The biggest identification challenge in this group is separating purple and Cassin's finches in the West. They rarely overlap, even in winter, but when they do, the females can be a tough call. The males are easily identified because of the Cassin's contrasting red cap and brown streaking below, but the females are very similar.

The best characters for separating female Cassin's and purple finches are the head pattern, the bill, and the undertail coverts, and absolute confidence sometimes requires seeing all of them. On average, female Cassin's have a duller face pattern than female purple finches, about halfway between the strong contrast of a purple and the plain face of a house. The eye line is present but not as distinct as it is on the purple, and the ear patch is not set off as strongly. The bill may be useful, but it

requires a close look and usually a direct comparison between the two —
and the difference is often not apparent. The bill of Cassin's is slightly
longer than the bill of purple, and the upper ridge appears quite straight.
The bill of purple finch is shorter, and the upper ridge is slightly curved.

The main character that separates the two females is the undertail
coverts, which can be hard to see (not as hard as on redpolls, though).
The undertail coverts of Cassin's finches are heavily streaked with brown,
and the undertail coverts of purple finches are white and contrast with
the rest of the underparts. Even if you don't get a great look, the difference in this area should be relatively obvious.

PINE SISKIN

The pine siskin is a small, brown, streaky finch that superficially resembles females of some of the other small finches. It is smaller than any
female finch it might be confused with. It also has wing bars, mostly
white but sometimes tinged with yellow, and a yellow patch on the wing
and at the base of the tail. The most striking feature is the bill, which is
so small and thin that it is hard to believe that the pine siskin is actually
a finch.

True to their finch nature, siskins are also irruptive. Some years they
are in short supply, and some years they seem to be everywhere. In winter they usually travel in flocks, and from below you can recognize them
as siskins by the bright pale stripe that shows on both sides (top and bottom) of the wing.

At feeders, they tend to associate with goldfinches and to prefer thistle
or Niger seed. When people pass over a siskin, it is usually because they
think it's a sparrow. But no sparrow has the yellow patch on the wing, and
most sparrows have a visibly larger bill than a siskin. Also, few sparrows
have the fluttery, quick, darting habits of a siskin. Siskins may feed on the
ground like sparrows, but they always seem to be on the move and usually prefer to stay in the trees. They almost always announce their presence with a loud rising *zzziiipp!!* call.

REDPOLLS

Redpolls are close to being most bird watchers' favorite winter finch.
Every few years they pour out of the Arctic in late fall, and rather than

stopping at the United States–Canada border they just keep going, in swirling flocks of tiny, pale, unwary, chittering birds that gather in fields, on roadsides, and at feeders. Waking to find a flock of redpolls at the feeder makes the winter for most people.

It is not difficult to decide that you have redpolls. Telling which kind is a task for the truly dedicated.

The only birds you are likely to confuse with redpolls are house finches. This confusion was more common when house finches were new to the East, but now that they are everywhere (and a pest as far as many people are concerned) the mistake is rarer. Redpolls are small, pale, red-capped, and have a black chin that contrasts against pale underparts. Some females and young birds are so heavily streaked below that they almost resemble house finches, but even on these birds the red cap is distinctive.

The bill is a dead giveaway. Redpolls have the smallest bills of any finch. In fact, they have, proportionately, the smallest bills of almost any bird you will see. The bill, along with the red cap (or "poll," which is where they get the name), gives them a dapper appearance that is not easily forgotten.

SO MUCH FOR THE EASY PART

Unfortunately, there are two kinds of redpolls. Actually, some scientists think there may be more. For the time being, two is more than enough.

As befits the name, the common redpoll is the common one, at least in the parts of North America that all but a few observers ever see. In winter, the vast majority of birds that move south are common redpolls.

Hoary redpolls are the more consistently northern, but a few birds do come south with their cousins, and this is when identification gets tough. Separating common and hoary redpolls is a massively difficult problem, confounded by age, feather wear, sex, subspecies, and variation. Ten-page technical articles have been written on the problem, and even if you've read (and understood) them, there are birds that refuse to be easily categorized.

The problem is picking out the occasional hoary redpoll from the flock of commons. There are a few general guidelines and one very-hard-to-discern character.

As a rule, hoary redpolls are bigger than common repolls. The difference may be only a quarter of an inch on average, but on a bird 5 inches long, it shows. Of course, all redpolls vary in size.

Hoary redpolls are also typically paler than commons. Many commons are dark (almost as dark as house finches) but some male commons can be quite pale. The palest male hoary redpolls are nearly white all over, with just a faint blush of red on the breast, a condition rarely achieved by common redpolls. In general, hoary redpolls are less heavily streaked on their sides and flanks than commons.

The bills of common redpolls are small, but the bills of hoary redpolls are just plain tiny — so short that they give the face a punched-in look, which is usually, but not always, evident.

Although there is overlap in all characters, any big frosty-looking redpoll with a ridiculously small bill is probably a hoary. To get past "probably," you have to see the undertail coverts. Seeing the undertail coverts can be easier than you think, because redpolls sit upright on the feeder and on small branches. If you get a good look, you will notice that the undertail coverts of common redpolls are streaked and the undertail coverts of hoary redpolls are plain. This is the deciding character, but even here, caution is in order. Common redpolls may have only one or two streaks on the undertail coverts, and hoaries may have a single streak. Some hoaries can even have more than one streak, and those birds are almost always passed off as common redpolls, even by experts.

There is no simple way to solve the redpoll problem. If you think you have a hoary, and really want to be sure, you need to search a good library for articles about redpoll identification (and search the Internet for hoary red poll photos) and plan to settle in for some intensive study.

Finches are a highlight for many bird watchers, the reward for enduring the long slow days of winter. They are unexpected, a treat that comes without warning and leaves just as quickly. They are nomads, reminding us that there is more to the mystery of migration than a hummingbird flying across the Gulf of Mexico or a warbler making it from the northern boreal forests to the tropics. There is something determined, almost humorless, in the demeanor of the birds that leave us in the fall. Then winter comes, the snow falls, the wind whips, and the finches arrive, chattering gangs swirling and dodging. Their cheerfulness in the face of the worst nature can offer lifts our own spirits as well.

ORGANIZATIONS FOR BIRD WATCHERS

American Birding Association
  P.O. Box 6599
  Colorado Springs, CO
    80934-6599
  800-850-2473
  www.americanbirding.org

American Bird Conservancy
  P.O. Box 249
  The Plains, VA 20198
  540-253-5780
  www.abcbirds.org

Cornell Laboratory of Ornithology
  159 Sapsucker Woods Road
  Ithaca, NY 14850
  800-843-2473
  www.birds.cornell.edu

National Wildlife Federation
  11100 Wildlife Center Drive
  Reston, VA 20190-5362
  800-822-9919
  www.nwf.org

National Audubon Society
  700 Broadway
  New York, NY 10003
  212-979-3000
  www.audubon.org

The Nature Conservancy
  4245 North Fairfax Drive,
    Suite 100
  Arlington, VA 22203-1606
  800-628-6860
  www.tnc.org

GENERAL REFERENCES

The Birder's Handbook: A Field Guide to the Natural History of North American Birds. Ehrlich, Paul R., David S. Dobkin, and Darryl Wheye. 1988. New York: Simon and Schuster Fireside.

Lives of North American Birds. Kaufman, Kenn. 1996. Boston: Houghton Mifflin.

Identification Guide to North American Birds. Pyle, Peter. Revised 1997. Bolinas, CA: Slate Creek Press.

FIELD GUIDES TO BIRDS

All the Birds of North America. Griggs, Jack L. 2002. New York: Harper Collins.

Birds of North America: A Guide to Field Identification (Golden Field Guide series), rev. ed. Robbins, Chandler S., et al. 2001. New York: Golden Press.

Kaufman Field Guide to Birds of North America. Kaufman, Kenn. 2000. Boston: Houghton Mifflin.

National Geographic Field Guide to the Birds of North America, 4th ed. National Geographic Society. 2002. Washington, D.C.: National Geographic.

PETERSON FIELD GUIDES

A Field Guide to the Birds of Eastern and Central North America, 5th ed. Peterson, Roger Tory, and Virginia Marie Peterson. 2002. Boston: Houghton Mifflin.

A Field Guide to Western Birds, 3rd ed. Peterson, Roger Tory. 1990. Boston: Houghton Mifflin.

SIBLEY GUIDES

The Sibley Guide to Birds. Sibley, David Allen. 2000. New York: Alfred A. Knopf, Inc.

The Sibley Field Guide to Birds of Eastern North America. Sibley, David Allen. 2003. New York: Alfred A. Knopf, Inc.

The Sibley Field Guide to Birds of Western North America. Sibley, David Allen. 2003. New York: Alfred A. Knopf, Inc.

STOKES GUIDES

Stokes Field Guide to Birds: Eastern Region. Stokes, Donald, and Lillian Stokes. 1996. Boston: Little, Brown and Co.

Stokes Field Guide to Birds: Western Region. Stokes, Donald, and Lillian Stokes. 1994. Boston: Little, Brown and Co.

SPECIFIC IDENTIFICATION REFERENCES

Sparrows of the United States and Canada: A Photographic Guide. Beadle, David D., and James D. Rising. 2001. San Diego: Academic Press.

Buntings and Sparrows: A Guide to the Buntings and North American Sparrows. Byers, Clive, Urban Olsson, and Jan Cursion. 1995. Tonbridge, UK: Pica Press.

Peterson Field Guide to Hawks of North America, 2nd ed. Clark, William S., and Brian K. Wheeler. 2001. Boston: Houghton Mifflin Co.

Warblers of the Americas: An Identification Guide. Curson, Jon, illustrated by David Quinn and David Beadle. 1994. Boston: Houghton Mifflin.

Peterson Field Guide to Warblers of North America. Dunn, Jon, and Kimball Garrett. 1997. Boston: Houghton Mifflin.

Gulls: A Guide to Identification. 2nd ed. Grant, Peter J. 1986. New York: Academic Press.

Seabirds: An Identification Guide. Harrison, Peter. Revised 1985. Boston: Houghton Mifflin.

Shorebirds: An Identification Guide to the Waders of the World. Hayman, Peter, John Marchant, and Tony Prater. 1986. Boston: Houghton Mifflin.

Hummingbirds of North America. Howell, Steve N. G. 2001. San Diego: Academic Press.

Waterfowl: An Identification Guide to the Ducks, Geese, and Swans of the World. Madge, Steve, and Hilary Burn. 1988. Boston: Houghton Mifflin.

Shorebirds: Beautiful Beachcombers. Morris, Arthur. 1996. Mechanicsburg, PA: Stackpole Books.

Gulls of North America, Europe, and Asia. Olsen, Klaus Malling, and Hans Larsson. 2004. Princeton, NJ: Princeton University Press.

Terns of Europe and North America. Olsen, Klaus Malling, and Hans Larsson. 1995. Princeton, NJ: Princeton University Press.

Hawks in Flight: The Flight Identification of North American Migrant Raptors. Sutton, Clay, Pete Dunne, and David Allen Sibley. 1989. Boston: Houghton Mifflin.

Handbook of Waterfowl Identification. Todd, Frank S. 1997. Temecula, CA: Ibis Publishing Co.

Raptors of Eastern North America: The Wheeler Guides. Wheeler, Brian K. 2003. Princeton, NJ: Princeton University Press.

Raptors of Western North America: The Wheeler Guides. Wheeler, Brian K. 2003. Princeton, NJ: Princeton University Press.

Peterson Field Guide to Hummingbirds of North America. Williamson, Sheri L. 2002. Boston: Houghton Mifflin.

AUDIO RESOURCES FOR BIRDERS

Know Your Bird Sounds, Volume 1: Yard, Garden, and City Birds. Elliott, Lang. 2004. Mechanicsburg, PA: Stackpole Books.
Know Your Bird Sounds, Volume 2: Birds of the Countryside. Elliott, Lang. 2004. Mechanicsburg, PA: Stackpole Books.
The Singing Life of Birds: The Art and Science of Listening to Birdsong. Kroodsma, Donald. 2005. Boston: Houghton Mifflin.

PETERSON FIELD GUIDE AUDIOS

A Field Guide to Bird Songs: Eastern and Central North America, rev. ed. Cornell Laboratory of Ornithology and Interactive Media. 2002. Boston: Houghton Mifflin.
A Field Guide to Western Bird Songs. Cornell Laboratory of Ornithology and Interactive Media. 1999. Boston: Houghton Mifflin.
Birding by Ear: Eastern and Central North America, rev. ed. (Peterson Field Guide Audio Series). Walton, Richard K., and Robert W. Lawson. 2002. Boston: Houghton Mifflin.
Birding by Ear: Western North America (Peterson Field Guide Audio Series). Walton, Richard K., and Robert W. Lawson. 1999. Boston: Houghton Mifflin.
More Birding by Ear: Eastern and Central North America (Peterson Field Guide Audio Series). Walton, Richard K., and Robert W. Lawson. 2002. Boston: Houghton Mifflin.

STOKES FIELD GUIDE AUDIOS

Stokes Field Guide to Bird Songs: Eastern Region. Stokes, Donald, Lillian Stokes, and Lang Elliott. 1997. New York: Time Warner Audio Books.
Stokes Field Guide to Bird Songs: Western Region. Stokes, Donald, Lillian Stokes, and Kevin Colver. 1999. New York: Time Warner Audio Books.

PERIODICALS FOR BIRD WATCHERS

Birding
>American Birding Association
>P.O. Box 6599
>Colorado Springs, CO 80934-6599
>800-850-2473
>www.americanbirding.org

Bird Watcher's Digest
>P.O. Box 110
>Marietta, OH 45750
>800-879-2473
>www.birdwatchersdigest.com

Living Bird
>Cornell Laboratory of Ornithology
>159 Sapsucker Woods Road
>Ithaca, NY 14850
>800-843-2473
>www.birds.cornell.edu

The Backyard Bird Newsletter
>P.O. Box 110
>Marietta, OH 45750
>800-879-2473
>www.birdwatchersdigest.com

MULTIMEDIA RESOURCES

>*Watching Waders: A Video Guide to the Waders of North America*. Male, Michael, and Judy Feith. 1999. Locustville, VA: Blue Earth Films.
>*Watching Warblers: A Video Guide to the Warblers of North America*. Male, Michael, and Judy Feith. 1996. Locustville, VA: Blue Earth Films.
>*Watching Sparrows*. Male, Michael, and Judy Feith. 2002. Locustville, VA: Blue Earth Films.

Watching Hummingbirds. Nature Science Network. 1999. Ark Media Group.

Lanius North American Bird Reference Book (CD-ROM). Robinson, John C. 2001. Fairfield, CA: LANIUS Software.

The Small Gulls of North America. Vanderpoel, John. 1999. Niwot, CO: Peregrine Video Productions.

The Large Gulls of North America. Vanderpoel, John. 1997. Niwot, CO: Peregrine Video Productions.

Shorebirds: A Guide to Shorebirds of Eastern North America. Walton, Richard K., and Greg Dodge. Hillsborough, NC: Brownbag Productions.

Hawk Watch: A Video Guide to Eastern Raptors. Walton, Richard K., and Greg Dodge. 1998. Hillsborough, NC: Brownbag Productions.

BIRD IDENTIFICATION WEB SITES

Bird Watcher's Digest   www.birdwatchersdigest.com

Cornell Laboratory of Ornithology   www.birds.cornell.edu

National Wildlife Federation   www.enature.com

Patuxent Wildlife Research Center   www.pwrc.usgs.gov

CONTRIBUTOR BIOGRAPHIES & CREDITS

BILL THOMPSON III

Bill Thompson III began watching birds at the age of eight. When his parents started *Bird Watcher's Digest* in 1978, Bill (by then a high school student) knew he had found his future profession. After a short stint working in advertising in New York City, Bill joined the staff of *Bird Watcher's Digest* in 1988 and became the magazine's editor in 1995. He has traveled to many of the world's best birding spots, but his all-time favorite is the bird watching tower he and his wife, author/illustrator Julie Zickefoose, built onto their southeastern Ohio home. Bill and Julie have recorded more than 180 bird species on their property.

Credits: Introduction (page xiv), Getting Started (page xvii), Grebes (page 15), Winter Loons (page 40), Dark Ibises (page 61), Basics of Hawk ID (page 66), Basics of Shorebird ID (page 102), Yellowlegs (page 109), Basics of Gull ID (page 134), Basics of Swallow ID (page 219), Green Swallows (page 221), Drab Swallows (page 232), Brown Thrushes (page 265), Basics of Warbler ID (page 279), Confusing Spring Warblers (page 283), Confusing Fall Warblers (page 292), Basics of Sparrow ID (page 319), *Ammodramus* Sparrows (page 334)

JULIE ZICKEFOOSE

Julie Zickefoose began working as a freelance illustrator in 1980 after graduating from Harvard University. She splits her time between writing for *Bird Watcher's Digest* and her illustration work, detailing her field experiences with wild birds, and interpreting and placing those experiences in a larger ecological and spiritual context. Julie lives with her husband, Bill Thompson III (Editor of *Bird Watcher's Digest*) and their two children on Indigo Hill, an 80-acre Appalachian sanctuary in southeastern Ohio.

Credits: All illustrations, Grebes (page 15), Streaky Fall Warblers (page 296), Plain Fall Warblers (page 302)

EIRIK A. T. BLOM

Eirik A. T. "Rick" Blom was one of North America's leading experts on bird identification and birding. He was editor of *Birding* magazine, director of the Maryland Breeding Bird Atlas project, and a chief consultant on the *National Geographic Field Guide to the Birds of North America*. Rick was a longtime contributing editor to *Bird Watcher's Digest* and was the founding author of the "Identify Yourself" column upon which this book is based. Rick Blom contributed content, birding advice, and his unparalleled sense of humor to *BWD* until his death in December 2002.

Credits: Mergansers (page 1), Scoters (page 7), Grebes (page 15), Ring-necked Duck and Scaup (page 23), Brown Herons (page 47), Falcons (page 78), Accipiters (page 86), Basics of Shorebird ID (page 102), Yellowlegs (page 109), Basics of Gull ID (page 134), Cuckoos (page 160), Owls (page 170), Hairy and Downy Woodpeckers (page 177), Shrikes (page 189), Corvids (page 211), Green Swallows (page 221), Chickadees (page 237), Small Wrens (page 246), Kinglets (page 253), Bluebirds (page 260), Confusing Fall Warblers (page 292), Tanagers (page 307), Buntings (page 312), Small Red Finches (page 361)

JEFFREY A. GORDON

Jeffrey A. Gordon turned a lifelong fascination with birding and natural history into a career. He has worked as an interpretive naturalist for the National Park Service and led bird watching trips for Victor Emanuel Nature Tours for more than a decade. In 2002, Jeff became field editor for *Bird Watcher's Digest*, contributing numerous articles on birding skills, travel, and bird identification. He is an associate director of the Delaware Nature Society at Abbott's Mill Nature Center near Milford, Delaware.

Credits: Teal (page 34), White Herons (page 54), Soaring Buteos (page 71), Eagles (page 95), Plovers (page 117), Medium-sized Terns (page 149), Flycatchers (page 182), "Spectacular" Vireos (page 205), Rusty Swallows (page 228), Female Blackbirds (page 349), Female Orioles (page 355)

MARSHALL ILIFF

Marshall Iliff grew up in Maryland and currently lives in Costa Mesa, California. He works as a tour guide for Victor Emanuel Nature Tours, leading trips throughout the United States and Canada, as well as in Central America and Kenya.

Credits: Ring-necked Duck and Scaup (page 23), Medium Probing Shore-birds (page 124), Plain-winged Vireos (page 197), Waxwings (page 272)

GEORGE ARMISTEAD

George Armistead grew up birding in southern New Jersey, the Delmarva Peninsula, and the Outer Banks. After working for seven years in the ornithology department at the Academy of Natural Sciences of Philadelphia, he now leads birding tours for Field Guides, Inc.

Credits: Winter Loons (page 40), Dark Ibises (page 61), Hooded Gulls (page 141), Large Crested Terns (page 154), Song–like Sparrows (page 322), *Spizella* Sparrows (page 329), Crowned Sparrows (page 343)

Auriculars: the feathers on the sides of a bird's head that cover the ear openings.

Avifauna: the community of birds found in a given region or habitat type.

Axillars (or axillaries): the long stiff feathers on the underside of the wing where it joins the body.

Banding: the placing of bands (metal or plastic rings) on the legs of wild birds in order to trace their migration times and routes, population changes, and lifespans.

Brood parasitism: a behavioral habit characterized by birds laying their eggs in the nests of others.

Call note: brief, relatively simple sound uttered by birds in various social contexts (for example, location calls, food calls).

Cavity nester: a bird that nests inside an enclosed area, such as a hollow tree, an old woodpecker hole, or a nestbox.

Check-list: a list of bird species compiled from records in a specific geographic area.

Coverts: the small contour feathers on the upper part of a bird's wing that overlap the flight feathers. (See Parts of a Bird, page xxiv.)

Crepuscular: describes birds that are active at dawn and dusk.

Crest: a tuft of long feathers on the head of a bird that may be held erect.

Crown: the top of a bird's head. (See Parts of a Bird, page xxiv.)

Decurved: curved downward (refers to the bill).

Dihedral: describes the upward-angled or V-shaped position (rather than flat or horizontal) in which certain birds hold their wings.

Diurnal: active during daylight hours.

Edge habitat: a place where two or more habitats overlap, such as an old meadow near woodlands. Edge habitat typically offers a rich diversity of birds.

Endemic: any breeding species unique to a specific geographical region.

Extinct: no longer existing.

Extirpated: no longer present in a given area (though still existing in others).

Eye line: the line over or through a bird's eye, often used as a field mark for identification.

Eye-ring: a ring of feathers, usually lighter than the head color, that encircles a bird's eye. A broken eye-ring is one that is not continuous, or does not completely encircle the eye.

Field mark: an obvious visual clue to a bird's identification, such as bill shape or plumage.

Flank: a bird's sides below the wings on either side of the belly. (See Parts of a Bird, page xxiv.)

Fledgling: a young bird that has left the nest, but may still be receiving care and feeding from a parent.

Hotspot: a location or habitat that is particularly good for bird watching on a regular basis.

Juvenal: plumage of a juvenile bird.

Juvenile: a bird that has not yet reached breeding age.

Life bird: a bird seen by a bird watcher for the first time, often recorded on a life list.

Life list: a record of all the birds a birder has seen at least once.

Lores: the area between a bird's bill and its eyes. (See Parts of a Bird, page xxiv.)

Malar: the area on the side of a bird's face, below the bill and eye, between the cheek and the throat. (See Parts of a Bird, page xxiv.)

Malar stripes: stripes in the malar or cheek area, often referred to as "the mustache."

Mantle: the upper back just behind the nape. (See Parts of a Bird, page xxiv.)

Migrant: a bird that travels from one region to another in response to changes of season, breeding cycles, food availability, or extreme weather.

Mimic: a bird that imitates other birds' sounds and songs.

Molt: the periodic shedding of old feathers and their replacement by new ones.

Morph: a genetically fixed color variation within a species, such as the blue morph of snow goose. (The term is only correct when both color variations occur in the same population. "Blue" morph snow geese breed side by side with white birds. The word "morph" is not applied to differently colored subspecies.)

Nape: the back of a bird's neck. (See Parts of a Bird, page xxiv.)

Neotropical migrant: refers to migratory birds of the New World, primarily those that travel seasonally between North, Central, and South America.

Nestling: a bird that has hatched from its egg but is still being cared for in the nest.

Peeps: a generic term for confusingly similar small sandpipers.

Pelagic: refers to birds of the ocean, rarely seen from land.

Pishing (or spishing): a sound made by bird watchers to attract curious birds into the open, made by repeating the sounds *spshhh* or *pshhh* through clenched teeth.

Plumage: collective reference to a bird's feathers, which change both color and shape during seasonal molts. Breeding plumage is often the most colorful. Nonbreeding or winter plumage, worn during fall and winter, is often less colorful than breeding plumage.

Primary feathers (or primaries): the nine or more long flight feathers at the end of a bird's wing. (See Parts of a Bird, page xxiv.)

Raptors: birds of prey.

Recurved: curved upward (refers to bill).

Resident: a nonmigratory species that is present in the same region all year.

Rump patch: a patch of color located above the point at which a bird's tail connects to the body. (See Parts of a Bird, page xxiv.)

Scapulars: the row of feathers lying just above a bird's folded wing; the lowest group of feathers on the mantle. (See Parts of a Bird, page xxiv.)

Secondary feathers (or secondaries): the medium-length inner flight feathers located on the wing. Secondaries form most of the wing's inner surface. (See Parts of a Bird, page xxiv.)

Shorebirds: refers to sandpipers, plovers, and related birds (but does not include herons, gulls, terns, and other birds found in coastal areas).

Song: a complex series of sounds, with elaborate note patterns, usually associated with courtship or territoriality.

Subadult: a bird that is not yet adult but more than one year old.

Supercilium: the area above a bird's eye, sometimes called the eyebrow. (See Parts of a Bird, page xxiv.)

Tail spots: spots of contrasting color (usually white) on a bird's tail, often used as a field mark.

Territoriality: behavior associated with the aggressive defense of a particular area or territory.

Tertial feathers (or tertials): the three innermost secondary feathers on a bird's wing (the closest feathers to the bird's body). Tertials are often distinctly visible and used in identification. (See Parts of a Bird, page xxiv.)

Underparts: the lower half of a bird (breast, belly, undertail), often used as a field mark.

Upperparts: the upper half of a bird (crown, back, top of tail), often used as a field mark.

Vagrant: a bird that wanders far from its normal range.

Vent: the feathered area under the tail and below the legs, sometimes used as a field mark. (See Parts of a Bird, page xxiv.)

Waders: herons, egrets, and related birds, including storks.

Wing bars: obvious areas of contrasting color, often white, across the central portion ("shoulder") of a bird's wings.

COMMON AND SCIENTIFIC NAMES OF BIRDS

Listed below are all of the birds included in this book, in taxonomic order.

COMMON NAME	SCIENTIFIC NAME
Pacific Loon	*Gavia pacifica*
Red-throated Loon	*Gavia stellata*
Common Loon	*Gavia immer*
Arctic Loon	*Gavia arctica*
Yellow-billed Loon	*Gavia adamsii*
Pied-billed Grebe	*Podilymbus podiceps*
Red-necked Grebe	*Podiceps grisegena*
Eared Grebe	*Podiceps nigricollis*
Horned Grebe	*Podiceps auritus*
American Bittern	*Botaurus lentiginosus*
Least Bittern	*Ixobrychus exilis*
Great Blue Heron	*Ardea herodias*
Great Egret	*Ardea alba*
Snowy Egret	*Egretta thula*
Reddish Egret	*Egretta rufescens*
Little Blue Heron	*Egretta caerulea*
Tricolored Heron	*Egretta tricolor*
Cattle Egret	*Bubulcus ibis*
Green Heron	*Butorides virescens*
Black-crowned Night-Heron	*Nycticorax nycticorax*
Yellow-crowned Night-Heron	*Nyctanassa violacea*
White Ibis	*Eudocimus albus*
Glossy Ibis	*Plegadis falcinellus*
White-faced Ibis	*Plegadis chihi*
Black Vulture	*Coragyps atratus*
Turkey Vulture	*Cathartes aura*
Blue-winged Teal	*Anas discors*
Green-winged Teal	*Anas crecca*
Cinnamon Teal	*Anas cyanoptera*
Northern Shoveler	*Anas clypeata*
Greater Scaup	*Aythya marila*
Ring-necked Duck	*Aythya collaris*

Common Name	Scientific Name
Lesser Scaup	*Aythya affinis*
Black Scoter	*Melanitta nigra*
Surf Scoter	*Melanitta perspicillata*
White-winged Scoter	*Melanitta fusca*
Bufflehead	*Bucephala albeola*
Hooded Merganser	*Lophodytes cucullatus*
Common Merganser	*Mergus merganser*
Red-breasted Merganser	*Mergus serrator*
Osprey	*Pandion haliaetus*
Bald Eagle	*Haliaeetus leucocephalus*
Northern Harrier	*Circus cyaneus*
Sharp-shinned Hawk	*Accipiter striatus*
Cooper's Hawk	*Accipiter cooperii*
Northern Goshawk	*Accipiter gentilis*
Red-shouldered Hawk	*Buteo lineatus*
Swainson's Hawk	*Buteo swainsoni*
Red-tailed Hawk	*Buteo jamaicensis*
Broad-winged Hawk	*Buteo platypterus*
Ferruginous Hawk	*Buteo regalis*
Rough-legged Hawk	*Buteo lagopus*
Golden Eagle	*Aquila chrysaetos*
Merlin	*Falco columbarius*
Peregrine Falcon	*Falco peregrinus*
Prairie Falcon	*Falco mexicanus*
American Kestrel	*Falco sparverius*
Gyrfalcon	*Falco rusticolus*
Common Ringed Plover	*Charadrius hiaticula*
Killdeer	*Charadrius vociferus*
Snowy Plover	*Charadrius alexandrinus*
Semipalmated Plover	*Charadrius semipalmatus*
Wilson's Plover	*Charadrius wilsonia*
Piping Plover	*Charadrius melodus*
Lesser Yellowlegs	*Tringa flavipes*
Greater Yellowlegs	*Tringa melanoleuca*
Solitary Sandpiper	*Tringa solitaria*
Willet	*Catoptrophorus semipalmatus*
Stilt Sandpiper	*Calidris himantopus*
Sanderling	*Calidris alba*
Western Sandpiper	*Calidris mauri*
Least Sandpiper	*Calidris minutilla*

COMMON NAME	SCIENTIFIC NAME
Curlew Sandpiper	*Calidris ferruginea*
Short-billed Dowitcher	*Limnodromus griseus*
Long-billed Dowitcher	*Limnodromus scolopaceus*
Wilson's Phalarope	*Phalaropus tricolor*
Laughing Gull	*Larus atricilla*
Black-headed Gull	*Larus ridibundus*
Franklin's Gull	*Larus pipixcan*
Bonaparte's Gull	*Larus philadelphia*
Little Gull	*Larus minutus*
Heermann's Gull	*Larus heermanni*
Ring-billed Gull	*Larus delawarensis*
Herring Gull	*Larus argentatus*
Sabine's Gull	*Xema sabini*
Black-legged Kittiwake	*Rissa tridactyla*
Ross's Gull	*Rhodostethia rosea*
Royal Tern	*Sterna maxima*
Roseate Tern	*Sterna dougallii*
Forster's Tern	*Sterna forsteri*
Gull-billed Tern	*Sterna nilotica*
Elegant Tern	*Sterna elegans*
Common Tern	*Sterna hirundo*
Least Tern	*Sterna antillarum*
Caspian Tern	*Sterna caspia*
Sandwich Tern	*Sterna sandvicensis*
Arctic Tern	*Sterna paradisaea*
Black Tern	*Chlidonias niger*
Mangrove Cuckoo	*Coccyzus minor*
Black-billed Cuckoo	*Coccyzus erythropthalmus*
Yellow-billed Cuckoo	*Coccyzus americanus*
Barn Owl	*Tyto alba*
Long-eared Owl	*Asio otus*
Short-eared Owl	*Asio flammeus*
Downy Woodpecker	*Picoides pubescens*
Hairy Woodpecker	*Picoides villosus*
Olive-sided Flycatcher	*Contopus cooperi*
Eastern Wood-Pewee	*Contopus virens*
Least Flycatcher	*Empidonax minimus*
Alder Flycatcher	*Empidonax alnorum*
Eastern Phoebe	*Sayornis phoebe*
Loggerhead Shrike	*Lanius ludovicianus*

COMMON NAME	SCIENTIFIC NAME
Northern Shrike	*Lanius excubitor*
Yellow-throated Vireo	*Vireo flavifrons*
Blue-headed Vireo	*Vireo solitarius*
Philadelphia Vireo	*Vireo philadelphicus*
White-eyed Vireo	*Vireo griseus*
Plumbeous Vireo	*Vireo plumbeus*
Red-eyed Vireo	*Vireo olivaceus*
Cassin's Vireo	*Vireo cassinii*
Warbling Vireo	*Vireo gilvus*
American Crow	*Corvus brachyrhynchos*
Fish Crow	*Corvus ossifragus*
Northwestern Crow	*Corvus caurinus*
Chihuahuan Raven	*Corvus cryptoleucus*
Common Raven	*Corvus corax*
Purple Martin	*Progne subis*
Violet-green Swallow	*Tachycineta thalassina*
Tree Swallow	*Tachycineta bicolor*
Northern Rough-winged Swallow	*Stelgidopteryx serripennis*
Bank Swallow	*Riparia riparia*
Cliff Swallow	*Petrochelidon pyrrhonota*
Cave Swallow	*Petrochelidon fulva*
Barn Swallow	*Hirundo rustica*
Carolina Chickadee	*Poecile carolinensis*
Black-capped Chickadee	*Poecile atricapillus*
Carolina Wren	*Thryothorus ludovicianus*
Bewick's Wren	*Thryomanes bewickii*
House Wren	*Troglodytes aedon*
Winter Wren	*Troglodytes troglodytes*
Golden-crowned Kinglet	*Regulus satrapa*
Ruby-crowned Kinglet	*Regulus calendula*
Eastern Bluebird	*Sialia sialis*
Western Bluebird	*Sialia mexicana*
Mountain Bluebird	*Sialia currucoides*
Bicknell's Thrush	*Catharus bicknelli*
Veery	*Catharus fuscescens*
Swainson's Thrush	*Catharus ustulatus*
Gray-cheeked Thrush	*Catharus minimus*
Hermit Thrush	*Catharus guttatus*
Wood Thrush	*Hylocichla mustelina*
Bohemian Waxwing	*Bombycilla garrulus*

COMMON NAME	SCIENTIFIC NAME
Cedar Waxwing	*Bombycilla cedrorum*
Nashville Warbler	*Vermivora ruficapilla*
Lucy's Warbler	*Vermivora luciae*
Tennessee Warbler	*Vermivora peregrina*
Blue-winged Warbler	*Vermivora pinus*
Orange-crowned Warbler	*Vermivora celata*
Yellow Warbler	*Dendroica petechia*
Cape May Warbler	*Dendroica tigrina*
Bay-breasted Warbler	*Dendroica castanea*
Chestnut-sided Warbler	*Dendroica pensylvanica*
Black-throated Blue Warbler	*Dendroica caerulescens*
Prairie Warbler	*Dendroica discolor*
Blackpoll Warbler	*Dendroica striata*
Magnolia Warbler	*Dendroica magnolia*
Yellow-rumped Warbler	*Dendroica coronata*
Black-throated Green Warbler	*Dendroica virens*
Blackburnian Warbler	*Dendroica fusca*
Pine Warbler	*Dendroica pinus*
Palm Warbler	*Dendroica palmarum*
Cerulean Warbler	*Dendroica cerulea*
Black-and-white Warbler	*Mniotilta varia*
American Redstart	*Setophaga ruticilla*
Prothonotary Warbler	*Protonotaria citrea*
Worm-eating Warbler	*Helmitheros vermivorum*
Swainson's Warbler	*Limnothlypis swainsonii*
Ovenbird	*Seiurus aurocapilla*
Northern Waterthrush	*Seiurus noveboracensis*
Louisiana Waterthrush	*Seiurus motacilla*
Common Yellowthroat	*Geothlypis trichas*
Summer Tanager	*Piranga rubra*
Scarlet Tanager	*Piranga olivacea*
Hepatic Tanager	*Piranga flava*
Western Tanager	*Piranga ludoviciana*
Clay-colored Sparrow	*Spizella pallida*
Black-chinned Sparrow	*Spizella atrogularis*
American Tree Sparrow	*Spizella arborea*
Brewer's Sparrow	*Spizella breweri*
Chipping Sparrow	*Spizella passerina*
Field Sparrow	*Spizella pusilla*
Vesper Sparrow	*Pooecetes gramineus*

COMMON NAME	SCIENTIFIC NAME
Savannah Sparrow	*Passerculus sandwichensis*
Henslow's Sparrow	*Ammodramus henslowii*
Saltmarsh Sharp-tailed Sparrow	*Ammodramus caudacutus*
Grasshopper Sparrow	*Ammodramus savannarum*
Le Conte's Sparrow	*Ammodramus leconteii*
Seaside Sparrow	*Ammodramus maritimus*
Baird's Sparrow	*Ammodramus bairdii*
Nelson's Sharp-tailed Sparrow	*Ammodramus nelsoni*
Fox Sparrow	*Passerella iliaca*
Swamp Sparrow	*Melospiza georgiana*
Song Sparrow	*Melospiza melodia*
Lincoln's Sparrow	*Melospiza lincolnii*
White-crowned Sparrow	*Zonotrichia leucophrys*
White-throated Sparrow	*Zonotrichia albicollis*
Golden-crowned Sparrow	*Zonotrichia atricapilla*
Harris's Sparrow	*Zonotrichia querula*
Blue Bunting	*Cyanocompsa parellina*
Blue Grosbeak	*Guiraca caerulea*
Lazuli Bunting	*Passerina amoena*
Painted Bunting	*Passerina ciris*
Indigo Bunting	*Passerina cyanea*
Varied Bunting	*Passerina versicolor*
Red-winged Blackbird	*Agelaius phoeniceus*
Yellow-headed Blackbird	*Xanthocephalus xanthocephalus*
Rusty Blackbird	*Euphagus carolinus*
Brewer's Blackbird	*Euphagus cyanocephalus*
Common Grackle	*Quiscalus quiscula*
Brown-headed Cowbird	*Molothrus ater*
Scott's Oriole	*Icterus parisorum*
Orchard Oriole	*Icterus spurius*
Bullock's Oriole	*Icterus bullockii*
Hooded Oriole	*Icterus cucullatus*
Baltimore Oriole	*Icterus galbula*
Purple Finch	*Carpodacus purpureus*
Cassin's Finch	*Carpodacus cassinii*
House Finch	*Carpodacus mexicanus*
Hoary Redpoll	*Carduelis hornemanni*
Pine Siskin	*Carduelis pinus*
Common Redpoll	*Carduelis flammea*